Essentials of Psychological Assessment Series

M000200031

Everything you need to know to administer, score, and interpret the major psychological tests.

I'd like to order the following *Essentials of Psychological Assessment*:

- ❑ WAIS®-IV Assessment (w/CD-ROM) / 978-0-471-73846-6 • $48.95
- ❑ WJ III™ Cognitive Abilities Assessment, Second Edition / 978-0-470-56664-0 • $38.95
- ❑ Cross-Battery Assessment, Second Edition (w/CD-ROM) / 978-0-471-75771-9 • $48.95
- ❑ Nonverbal Assessment / 978-0-471-38318-5 • $38.95
- ❑ PAI® Assessment / 978-0-471-08463-1 • $38.95
- ❑ CAS Assessment / 978-0-471-29015-5 • $38.95
- ❑ MMPI®-2 Assessment, Second Edition / 978-0-470-92323-8 • $38.95
- ❑ Myers-Briggs Type Indicator® Assessment, Second Edition / 978-0-470-34390-6 • $38.95
- ❑ Rorschach® Assessment / 978-0-471-33146-9 • $38.95
- ❑ Millon™ Inventories Assessment, Third Edition / 978-0-470-16862-2 • $38.95
- ❑ TAT and Other Storytelling Assessments, Second Edition / 978-0-470-28192-5 • $38.95
- ❑ MMPI-A™ Assessment / 978-0-471-39815-8 • $38.95
- ❑ NEPSY®-II Assessment / 978-0-470-43691-2 • $38.95
- ❑ Neuropsychological Assessment, Second Edition / 978-0-470-43747-6 • $38.95
- ❑ WJ III™ Tests of Achievement Assessment / 978-0-471-33059-2 • $38.95
- ❑ Evidence-Based Academic Interventions / 978-0-470-20632-4 • $38.95
- ❑ WRAML2 and TOMAL-2 Assessment / 978-0-470-17911-6 • $38.95
- ❑ WMS®-IV Assessment / 978-0-470-62196-7 • $38.95
- ❑ Behavioral Assessment / 978-0-471-35367-6 • $38.95
- ❑ Forensic Psychological Assessment, Second Edition / 978-0-470-55168-4 • $38.95
- ❑ Bayley Scales of Infant Development II Assessment / 978-0-471-32651-9 • $38.95
- ❑ Career Interest Assessment / 978-0-471-35365-2 • $38.95
- ❑ WPPSI™-III Assessment / 978-0-471-28895-4 • $38.95
- ❑ 16PF® Assessment / 978-0-471-23424-1 • $38.95
- ❑ Assessment Report Writing / 978-0-471-39487-7 • $38.95
- ❑ Stanford-Binet Intelligence Scales (SB5) Assessment / 978-0-471-22404-4 • $38.95
- ❑ WISC®-IV Assessment, Second Edition (w/CD-ROM) / 978-0-470-18915-3 • $48.95
- ❑ KABC-II Assessment / 978-0-471-66733-9 • $38.95
- ❑ WIAT®-III and KTEA-II Assessment (w/CD-ROM) / 978-0-470-55169-1 • $48.95
- ❑ Processing Assessment / 978-0-471-71925-0 • $38.95
- ❑ School Neuropsychological Assessment / 978-0-471-78372-5 • $38.95
- ❑ Cognitive Assessment with KAIT & Other Kaufman Measures / 978-0-471-38317-8 • $38.95
- ❑ Assessment with Brief Intelligence Tests / 978-0-471-26412-5 • $38.95
- ❑ Creativity Assessment / 978-0-470-13742-0 • $38.95
- ❑ WNV™ Assessment / 978-0-470-28467-4 • $38.95
- ❑ DAS-II® Assessment (w/CD-ROM) / 978-0-470-22520-2 • $48.95
- ❑ Executive Function Assessment / 978-0-470-42202-1 • $38.95
- ❑ Conners Behavior Assessments™ / 978-0-470-34633-4 • $38.95
- ❑ Temperament Assessment / 978-0-470-44447-4 • $38.95
- ❑ Response to Intervention / 978-0-470-56663-3 • $38.95
- ❑ Specific Learning Disability Identification / 978-0-470-58760-7 • $38.95
- ❑ IDEA for Assessment Professionals (w/CD-ROM) / 978-0-470-87392-2 • $48.95
- ❑ Dyslexia Assessment and Intervention / 978-0-470-92760-1 • $38.95
- ❑ Autism Spectrum Disorders Evaluation and Assessment / 978-0-470-62194-3 • $38.95

Please complete the order form on the back.
To order by phone, call toll free 1-877-762-2974
To order online: www.wiley.com/essentials
To order by mail: refer to order form on next page

Essentials

of **Psychological Assessment** Series

ORDER FORM

Please send this order form with your payment (credit card or check) to:
John Wiley & Sons, Attn: J. Knott, 111 River Street, Hoboken, NJ 07030-5774

QUANTITY	TITLE	ISBN	PRICE

Shipping Charges:	Surface	2-Day	1-Day
First item	$5.00	$10.50	$17.50
Each additional item	$3.00	$3.00	$4.00

For orders greater than 15 items,
please contact Customer Care at 1-877-762-2974.

ORDER AMOUNT _____

SHIPPING CHARGES _____

SALES TAX _____

TOTAL ENCLOSED _____

NAME_____

AFFILIATION_____

ADDRESS_____

CITY/STATE/ZIP _____

TELEPHONE _____

EMAIL_____

❑ Please add me to your e-mailing list

PAYMENT METHOD:

❑ Check/Money Order   ❑ Visa   ❑ Mastercard   ❑ AmEx

Card Number _____ Exp. Date _____

Cardholder Name *(Please print)* _____

Signature _____

*Make checks payable to **John Wiley & Sons**. Credit card orders invalid if not signed.*
All orders subject to credit approval. • Prices subject to change.

To order by phone, call toll free 1-877-762-2974
To order online: www.wiley.com/essentials

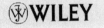

Essentials of Autism Spectrum Disorders Evaluation and Assessment

Essentials of Psychological Assessment Series
Series Editors, Alan S. Kaufman and Nadeen L. Kaufman

Essentials of 16 PF R Assessment
by Heather E.-P. Cattell and James M. Schuerger

Essentials of Assessment Report Writing
by Elizabeth O. Lichtenberger, Nancy Mather, Nadeen
L. Kaufman, and Alan S. Kaufman

Essentials of Assessment with Brief Intelligence Tests
by Susan R. Homack and Cecil R. Reynolds

Essentials of Autism Spectrum Disorders Evaluation and Assessment
by Celine A. Saulnier and Pamela E. Ventola

Essentials of Bayley Scales of Infant Development–II Assessment
by Maureen M. Black and Kathleen Matula

Essentials of Behavioral Assessment
by Michael C. Ramsay, Cecil R. Reynolds, and R. W. Kamphaus

Essentials of Career Interest Assessment
by Jeffrey P. Prince and Lisa J. Heiser

Essentials of CAS Assessment
by Jack A. Naglieri

Essentials of Cognitive Assessment with KAIT and Other Kaufman Measures
by Elizabeth O. Lichtenberger, Debra Broadbooks,
and Alan S. Kaufman

Essentials of Conners Behavior Assessments™
by Elizabeth P. Sparrow

Essentials of Creativity Assessment
by James C. Kaufman, Jonathan A. Plucker, and John Baer

Essentials of Cross-Battery Assessment, Second Edition
by Dawn P. Flanagan, Samuel O. Ortiz, and Vincent C. Alfonso

Essentials of DAS-II R Assessment
by Ron Dumont, John O. Willis, and Colin D. Elliot

Essentials of Dyslexia Assessment and Intervention
by Nancy Mather and Barbara J. Wendling

Essentials of Evidence-Based Academic Interventions
by Barbara J. Wendling and Nancy Mather

Essentials of Forensic Psychological Assessment, Second Edition
by Marc J. Ackerman

Essentials of IDEA for Assessment Professionals
by Guy McBride, Ron Dumont, and John O. Willis

Essentials of Individual Achievement Assessment
by Douglas K. Smith

Essentials of KABC-II Assessment
by Alan S. Kaufman, Elizabeth O. Lichtenberger, Elaine
Fletcher-Janzen, and Nadeen L. Kaufman

Essentials of Millon™ Inventories Assessment, Third Edition
by Stephen Strack

Essentials of MMPI-A™ Assessment
by Robert P. Archer and Radhika Krishnamurthy

Essentials of MMPI-2 R Assessment, Second Edition
by David S. Nichols

Essentials of Myers-Briggs Type Indicator R Assessment, Second Edition
by Naomi Quenk

Essentials of NEPSY R -II Assessment
by Sally L. Kemp and Marit Korkman

Essentials of Neuropsychological Assessment, Second Edition
by Nancy Hebben and William Milberg

Essentials of Nonverbal Assessment
by Steve McCallum, Bruce Bracken, and John Wasserman

Essentials of PAI R Assessment
by Leslie C. Morey

Essentials of Processing Assessment
by Milton J. Dehn

Essentials of Response to Intervention
by Amanda M. VanDerHeyden and Matthew K. Burns

Essentials of Rorschach R Assessment
by Tara Rose, Nancy Kaser-Boyd, and Michael P. Maloney

Essentials of School Neuropsychological Assessment
by Daniel C. Miller

Essentials of Specific Learning Disability Identification
by Dawn Flanagan and Vincent C. Alfonso

Essentials of Stanford-Binet Intelligence Scales (SB5) Assessment
by Gale H. Roid and R. Andrew Barram

Essentials of TAT and Other Storytelling Assessments, Second Edition
by Hedwig Teglasi

Essentials of Temperament Assessment
by Diana Joyce

Essentials of WAIS R -IV Assessment
by Elizabeth O. Lichtenberger and Alan S. Kaufman

Essentials of WIAT R -III and KTEA-II Assessment
by Elizabeth O. Lichtenberger and Kristina C. Breaux

Essentials of WISC R -IV Assessment, Second Edition
by Dawn P. Flanagan and Alan S. Kaufman

Essentials of WJ III™ Cognitive Abilities Assessment, Second Edition
by Fredrick A. Schrank, Daniel C. Miller, Barbara J. Wendling,
and Richard W. Woodcock

Essentials of WJ III™ Tests of Achievement Assessment
by Nancy Mather, Barbara J. Wendling,
and Richard W. Woodcock

Essentials of WMS R -IV Assessment
by Lisa Whipple Drozdick, James A. Holdnack,
and Robin C. Hilsabeck

Essentials of WNV ™ Assessment
by Kimberly A. Brunnert, Jack A. Naglieri,
and Steven T. Hardy-Braz

Essentials of WPPSI ™ -III Assessment
by Elizabeth O. Lichtenberger and Alan S. Kaufman

Essentials of WRAML2 and TOMAL-2 Assessment
by Wayne Adams and Cecil R. Reynolds

Essentials

of Autism Spectrum

Disorders Evaluation

and Assessment

Celine A. Saulnier and
Pamela E. Ventola

John Wiley & Sons, Inc.
WILEY

Published by John Wiley & Sons, Inc., Hoboken, New Jersey.
Published simultaneously in Canada.

Library of Congress Cataloging-in-Publication Data:
Saulnier, Celine A.
  Essentials of autism spectrum disorders evaluation and assessment / Celine A. Saulnier, Pamela E. Ventola.
    p. ; cm. — (Essentials of psychological assessment series)
  Includes bibliographical references and index.
  ISBN 978-0-470-62194-3 (pbk)
  ISBN 978-1-118-25903-0 (ebk)
  ISBN 978-1-118-23455-6 (ebk)
  ISBN 978-1-118-22077-1 (ebk)
  I. Ventola, Pamela E. II. Title. III. Series: Essentials of psychological assessment series.
  [DNLM: 1. Child Development Disorders, Pervasive–diagnosis. WS 350.8.P4]

  616.85'882—dc23
                                                                                    2011044316

10 9 8 7 6 5 4 3 2

To Tony, for your eternal love, support, and patience—
You are my everything; and to Lucienne and Vivienne,
for being the light of my life. ~ Celine

To Noah, you are an inspiration; your unfaltering strength,
love, and endless encouragement make it all possible; to Madelyn,
you are truly the center of my world. ~ Pam

This book has a very special dedication to our beloved
mentor and colleague, Dr. Sara Sparrow, for shaping our
knowledge of childhood assessments, particularly the critical
role of adaptive behavior in autism spectrum disorders.
Working with you was an honor, and
we miss you terribly. ~ Celine and Pam

TABLE OF CONTENTS

Series Preface   xiii

Acknowledgments   xv

One   Overview   1

Diagnostic Criteria   2

Asperger Syndrome   3

Pervasive Developmental Disorder, Not
Otherwise Specified   5

Rett's Disorder and Childhood Disintegrative Disorder   8

DSM-5   9

Two   Assessment of Level of Functioning   13

Selecting Instruments   14

Developmental and Early Cognitive Measures   16

Cognitive Assessments   19

Neuropsychological Assessments   28

Qualitative Observations   31

Summary   33

Test Yourself   36

Answers   37

Three   Speech, Language, and Communication Assessment   39

Receptive Language   42

Expressive Language   44

Pragmatic Language/Social Communication   47

Stages of Language Development   48

Formulation of Findings   51

	Summary	55
	Test Yourself	57
	Answers	58
Four	Assessment of Behavioral Profiles	59
	Standardized Assessments of Behavior	60
	Functional Behavior Assessment	61
	Assessment of Adaptive Behavior	64
	Summary	70
	Test Yourself	72
	Answers	73
Five	Clinical Interview and Record Review	75
	Clinical Interview	76
	Methods of Collecting Information on Current and Historical Presentation	87
	Summary	94
	Test Yourself	97
	Answers	98
Six	Direct Diagnostic Assessment	99
	Direct Observation	99
	Diagnostic Assessment	100
	Semistructured Measures for Diagnostic Assessment	116
	Summary	119
	Test Yourself	120
	Answers	122
Seven	Diagnostic Differentials and Comorbidity	123
	Intellectual Disability	124
	Learning Profiles	130
	Specific Language Impairment	134
	Attention Deficit Hyperactivity Disorder	135
	Anxiety and Tic Disorders	137
	Mood Disorders	141
	Psychiatric Conditions in Adulthood	143
	Summary	146

Test Yourself 150
Answers 151

Eight Case Conceptualization and
Integrated Report Writing 153
The Parent Conference 153
The Written Report 154
Case Samples 155
Case Sample: Initial Diagnosis—Toddler 156
Case Sample: School-Aged Child With ASD 171

Annotated Bibliography 197

About the Authors 201

Author Index 203

Subject Index 207

SERIES PREFACE

I n the *Essentials of Psychological Assessment* series, we have attempted to provide the reader with books that will deliver key practical information in the most efficient and accessible style. The series features instruments in a variety of domains, such as cognition, personality, education, and neuropsychology. For the experienced clinician, books in the series will offer a concise yet thorough way to master utilization of the continuously evolving supply of new and revised instruments, as well as a convenient method for keeping up to date on the tried-and-true measures. The novice will find here a prioritized assembly of all the information and techniques that must be at one's fingertips to begin the complicated process of individual psychological diagnosis.

Wherever feasible, visual shortcuts to highlight key points are utilized alongside systematic, step-by-step guidelines. Chapters are focused and succinct. Topics are targeted for an easy understanding of the essentials of administration, scoring, interpretation, and clinical application. Theory and research are continually woven into the fabric of each book, but always to enhance clinical inference, never to sidetrack or overwhelm. We have long been advocates of "intelligent" testing—the notion that a profile of test scores is meaningless unless it is brought to life by the clinical observations and astute detective work of knowledgeable examiners. Test profiles must be used to make a difference in the child's or adult's life, or why bother to test?

We want this series to help our readers become the best intelligent testers they can be.

In *Essentials of Autism Spectrum Disorders Evaluation and Assessment*, the authors illustrate a comprehensive developmental model for multi-disciplinary diagnostic evaluations. They derived this model from years of experience in conducting diagnostic evaluations for ASD following standards of best practice. Given the neurodevelopmental nature of ASD, symptoms unfold over the course of early development and subsequently affect multiple areas of functioning. For these reasons, the developmental skills that need to be assessed often require clinicians with different disciplinary expertise. Thus, in this Essentials text, the authors outline the components of a state-of-the-art diagnostic evaluation for ASD and also highlight the necessity of integrating findings from multiple sources. The end goal is to provide one comprehensive and cohesive diagnostic formulation for an individual's optimal care.

Alan S. Kaufman, Ph.D., and
Nadeen L. Kaufman, Ed.D., Series Editors
Yale University School of Medicine

ACKNOWLEDGMENTS

The completion of this book would not have been possible without the help and support from a host of people. This publication exemplifies the knowledge and expertise in autism spectrum and related disorders, diagnostic evaluation, and childhood development that was acquired over many years thanks to the teachings and collaborations of our incredible mentors and colleagues. They include, but are certainly not limited to, the following:

Ami Klin, Ph.D., our extraordinary leader—A million thanks for teaching us the art of the comprehensive developmental approach to diagnostic evaluations in ASD. We have been incredibly fortunate to witness and learn from your clinical magic firsthand. This book hopefully embodies your approach to fully understanding the unique needs and gifts of the children that we serve each day. Your leadership, mentorship, and most importantly support of our careers are unparalleled. You are and continue to be an inspiration. *Muito obrigado!*

Deborah Fein, Ph.D., and Marianne Barton, Ph.D., our beloved graduate school advisors, mentors, and friends from the University of Connecticut—Words cannot express our gratitude and appreciation for all that you have taught us. You both are undeniably responsible for shaping our knowledge of autism and diagnostic assessment, and for single-handedly launching our careers. We will never forget the nest from which we came!

Julie Wolf, Ph.D., and Leah Booth, MA, CCC-SLP, our dear friends and colleagues—We cannot thank you enough for your generous contributions to the chapters on diagnostic differentials and speech, language, and communication. We are privileged to have your respective areas of expertise reflected in this book. The opportunity to work alongside both of you for years has been an absolute gift, and one of these authors misses you both very much!

To Michelle Levine, Kelly Caravella, and Yael Stern, our bourgeoning experts in autism—Thank you for your efforts in helping us to put the finishing touches on this book at the 11th hour! We could never have reached our deadline without you. We look forward to saying we knew you when.

To our colleagues and mentors at the Yale Child Study Center, Kasia Chawarska, Ph.D.; Karyn Bailey, LCSW; Rhea Paul, CCC-SLP, Ph.D.; Kathy Koenig, MSN; Fred Volkmar, MD; and Domenic Cicchetti, Ph.D.—Your teachings, clinical expertise, and guidance are not only reflected throughout this book, but will continue to influence the work that we do on a daily basis. Forever thanks.

A very special thank you to our editors, Marquita Flemming and Kim Nir—without your patience, tolerance, and support throughout this entire process, this book would never have become a reality. Numerous obstacles on our end made any deadline seem impossible; thus, we thank you for your faith in us and your willingness to see this book through to fruition. Furthermore, we are indebted to Wiley and Alan and Nadeen Kaufman for recognizing the utility and necessity for including the topic of autism assessments within the *Essentials* series. We believe that this will offer a unique contribution to clinicians in the field, and we are honored to be a part of it.

Finally, our overwhelming gratitude to the children and families from whom we learn every day. Thank you for sharing your lives with us.

One

Autism spectrum disorders (ASD) are among the most common childhood disorders, with prevalence rates reaching near 1% of the population (CDC, 2007a, 2007b). Defined as a lifelong neurodevelopmental disorder with a complex genetic etiology, ASD's symptoms tend to unfold over the course of early development. Research indicates that 80% to 90% of parents report their first concerns about their child's development by the second birthday and often earlier. However, the mean age of diagnosis continues to be well over the age of three despite these concerns (Chawarska et al., 2007). Moreover, when experienced clinicians make a diagnosis of ASD at 18 to 24 months, the stability of diagnosis is quite strong, also around 80% to 90% (Chawarska et al., 2009). This highlights an extremely concerning gap between when first concerns are raised and when something is actually done to help the child; often because of a limited awareness of the early markers of ASD by professionals on the front line. These facts underscore the necessity for clinicians of all disciplines to learn about and

> ## CAUTION
>
> Most parents of children who develop ASD express concerns regarding their child's development prior to the second birthday, well over a year before diagnostic evaluations take place, on average. Professionals need to be extra vigilant in not only validating concerns, but also in taking immediate action to assess and identify potential risk for ASD.

be vigilant for the early signs of ASD, so that children can be effectively evaluated and efficiently diagnosed. Only then can these children subsequently receive the critical early and intensive intervention that is associated with optimal outcome (National Research Council, 2001).

DIAGNOSTIC CRITERIA

Although the causes of ASD are likely neurobiological in nature, the spectrum of disorders still requires diagnosis based on behavioral symptomatology. The current diagnostic criteria put forth in the *Diagnostic and Statistical Manual, Fourth Edition, Text Revision* (DSM-IV-TR; APA, 2000) fall under the category of Pervasive Developmental Disorders (PDD), which includes Autistic Disorder, or autism; Asperger's Disorder, or Asperger syndrome, Rett's Disorder, Childhood Disintegrative Disorder (CDD), and Pervasive Developmental Disorder, Not Otherwise Specified (PDD-NOS). The behavioral features of all five PDDs fall within the following subcategories: (1) impairments in social interaction; (2) impairments in communication; and (3) restricted, repetitive, and stereotyped patterns of behavior, interests, and activities. A diagnosis of Autistic Disorder, the most prototypical of the PDDs, requires onset of delays or deviance in development prior to the age of three and a total of at least six impairments in all subcategories, with at least two falling within the area of social interaction.

≡ *Rapid Reference 1.1*

Pervasive Developmental Disorders in the DSM-IV-TR
Autistic Disorder
Asperger's Disorder
Rett's Disorder
Childhood Disintegrative Disorder
Pervasive Developmental Disorder, Not Otherwise Specified

ASPERGER SYNDROME

The description of Asperger syndrome is more complicated. The *DSM-IV-TR* defines the disorder as having impairment in at least two areas of social interaction and one restricted, repetitive, and stereotyped pattern of behavior, but not meeting full criteria for Autistic Disorder. The criteria further stipulate that there can be no clinically significant delays in the development of language, cognition, and self-help adaptive skills *during the first three years of life* (APA, 2000). However, many clinicians overlook the text of the *DSM-IV-TR* and resort only to the charts. In this case, the text signifying "during the first three years of life" would be missed, resulting in misdiagnoses of older individuals with Asperger syndrome who most certainly do present with areas of deficit in cognitive, adaptive, and language abilities (e.g., Klin et al., 2007; Saulnier & Klin, 2007).

Furthermore, if one refers only to the charts and not the text, the description of circumscribed interests—the all-encompassing preoccupations with topics of interest that tend to be more specific to Asperger syndrome than the other PDDs—would be similarly overlooked. These criteria have generated a great deal of controversy, resulting in tremendous variation in the diagnosis of Asperger syndrome, both clinically and in research. This variability and lack of consistency in defining the disorder has ultimately resulted in removal of the subtype from the forthcoming *DSM-5* (APA, 2010), which is not without controversy (e.g., Wing, Gould, & Gillberg, 2011).

Clinicians and researchers who have closely studied and worked with individuals with Asperger syndrome invariably view this subtype as qualitatively distinct from the other

> **CAUTION**
>
> Clinicians are cautioned against merely relying on the *DSM-IV-TR* charts for determining diagnostic criteria for the PDDs, as the descriptions of the most differentiating features of Asperger syndrome are included within the text of the *DSM-IV-TR* but not within the charts.

CAUTION

....

Common misconceptions of Asperger Syndrome include the following characteristics interpreted in isolation:

- Individuals with ASD without cognitive impairment
- Individuals with ASD who have higher verbal than nonverbal IQ scores
- Individuals with ASD who have social intent and motivation to interact with others
- Asperger Syndrome is "mild autism"

PDDs, given the verbosity, social motivation, and fixation on topics of interest in these individuals. Ironically, these same symptoms can cause the most confusion in differential diagnosis. Common misconceptions propose those with Asperger's to be individuals without cognitive impairment; individuals with higher verbal than nonverbal IQ scores; individuals who have social intent; individuals who have mild or subtle social impairments; or individuals with perseverative interests, such as *Thomas the Tank Engine*— confusing getting "stuck" on a character or video rather than wanting to obsessively collect details about the topic of, for instance, trains. These misconceptions can have negative implications on outcome for individuals with Asperger syndrome because they are assumed to be less impaired and more able to navigate the world without supports— which is certainly not the case for many individuals.

It is not one of these behaviors, in isolation, that defines Asperger syndrome, but the overall profile of behavior, including developmental history. In early childhood, the social vulnerabilities of toddlers with Asperger syndrome are often masked by their relative strengths in other areas—such as their often precocious language; fixation on numbers and letters to the point of self-reading; and bourgeoning circumscribed interests. It is typically not until these children are immersed in social settings, where the social demands far outweigh their capacity to engage, that red flags are raised.

During the school-age years, individuals with Asperger syndrome tend to have more social motivation to interact with their peers, often inserting themselves into interactions inappropriately and/or lacking

CAUTION

Unlike autism, Asperger syndrome is often not detected in the first few years of life because in early childhood, the social vulnerabilities of toddlers with Asperger syndrome are often masked by their precocious language, affinity for numbers and letters, and regurgitation of facts on topics of interest. It is not until these children are immersed in social settings, such as preschool, that their true social impairments are recognized. For this reason, clinicians need to be extra vigilant in screening for social impairments in young children who have strong language and cognitive skills.

the appropriate social awareness to effectively navigate an interaction. Yet, they can have just enough awareness to understand the failed nature of their attempts, placing them at great risk for anxiety, depression, and isolation. In autism, individuals tend to be more socially passive; they certainly may respond to direct interaction, often even appropriately, but they are less likely to initiate interactions with their peers. Furthermore, self-awareness in autism can be more impaired, acting as a buffer in that individuals might not be as cognizant of their failed social experiences. Nevertheless, as stressed previously, social motivation should not be interpreted in isolation when distinguishing Asperger syndrome from other PDDs.

PERVASIVE DEVELOPMENTAL DISORDER, NOT OTHERWISE SPECIFIED

A diagnosis of PDD-NOS requires impairment in reciprocal social interaction (i.e., symptoms in subcategory 1) with associated

DON'T FORGET

Individuals with ASD, particularly those with Asperger Syndrome who tend to have a modicum of social awareness, are at great risk for mood disorders such as anxiety and depression. These symptoms can emerge as early as school age, but are most prominent in adolescents and adults and, therefore, should be monitored and treated accordingly.

≡ Rapid Reference 1.2

Distinctions Between Asperger Syndrome and Other PDDs

Asperger Syndrome	Autism, PDD-NOS
• Early history marked by intact or precocious speech development	• Early history marked by significant language delays/impairments
• Extreme verbosity and one-sided conversations	• Limited speech and/or stereotyped language (e.g., echolalia, scripting)
• Social motivation in the absence of ability to effectively navigate social interactions	• Social passivity—more apt to monitor peers rather than initiate interaction
• May have stronger rote verbal than nonverbal cognitive scores—*though not diagnostic!*	• Tend to have stronger rote nonverbal than verbal cognitive scores
• Circumscribed interests—all-absorbing interest on a topic, including collecting facts on the topic, and this interest pervades and dominates conversations	• Perseverative interests—fixations on objects/movies/activities that become overly repetitive, and the individual has difficulty disengaging from the interest

impairments in at least one of the remaining two subcategories. Therefore, under the current taxonomy, an individual does not necessarily have to present with stereotypical behaviors (i.e., symptoms falling under subcategory 3) to carry a diagnosis of PDD-NOS. The proposed diagnostic criteria for a *DSM-5* diagnosis of ASD, however, require *at least two* stereotyped behaviors (see Table 1.1). This will most certainly impact many individuals who currently hold the label of PDD-NOS, as it raises the question as to what label, if any, will be appropriate to merit the same degree of services for these individuals.

**Table 1.1. Comparison Between *DSM-IV* and Proposed *DSM-5*
Diagnostic Criteria for Autism Spectrum Disorders**

	DSM-IV	DSM-5
Category	*Pervasive Developmental Disorders*	*Autism Spectrum Disorder*
Category Subtypes	1. Autistic Disorder 2. Asperger's Disorder 3. Pervasive Developmental Disorder, Not Otherwise Specified (PDD-NOS) 4. Rett's Disorder 5. Childhood Disintegrative Disorder	None
Symptom Subcategories	1. Impairments in Social Interaction 2. Impairments in Communication 3. Restricted, Repetitive, and Stereotyped Patterns of Behavior, Interests, and Activities	1. Deficits in Social Communication and Social Interaction 2. Restricted, Repetitive Patterns of Behavior, Interests, or Activities
Diagnostic Criteria	1. *Autistic Disorder* = at least six total symptoms across all three subcategories, at least two of which are in social interaction 2. *Asperger's Disorder* = symptoms in social interaction and restricted behaviors, with no delays in the development of language, cognition, or adaptive self-help skills in first three years of life; but not to full criteria for Autistic Disorder 3. *PDD-NOS* = social impairments _and_ symptoms in either communication and/or restricted behaviors; but not to full criteria for Autistic Disorder	1. *ASD* = three required criteria in social communication and social interaction _and_ at least two out of four restricted and repetitive patterns of behavior 2. Symptoms must be present in early childhood (even if not fully manifested until social demands exceed the child's level of social functioning)

DON'T FORGET

Rett's syndrome is differentiated by ASD in that it is more prevalent in girls than boys; it is associated with a mutation in the MECP2 gene; there is early regression of psychomotor development in the first year of life; and there is a deceleration of head circumference.

RETT'S DISORDER AND CHILDHOOD DISINTEGRATIVE DISORDER

Rett's Disorder and CDD are rare, regressive-type disorders where at the outset of the respective regressions in development, the individual's behavioral presentation is similar to autism. In Rett's Disorder, pre- and perinatal development are apparently normal, followed by a regression in psychomotor development and social engagement between the ages of 5 and 48 months. There is also a deceleration of head circumference and progression of hand washing/hand wringing mannerisms. What differentiates Rett's from all other PDDs is that Rett's, to date, is predominantly prevalent in females, whereas the remaining PDDs are, overall, four to five times more prevalent in males. A genetic mutation on the MECP2 gene has also been identified in the majority of Rett's cases (Van Acker, Loncola, & Van Acker, 2005).

In CDD, early development is spared for the first two to three years, after which there is a clinically significant loss of previously acquired skills in at least two of the following areas: receptive or expressive language, social skills, adaptive skills, toileting skills, play skills, or motor development. The regression must take place before age 10, but in most cases, the regression occurs between ages 2 and 3 (Volkmar, Koenig, & State, 2005). At the outset of the regression, individuals with CDD often are afflicted with severe or profound intellectual disability in addition to the autism symptomatology. Very little is known about the etiology of CDD or the triggers of the regression, although research suggests that triggers can be associated with (but not caused by) psychosocial stressors, such as those that are common to preschool-age children. These could include birth of a sibling, death of a family member, or a significant hospitalization

(Volkmar, Koenig, & State, 2005). CDD should not be confused with regressive autism, which occurs in about 10% of cases of ASD and where there is a reported loss of or plateau in development of skills prior to the age of 2. Children with regressive autism do not appear to be as impaired as children with CDD at the outset of their regression; yet, just as little is

> **DON'T FORGET**
> ....
> Childhood Disintegrative Disorder is distinct from regressive autism in that the regression of skills in CDD occurs after the age of 2, and substantial delays are evident at the outset of the regression in CDD in many areas of development, including language, social functioning, self-help skills, motor skills, and play skills.

known about regressive autism and how it is differentiated from autism without regression. To reiterate, ASD is a neurodevelopmental disorder and, as such, the symptoms unfold over the first few years of life. Thus, deviance in the developmental course of social communication and behavioral skills around 18 to 24 months of age is anticipated in ASD but can often be misconstrued as regression.

DSM-5

Recent nomenclature has moved in the direction of considering the PDDs a spectrum of disorders; that is, taking more of a dimensional rather than categorical approach to diagnostic conceptualization. Thus, more common terminology refers to Autism Spectrum Disorders (ASD), typically signifying Autistic Disorder, Asperger syndrome, and PDD-NOS (given the rarity and relatively limited public awareness of Rett's

> **CAUTION**
> ....
> Autism is a neurodevelopmental disorder where symptoms (i.e., deviance in behavioral development) tend to manifest in the second year of life. This unfolding of symptomatology can be misinterpreted as a regression in the development of skills.

DON'T FORGET

Despite the vast heterogeneity observed between individuals across the autism spectrum, the common thread among the five Pervasive Developmental Disorders is that they are all *social disabilities*.

Disorder and CDD). The *DSM-5*, slated to be published in 2013, is proposing to change the diagnostic category to *Autism Spectrum Disorder*, eliminating the subtypes altogether (see Table 1.1; APA, 2010). Given these forthcoming changes, this book will focus on the broad spectrum of autism rather than on specific subtypes. Nevertheless, the authors will highlight when specific features that are more relevant to one subtype than another merit analysis (e.g., in Asperger syndrome).

No two individuals under the umbrella of the autism spectrum have identical presentations. There is more heterogeneity than similarity of symptom expression, which has resulted in a host of theories as to what the causes might be. Nonetheless, the common thread of all five PDDs, or ASDs, is the resulting social disability and the limited capacity to independently navigate the social world, whether expressed as substantial deficits in rudimentary social skills, more subtle vulnerabilities in interpreting the nuances of social interactions, or any variation in between. These social impairments are qualitatively different from and more severe than the vulnerabilities in social development that can be observed in other developmental disorders.

With the following book, we present a model process for identifying the symptoms of ASD while accurately differentiating the nature of social disabilities from mere delays in social development. As such, the focus is more on the differentials between ASD and other neurodevelopmental disorders rather than on distinguishing among the ASD subtypes, especially given the aforementioned *DSM-5* changes. Having obtained extensive experience in multidisciplinary diagnostic evaluations, we adopt the comprehensive developmental approach to assessment, diagnosis, interpretation, and report writing. Beginning with Chapter 2, the necessity for obtaining a baseline of cognitive and developmental functioning is discussed. Because the essence of social interaction is communication, Chapter 3 then outlines how the speech, language, and communication assessment informs the diagnostic process. This naturally transitions to Chapter 4, where aberrant or problematic behaviors are often the result of impaired communicative functioning, thus highlighting the need to functionally assess these behaviors and then replace them with more adaptive means of communicating.

Chapters 5 and 6 collectively outline the diagnostic assessment, which entails the gathering of historic information, observing the individual in natural contexts, and directly assessing behaviors through interaction and play. Chapter 7 focuses on the common differentials and comorbidities that arise through referrals for diagnostic evaluations in ASD throughout the life span. Finally, Chapter 8 ties the process together with two samples of integrated reports from model comprehensive diagnostic evaluations—one of a toddler and one of a school-aged child. Our hope is that this model will be useful in informing both burgeoning clinicians just starting out in the field, as well as seasoned professionals who are experiencing an increased exposure to ASDs and, subsequently, are seeking knowledge of how to effectively identify, diagnose, and/or refer patients at risk.

REFERENCES

American Psychiatric Association. (2000). *Diagnostic and statistical manual of mental disorders* (4th ed., text rev.). Washington, DC: Author.

American Psychiatric Association. (2010). *DSM-5 development: Autism spectrum disorder*. Retrieved September 28, 2011 from http://www.dsm5.org/ProposedRevision/Pages/proposedrevision.aspx?rid=94

Centers for Disease Control and Prevention. (2007a). Prevalence of autism spectrum disorders: Autism and developmental disabilities monitoring network, 6 sites, United States, 2000. *MMWR Surveillance Summaries* 56:1–11.

Centers for Disease Control and Prevention. (2007b). Prevalence of autism spectrum disorders: Autism and developmental disabilities monitoring network, 14 sites, United States, 2002. *MMWR Surveillance Summaries* 56:12–28.

Chawarska, K., Klin, A., Paul, R., Macari, S., & Volkmar, F. (2009). A prospective study of toddlers with ASD: Short-term diagnostic and cognitive outcomes. *Journal of Child Psychology and Psychiatry*, 50(10), 1235–1245.

Chawarska, K., Paul, R., Klin, A., Hannigen, S., Dichtel, L. E., & Volkmar, F. (2007). Parental recognition of developmental problems in toddlers with autism spectrum disorders. *Journal of Autism and Developmental Disorders, 37*(1), 62–73.

Klin, A., Saulnier, C. A., Sparrow, S. S., Cicchetti, D. V., Volkmar, F. R., & Lord, C. (2007). Social and communication abilities and disabilities in higher functioning individuals with autism spectrum disorders: The Vineland and the ADOS. *Journal of Autism and Developmental Disorders, 37,* 748–759.

National Research Council. (2001). *Educating children with autism.* Washington, DC: National Academy Press.

Saulnier, C. A., & Klin, A. (2007). Brief report: Social and communication abilities and disabilities in higher functioning individuals with autism and Asperger syndrome. *Journal of Autism and Developmental Disorders, 37,* 788–793.

Van Acker, R., Loncola, J. A., & Van Acker, E. Y. (2005). Rett syndrome: A pervasive developmental disorder. In F. R. Volkmar, R. Paul, A. Klin, & D. Cohen (Eds.), *Handbook of autism and pervasive developmental disorders* (pp. 126–164). Hoboken, NJ: Wiley.

Volkmar, F. R., Koenig, K., & State, M. (2005). Childhood disintegrative disorder. In F. R. Volkmar, R. Paul, A. Klin, & D. Cohen (Eds.), *Handbook of autism and pervasive developmental disorders* (pp. 70–87). Hoboken, NJ: Wiley.

Wing, L., Gould, J., & Gillberg, C. (2011). Autism spectrum disorders in the DSM-V: Better or worse than the DSM-IV? *Research in Developmental Disabilities, 32*(2), 768–773.

Two

ASSESSMENT OF LEVEL OF FUNCTIONING

The assessment of an individual's level of functioning across areas of development is a seminal component to the diagnostic evaluation. A clinician needs to have comprehensive knowledge of an individual's profile of abilities—both strengths and weaknesses—in order to inform the diagnosis and, more importantly, to inform recommendations for treatment and intervention.

A striking aspect of the clinical presentation of individuals with ASD is the variability in levels of functioning, including developmental, cognitive, behavioral, and neuropsychological profiles that can change throughout the course of life. It therefore becomes essential to thoroughly evaluate each individual's profile of skills at various stages of development, particularly when approaching pivotal transitions (e.g., upon initial concern/diagnosis; entering/exiting academic environments/schools;

≡ *Rapid Reference 2.1*

When Comprehensive Evaluations Are Indicated

- Upon initial concern or when diagnostic clarification is needed
- Entering or exiting academic environments/schools
- Upon significant behavioral change
- Puberty/adolescence
- Transition into adulthood

upon significant behavioral change; during puberty/adolescence; transition into adulthood). Identifying the individual's personal strengths and weaknesses will help inform treatment and intervention approaches that are best matched to one's ability at a given point in time.

SELECTING INSTRUMENTS

When evaluating an individual with ASD, it is important to select the appropriate instrument that is catered to the individual's overall level of functioning. Factors to consider include the level of language skills required to both comprehend and respond to instructions; the degree of complexity of instructions; the level of structure and support needed to obtain optimal attention and performance; time and motor demands of tasks; and the extent to which social demands impede performance. Results need to elucidate the individual's optimal skills without the administration causing undue stress.

Within the field of psychology, there is a dearth of instruments suitable for measuring substantial cognitive delays using standardized instruments that have normative data on lower levels of intellectual ability. Thus, it is important for the clinician to have knowledge of the norms of each instrument, including the reliability and validity of the measure. When testing individuals with significant cognitive and/or language impairments, it is often not possible to obtain standard scores

≡ Rapid Reference 2.2

....

Challenges to Assessment in ASD

- Broad range of symptom expression
- Varied levels of functioning
- Varied profiles of functioning
- Inconsistency in presentation and performance across settings, people, and level of structure
- Changes in profiles of functioning over time

Table 2.1. Developmental, Cognitive, and Neuropsychological Processes

Developmental	Cognitive	Neuropsychological
Receptive Language	Verbal Reasoning	Attention: Shifting, Sustaining
Expressive Language	Spatial Reasoning	Executive Functioning
Visual Reasoning	Perceptual Reasoning	Impulse Control
Visual Memory	Processing Speed	Auditory Memory
Fine Motor	Visual Scanning	Visual Memory
Gross Motor		Working Memory
		Psychomotor Coordination
		Sensory Perception
		Visual Learning
		Verbal Learning

or an overall IQ score. Nevertheless, identifying an individual's strengths and weaknesses is still possible by ascertaining skill sets and mental ages that can certainly inform treatment and education planning. Table 2.1 outlines the skills that are often assessed as part of a developmental, cognitive, or neuropsychological assessment. It should be noted that although the behaviors listed under the neuro-psychological section can certainly be assessed during a diagnostic evaluation, a comprehensive neuropsychological evaluation, in and of itself, is not necessarily indicated for every individual with ASD.

In order to gauge an individual's level of functioning, it is useful to collect information before testing. This can be done by interviewing parents, obtaining reports from any previous evaluations, speaking with school and/or service providers, or directly observing the individual— descriptions of which are provided in subsequent chapters of this book. Even given this information, the actual testing demands in vivo can be so overwhelming that clinicians need to be prepared to possibly switch instruments mid-assessment and/ or draw upon subtests from various instruments.

The following sections outline the process of conducting developmental, cognitive, and neuropsychological assessments as part of the diagnostic evaluation. This chapter is not meant to provide detailed descriptions of the psychometric properties of each measure, but rather to offer an overview of the instruments that have been found to be clinically and scientifically useful in assessing individuals with ASD, and the common profiles of strengths and weaknesses observed within each.

DEVELOPMENTAL AND EARLY COGNITIVE MEASURES

Developmental assessments are typically used to assess skills in very young children (i.e., infants, toddlers, and preschool-aged children). Skills assessed include sensory, motor, language, perceptual reasoning, and visual memory skills. The most commonly used instruments are the *Mullen Scales of Early Learning* (Mullen, 1995) and the *Bayley Scales of Infant and Toddler Development, Third Edition* (Bayley, 2005). Because skill sets continue to change throughout early development, it is important to refrain from making any interpretations or predictions about future levels of functioning (i.e., cognition) based on early developmental profiles. Nevertheless, scores obtained (both standard scores and age-equivalent scores) can be useful for informing treatment programs as well as for tracking progress over time.

The *Mullen Scales* measure five areas of development, including receptive and expressive language, fine and gross motor abilities, and visual reception. All subdomains can be assessed from birth to 68 months, except for gross motor, which can be assessed up to 33 months of age. An overall Early Learning Composite can also be obtained, although, given the scatter typically observed across subdomain scores in ASD, this broader score is often less informative than domain-specific scores. The *Mullen* materials are user-friendly, with lots of manipulatives, and items are clearly organized within each domain, which is helpful for administration and scoring.

The *Mullen* has been widely used in clinical research on ASD to the degree that national data repositories (e.g., the National Database for Autism Research and the Simons Foundation Autism Research Initiative) have modeled the instrument for collaborative scientific data collection. Early detection studies on infants and toddlers with ASD have shown remarkable improvements in *Mullen* scores for children who were diagnosed as early as 24 months of age and followed up after the age of 4 (e.g., Chawarska et al., 2009; Klin et al., 2008). Children who were identified as having significant developmental and language delays upon diagnosis were able to close the gap in these delays prior to school age with targeted early intervention. Though the majority of these children still had ASD when assessed later in development, their prognosis drastically improved in that they were less likely to have cognitive impairment later in life. These results stress the importance of early detection and intensive intervention on positive outcome.

The *Bayley Scales* measure cognitive, language, motor, social-emotional, and adaptive development in children ages 1 month through 42 months. There is also a Screening Test to determine if a child requires additional testing, as well as a Caregiver Report that offers parents suggestions to help plan for their child. Like the *Mullen*, the materials in the *Bayley* are very child-friendly, and the Third Edition has simplified scoring criteria from the previous edition. However, the age range is not as high as the *Mullen*, and the Second Edition of the *Bayley* did not break down items by developmental level beyond differentiating motor from a broader mental index, which resulted in many clinicians and researchers resorting to the *Mullen* for obtaining more specialized developmental profiles in ASD. The *Bayley-III*, however, offers more differentiated scores.

The *Wechsler Preschool and Primary Scales of Intelligence, Third Edition* (WPPSI-III; Wechsler, 2002) measures early cognitive skills in preschool-age children. Starting at 2 years, 6 months and extending to age 7 years, 3 months, the WPPSI-III is not indicated for infants. It is also quite verbally demanding; thus, children within the age range need to have a moderate degree of language use and comprehension to successfully complete the tasks. If it possible to obtain valid basals on subtests, then the WPPSI-III provides valuable information about early verbal and nonverbal reasoning abilities, as well as speed of information processing; however, it would not provide the assessment of early motor skills that both the *Mullen* and *Bayley* scales measure.

≡ *Rapid Reference 2.3*

Developmental and Early Cognitive Measures

- *Mullen Scales of Early Learning* (Mullen, 1995)
- *Bayley Scales of Infant Toddler Development, Third Edition* (Bayley, 2005)
- *Wechsler Preschool and Primary Scales of Intelligence, Third Edition* (WPPSI-III; Wechsler, 2002)
- *Differential Ability Scales, Second Edition, Early Years* (DAS-II Early Years; Elliott, 2007)
- *Stanford-Binet Intelligence Scales for Early Childhood* (Early SB5; Roid, 2003)

When testing young children, it is important to keep in mind that few children are accustomed to sitting at a table and responding to a series of task demands for an extended period. Thus, it is often helpful to utilize strategies to enhance motivation and attention, such as offering natural reinforcers and providing frequent breaks. For many children with developmental disabilities, significant behavioral challenges can also impede a child's ability to comply with directives. These can

> ## DON'T FORGET
>
> No child is untestable! Challenging behaviors and significant delays might impede the ability to obtain standard scores, but valuable information regarding developmental profiles can still be obtained from the assessment. Additionally, in a child with significant behavioral difficulties, although the results of the testing may not reflect the child's true developmental/cognitive *potential*, they likely are representative of the child's *current* level of functioning and are extremely important for informing intervention programs.

include escape/avoidance behaviors, crying, screaming, tantrums, and self-injurious, explosive, or aggressive behaviors. In these instances, it is important to observe the behavioral triggers that likely involve communication impairments and low frustration tolerance. If examiners modify their language or task demands (e.g., use truncated language; more frequent reinforcement/contingencies), these behaviors can subside. Therefore, understanding, respecting, and addressing the child's needs becomes critical. It is very rarely the case that any child is "untestable"; rather, their level of functioning and/or behavioral challenges makes obtaining standard scores difficult, as outlined in Chapter 4.

COGNITIVE ASSESSMENTS

There are varying conceptualizations of how *cognition* is defined. Many batteries are based on the Cattell-Horn-Carroll (CHC; McGrew, 2005) theory of cognitive abilities, which is an overarching taxonomy of cognitive elements that includes three levels of cognition culminating in an overall general intelligence "g." The major components of the overall "g" include: fluid reasoning (inductive and deductive logic), knowledge, short-term memory, visual-spatial processing (e.g., the ability to transform visual images, sequence visual information, recognize visual patterns), and auditory processing (e.g., the ability to control auditory input and differentiate between salient and non-salient auditory input). In line with the dominant theories of cognition, most cognitive measures have subdomains or indices that assess processes, such as those listed previously.

The most commonly used cognitive instruments are the Wechsler scales: the *Wechsler Preschool and Primary Scales of Intelligence, Third Edition* (WPPSI-III, ages 2 years, 6 months to 7 years, 3 months); the *Wechsler Intelligence Scale for Children, Fourth Edition* (WISC-IV, ages 6 years to 16 years, 11 months); and the *Wechsler Adult Intelligence Scale, Fourth Edition* (WAIS-IV, 16 years to 89 years). The Wechsler scales organize cognitive abilities with the following indexes: Verbal Comprehension, Perceptual Organization/Reasoning, Freedom from Distractibility/Working Memory, and Processing Speed. Full Scale IQ scores can be obtained on all three measures, but similar to developmental composites, the variability across cognitive profiles in ASD often renders a generalized IQ score uninterpretable. When significant discrepancies are observed between Index scores and/or subtest scores, then it is recommended that when reporting the Full Scale IQ, clinicians provide a cautionary statement about making generalizations based on this overall score.

Although few cognitive instruments have direct measures of motor skills, many subtests involve a motor component. This needs to be recognized because many individuals with weak motor control perform poorly on certain cognitive tasks because of the motor demands rather than because they lack the skill (e.g., doing poorly on Block Design on a Wechsler scale because of fine motor impairments and not because of visual perception difficulties). This highlights the necessity for clinicians to make qualitative observations during testing to ensure that appropriate qualifications are made to the interpretation of findings.

Other commonly used measures of cognition include the *Stanford-Binet Intelligence Scales, Fifth Edition* (SB5; Roid, 2003), the *Differential Ability Scales, Second Edition* (DAS-II; Elliott, 2007), the *Kaufman Assessment Battery for Children, Second Edition* (KABC-II; Kaufman & Kaufman, 2004), the *Kaufman Adolescent and Adult Intelligence Test* (KAIT; Kaufman

DON'T FORGET

Given the variability observed within cognitive profiles, composite IQ scores (e.g., Full Scale IQ) are often less meaningful than an individual's profile of subtest scores. When significant discrepancies are observed between composite and/ or subtest scores, then a cautionary statement should be made about interpreting overall scores.

& Kaufman, 1993), and the *Woodcock-Johnson Tests of Cognitive Abilities, Third Edition* (WJ-III; Woodcock, McGrew, & Mather, 2001). Each measure has its important place in the assessment of abilities of individuals with ASD, although verbal and conceptual demands of all instruments can be obstacles in the successful administration of comprehensive batteries for many individuals across the spectrum, particularly the lower-functioning ones.

The DAS-II is unique in the field of cognitive tests in that the theoretical focus is on distinct subtest scores that elucidate profiles of cognitive strengths and weaknesses rather than an overall intelligence quotient or estimation of "g." The abilities that the DAS-II subtests assess are directly related to educational needs at each age range, which are useful in translating results into educational and treatment recommendations.

One benefit of the DAS-II over the more commonly used Wechsler scales is the inclusion of teaching items. Frequently, individuals with ASD are unable to complete a cognitive task not because of a lack of ability, but rather because of an inability to comprehend the standardized instructions. Thus, when an examiner is able to model and teach the task over successive items, as well as correct initial erroneous responses, individuals can better comprehend the task objective. Another benefit of the DAS-II is that both the Early Years and School-Age batteries have extended norms so that older,

≡ *Rapid Reference 2.4*

The *Differential Ability Scales, Second Edition,* has many benefits for use with individuals with ASD. These include:
- Teaching items that allow for modeling task objectives and for correcting errors
- Extended norms for both the Early Years and School-Age batteries
- Alternative stopping points

lower-functioning individuals and younger, higher-functioning individuals can be assessed using subtests that more appropriately match their capabilities. For instance, the Early Years battery has extended norms through age eight, and the School-Age battery has extended norms down to age five. Finally, the DAS-II offers alternative stopping points so that an examiner can choose to end a subtest either by reaching a ceiling point or by completing a set number of items. This alleviates frustration that often arises with designated ceiling rules.

≡ *Rapid Reference 2.5*

School-Age and Adult Cognitive Measures

Comprehensive Batteries
- *Wechsler Intelligence Scale for Children, Fourth Edition* (WISC-IV; Wechsler, 2003)
- *Wechsler Adult Intelligence Scale, Fourth Edition* (WAIS-IV; Wechsler, 2008)
- *Differential Ability Scales, Second Edition* (DAS-II; Elliott, 2007)
- *Kaufman Assessment Battery for Children, Second Edition* (KABC-II; Kaufman & Kaufman, 2004)
- *Kaufman Adolescent and Adult Intelligence Test* (KAIT; Kaufman & Kaufman, 1993)
- *Stanford-Binet Intelligence Scales, Fifth Edition* (SB5; Roid, 2003)

- *Woodcock-Johnson Tests of Cognitive Abilities, Third Edition* (WJ-III; Woodcock, McGrew, & Mather, 2001)

Measures of Nonverbal Intelligence
- *Leiter International Performance Scale, Revised* (Roid & Miller, 1997)
- *Test of Nonverbal Intelligence, Fourth Edition* (TONI-4; Brown, Sherbenou, & Johnsen, 2010)
- *Universal Nonverbal Intelligence Test* (UNIT; Bracken & McCallum, 1998)

The most research on cognitive profiles in ASD has been conducted using the Wechsler scales. Common Wechsler profiles across the autism spectrum include lower Freedom from Distractibility and Processing Speed Index scores compared to Verbal Comprehension and Perceptual Organization Index scores. Within the Verbal Comprehension domain, it is not surprising that Comprehension is often the lowest subtest score (e.g., Mayes & Calhoun, 2003), given that it measures social reasoning and problem solving. Comprehension scores typically fall significantly below scores on more rote verbal subtests, such as Information and Similarities. Information is often an area of relative strength, as it measures rote knowledge for information that never changes (e.g., identifying categorical relationships). Individuals with ASD can be extremely concrete and thus gravitate to learning and remembering rote facts. Similarities is a verbal association task (e.g., identifying categorical relationships), which is also a strength for individuals with ASD, as deductions can be made without requiring conceptual integration of multiple pieces of information, as is

DON'T FORGET

On the Wechsler scales, individuals with ASD tend to have a relative weakness on the Comprehension subtest, which measures the ability to solve common social problems. In contrast, they tend to fare well on rote verbal tasks, such as Information, which assesses for factual knowledge, and Similarities, which requires making rote associations between words.

the case on Word Reasoning. In Asperger syndrome, Vocabulary can be a relative strength, given the proneness to verbosity and focus on verbal details; in fact, when testing individuals with Asperger syndrome, it is not uncommon for clinicians to receive textbook definitions for words, including all varying meanings.

Within the Perceptual Reasoning index, scores can vary depending on the individual's profile. Matrix Reasoning and Block Design tend to be among the highest scores in prototypical autism, where parts-to-whole pattern completion and pattern construction are areas of strength. However, in Asperger syndrome, visual perception and visual-motor integration can be quite challenging, resulting in Block Design being a relatively lower score.

Scores within the Working Memory or Freedom from Distractibility indices vary according to the individual's personal strengths and weaknesses in recalling verbal information. Rote verbal memory skills can be relatively strong in ASD, resulting in higher scores on the Digit Span, Forward subtest than, for example, Digit Span, Backward or Arithmetic. However, if working memory skills are impoverished, then clinicians need to specifically look at Digit Span, Backward, Arithmetic, and Letter-Number Sequencing (LNS). A note of caution about LNS: the verbal instructions for LNS are extraordinarily cumbersome and often result in clinicians having to abort the subtest altogether, not because of an individual's poor memory skills but because of the language demands associated with comprehending the unwieldy instructions. In these instances, the Arithmetic subtest can be substituted. Scores on Arithmetic are more associated with relative math abilities, but they can certainly be negatively impacted by poor working

> ### CAUTION
> ....
> The verbal instructions for Letter-Number Sequencing are extremely cumbersome and can often result in failure to obtain an accurate basal, not because of an individual with ASD's impoverished working memory skills, but because of ASD-related deficits in verbal comprehension. When this is the case, the Arithmetic subtest is often substituted for LNS.

memory and auditory processing skills. Thus, qualitative observations become informative for all subtests within these indices. For instance, if an individual asks for a pencil and paper to "write out" an arithmetic problem, or uses their finger to "write" either on the table or in the air, then they are relying upon compensatory visual strategies to help problem-solve.

Interestingly, the Processing Speed index tends to be the lowest overall index of Wechsler profiles in ASD, with Coding being the lowest subtest across profiles of cognition—often even below Comprehension (Mayes & Calhoun, 2003). There could be individual differences as to why this might be the case, but it likely has to do with a combination of limited visual-motor skills coupled with a poor sense of the concept of time. Both Coding and Symbol Search require independently performing a task with speed and accuracy during a two-minute time constraint. Individuals with ASD are often extremely accurate in their performance across both tasks, but they pay little attention to the time constraint. Repeatedly instructing them to "work as quickly as you can" holds little meaningful value, resulting in the individual with ASD often becoming distracted and losing sight of the task objective. Moreover, given the graphomotor nature of the Coding task—having to recreate small symbols within boxes—individuals with perseverative tendencies can also become stuck on retracing and perfecting their writing rather than attending to the true task

CAUTION

Do not assume that low scores on Coding and Symbol Search automatically imply poor processing speed. It is often the case that individuals with ASD have limited awareness of time concepts and subsequently do poorly on timed tasks on which they are required to work independently (i.e., comprehending and following the instruction, "work as quickly as you can"). It is often *not* the case that their speed of processing is "slow." It is therefore important that clinicians make qualitative observations of task performance in order to parcel out and appropriately interpret areas of true vulnerability.

at hand. In these cases, when the Cancellation subtest is administered or substituted, this score is often higher than both Coding and Symbol Search, as the graphomotor and visual-motor integration demands are removed, with the focus being purely on visual scanning. With the time constraint on Cancellation being only 45 seconds, individuals also have less time to become distracted and veer off task.

Table 2.2 outlines common profiles of subtest scores on the WISC-IV observed in what is described as prototypical autism compared to Asperger syndrome. The term "sample" is used to reiterate that even within prototypical cases, there is always individual variation—there are no "norms" to represent a collective whole. Due to the vast differences in scores between individuals with and without cognitive impairment, two comparative samples for autism are provided.

Table 2.2. Common WISC-IV Profiles in Autism Versus Asperger Syndrome

	Prototypical Autism *With* Intellectual Disability (Sample)	Prototypical Autism *Without* Intellectual Disability (Sample)	Asperger Syndrome (Sample)
Verbal Comprehension			
Similarities	3	12	17
Vocabulary	2	10	18
Comprehension	1	7	11
Information	5	13	18
Perceptual Reasoning			
Block Design	6	13	9
Picture Concepts	5	12	10
Matrix Reasoning	8	16	12

Working Memory

Digit Span	3	10	15
Letter-Number Sequencing	—	8	13
Arithmetic	2	10	10

Processing Speed

Coding	1	6	7
Symbol Search	2	9	10
Cancellation	5	12	10

Scores denote scaled scores that have a mean of 10 and standard deviation of 3.

Less information is known about profiles of performance in ASD on other cognitive measures. One study using the original *Differential Ability Scales* (first edition) found greater gaps between verbal and nonverbal skills in ASD compared to a normative sample, with nonverbal skills being stronger and with more significant social impairments observed in individuals with ASD as the gap widened (Joseph, Tager-Flusberg, & Lord, 2002). In looking at specific subtypes of ASD, typical autism profiles tend to show higher nonverbal skills compared to verbal skills, with the opposite being true for Asperger syndrome (e.g., Klin, Volkmar, Sparrow, Cicchetti, & Rourke, 1995). However, clinicians are cautioned against making diagnostic inferences based solely on cognitive profiles.

Given the pervasive language impairments observed across the spectrum, clinicians often choose to administer a nonverbal test of intelligence to

CAUTION

Clinicians should avoid making diagnostic inferences based solely on cognitive profiles. For instance, if Verbal Comprehension scores are significantly greater than Perceptual Reasoning scores, this information alone does not indicate Asperger syndrome, and vice versa for autism.

CAUTION

Measures of nonverbal intelligence used in isolation can grossly overestimate an individual's true level of functioning, highlighting the need to assess a broad range of skills to fully understand an individual's profile of strengths *and* weaknesses.

estimate an individual's level of cognitive ability in the absence of language demands, such as the *Leiter International Performance Scale, Revised* (Roid & Miller, 1997), the *Test of Nonverbal Intelligence, Fourth Edition* (TONI-4; Brown, Sherbenou, & Johnsen, 2010), and the *Universal Nonverbal Intelligence Test* (UNIT; Bracken & McCallum, 1998). The subtests of these measures involve conceptual matching and visual reasoning skills, such as sequencing, pattern completion, figure-ground identification, and perceptual rotation. Individuals with ASD often do relatively well on these types of tasks; that is, in comparison to their more impoverished language and verbal reasoning abilities, these visual processing skills tend to be areas of relative strength. Caution should be taken, therefore, in interpreting results from nonverbal intelligence tests in isolation, particularly if generalizations are then made to the individual's broader level of functioning. This can have devastating real-life consequences if, for example, an individual is misplaced into an academic setting where the level of expectations far exceed the individual's true ability to successfully meet those demands.

NEUROPSYCHOLOGICAL ASSESSMENTS

Given the complex profiles in many individuals with ASD, comprehensive neuropsychological assessments are often quite helpful in illustrating the individual's complete profile of strengths and weaknesses. A comprehensive neuropsychological evaluation for ASD usually consists of tests measuring the following domains: sensorimotor, attention, memory, language, visual-spatial processing, executive functioning, and problem solving.

Several neuropsychological batteries are available for testing a broad range of skills. The *NEPSY, Second Edition,* for example, includes domains such as memory and learning (verbal and visual), language, sensory motor, and visual-spatial processing. The *Wechsler Intelligence Scales for Children, Fourth Edition, Integrated* (WISC-IV, Integrated; Kaplan, Fein, Kramer, Delis, & Morris, 2004), the *Luria-Nebraska,* and the *Halstead-Reitan* are also comprehensive batteries that assess a range of processes. Such batteries have common normative data across the various subtests, making comparisons among scores on varied processes more valid. Other widely used neuropsychological measures include the *California Verbal Learning Test* (CVLT; Delis, Kramer, Kaplan, & Ober, 2000) (verbal memory), *Wechsler Memory Scales* (verbal and visual memory), the *Rey-Osterreith Complex Figure* (Osterreith & Rey, 1944) (visual memory), *Continuous Performance Tests* (e.g., *Conners' Continuous Performance Test, Second Edition;* Conners, 2004) for sustained attention and inhibition, pegboards (e.g., *Purdue Pegboard*) for motor dexterity and control, and the *Beery-Buktenika Tests of Visual-Motor Integration* (VMI).

The VMI can be a useful measure for elucidating the visual-perception versus visual-motor integration questions that arise in the cognitive testing. For instance, as described previously, a WISC profile often shows relatively low Coding and Block Design scores, but the clinician's qualitative observations suggest that the low scores are more reflective of poor visual-motor than visual-processing abilities. The VMI has three subtests—the overall Visual-Motor Integration as well as Visual Perception and Motor Coordination. If an individual's score on Motor Coordination is significantly lower than that on Visual Perception, then the clinician's judgments were accurate. This is often the profile

DON'T FORGET

The Visual Perception and Motor Coordination subtests of the *Beery Buktenika Tests of Visual Motor Integration* can add useful information to the Visual-Motor Integration subtest in that visual perception skills can be highly discrepant from graphomotor abilities in many individuals with ASD.

observed in individuals with Asperger syndrome who have a corresponding Nonverbal Learning Disability profile (described in more detail in Chapter 7).

Executive functioning is also a crucial construct to consider when evaluating individuals with ASD. Executive functioning skills regulate and control more basic abilities and behaviors, and they are highly related to adaptive or independent living skills in individuals with ASD (Gilotty et al., 2002). Behaviors falling under the umbrella of executive functioning skills include organization, planning, emotional control, inhibition, flexibility, self-monitoring, and working memory.

A variety of measures are available to assess executive functioning skills directly, including the *Wisconsin Card Sorting Test* (Heaton, 1981), the *Delis-Kaplan Executive Functioning System* (Delis, Edith, & Kramer, 2001), and subtests from the *NEPSY-II* (Korkman, Kirk, & Kemp, 2007). These measures assess sustained attention, inhibition, concept formation, flexibility, and planning. The *Behavior Rating Inventory of*

≡ *Rapid Reference 2.6*

....

Neuropsychological Measures

- *Behavior Rating Inventory of Executive Functioning* (BRIEF; Gioia, Isquith, Guy, & Kenworthy, 2000)
- *Delis-Kaplan Executive Functioning System* (D-KEFS; Delis, Edith, & Kramer, 2001)
- *NEPSY-II* (Korkman, Kirk, & Kemp, 2007)
- *Rey Osterreith Complex Figure Test* (Rey-O; Osterreith & Rey, 1944)
- *California Verbal Learning Test (CVLT)* (Delis, Kramer, Kaplan, & Ober, 2000)
- *Continuous Performance Test (CPT)* (Conners, 2004)
- *Wisconsin Card Sorting Test (WCST)* (Heaton, 1981)
- *Wechsler Intelligence Scale for Children, Integrated* (Kaplan, Fein, Kramer, Delis, & Morris, 2004)

Executive Functioning (BRIEF; Gioia, Isquith, Guy, & Kenworthy, 2000) is a parent- and teacher-report instrument for children ages 6 to 18 (with a preschool edition for children ages 4 and 5), which includes items related to a variety of exec-

> # DON'T FORGET
>
> When conducting neuropsychological evaluations on individuals with ASD:
> - Provide frequent breaks
> - Alternate easy and more difficult tasks
> - Praise effort

utive functions and provides a wide breadth of information related to an individual's daily functioning. Additionally, measures of complex learning, such as the *Rey Osterreith Complex Figure* and CVLT, as listed previously, can be informative regarding an individual's practical application of executive functioning skills. For example, the CVLT, a list-learning task, provides information about a person's ability to organize and plan an approach to learning as well as to utilize efficient metacognitive strategies.

Importantly, neuropsychological assessments are comprehensive by nature, and as such, the testing tends to be quite lengthy. Therefore, when conducting neuropsychological assessments with individuals with ASD, it is important to provide frequent breaks (even if the test taker does not specifically request one), alternate easy and more difficult tasks, and provide the individual with regular praise for his or her effort.

QUALITATIVE OBSERVATIONS

The qualitative aspects of an individual's processing style are just as important to consider as standard scores on tests. Observing how an individual can self-regulate and self-advocate in the face of task demands is essential to understanding how this individual can benefit from instruction in intervention. Therefore, it is imperative to evaluate how well the individual can tolerate task demands, contingencies, mistakes, level of difficulty, sustain attention and shift focus between tasks, and how efficiently one can perform tasks.

≡ *Rapid Reference 2.7*

Important Qualitative Observations of Performance

- Self-regulation and frustration tolerance
- Self-monitoring ("Oops, I made a mistake!")
- Self-evaluation ("This is hard/easy!")
- Self-advocacy ("I need a break," "Could you repeat that?," "I don't know")
- Level of attention to tasks
- Ability to follow contingencies (First do this, then get this)
- Flexibility in response
- Response inhibition
- Perseveration (getting stuck on a task objective; repeating a response)
- Inefficiency (taking more steps than necessary to complete task)

Another significant aspect of the evaluation is the assessment of basic learning readiness skills, such as the individual's ability to sit, attend, follow adult instruction, and imitate the actions of others. Without these fundamental skills, it is not only challenging to successfully administer a standardized assessment, but the results rendered would be difficult to interpret meaningfully. Moreover, an individual's ability to learn new skills is greatly compromised if these rudimentary building blocks are absent.

≡ *Rapid Reference 2.8*

Learning Readiness Skills

- **Sitting** (ability to sit and tolerate adult-led activities)
- **Attention** (ability to focus on and tolerate adult-led activities)
- **Follow Instructions** (ability to follow adult-led activities)
- **Imitation** (ability to model another person's behavior/speech)

Tips to aid in the assessment of a individual who is lacking in learning-readiness skills are to provide clear rules and expectations for testing (e.g., a written/visual schedule); to establish a "ready-response" (e.g., "Look at me"; "Ready?"; "Sit nicely"); and to establish first-then contingencies (e.g., "First watch me, then you do it"; "My turn; Your turn").

> **DON'T FORGET**
> ....
> Qualitative/behavioral observations are just as important as quantitative scores!

In the event that an individual is unable to complete any portion of the standardized assessment battery, whether because of limited learning-readiness skills or interfering behaviors, clinicians should qualify scores in the report signifying that they may, in fact, be an underrepresentation of the individual's true abilities. Recommendations can then be made to address these skills and behaviors in intervention and then to reassess the individual's abilities after learning readiness skills have been established.

SUMMARY

A diagnostic evaluation of individuals with ASD is virtually impossible without having an understanding of the cognitive or developmental profile of that individual. It is the norm rather than the exception that profiles of skills will be extremely varied, with significant strengths and weaknesses observed across areas of development regardless of overall level of functioning. Common profiles include strengths in rote verbal and visual reasoning, with weaknesses in social cognition, conceptual reasoning, and often motor processing. Obtaining qualitative observations of performance is just as important as obtaining standard scores, because a host of aberrant behaviors can negatively impact an individual's ability to demonstrate his or her repertoire of skills. Limited learning-readiness skills are an example, such as limitations in sitting, attending to adult instruction, and imitating the actions of others. These skills are necessary for individuals to learn from others and their environment. If they are absent or impaired, there can be significant impacts on learning.

Choosing the appropriate measure for assessing skills is also essential. Many individuals with ASD, because of their social communication weaknesses, have difficulty comprehending task directives in the absence of models or demonstrations. For this reason, the *Differential Ability Scales, Second Edition* (Elliott, 2007), is often the cognitive measure of choice, as subtests include teaching items. Nevertheless, the Wechsler Scales (e.g., WISC-IV; Wechsler, 2003, and WAIS-IV; Wechsler, 2008) are the most common measures of cognition and offer extremely comprehensive score profiles if an individual is capable of tolerating the language demands of the tasks and instructions. Caution is given to using measures of nonverbal intelligence in isolation, as they offer only a snapshot of visual processing skills, which are often areas of strength in ASD.

Although not necessarily indicated for every individual with ASD, neuropsychological assessments offer extensive information on executive functioning, memory, sensorimotor processing, and attention that basic measures of cognition do not assess. Many individuals with ASD struggle with higher-order cognitive skills, including the ability to solve problems, plan ahead, integrate multiple sources of information effectively, and attend to salient details in the context of competing information. Neuropsychological assessments can clarify these vulnerabilities that often significantly impede an individual with ASD's ability to navigate not only an academic environment but a social one as well.

REFERENCES

Bayley, N. (2005). *Bayley Scales of Infant and Toddler Development, Third Edition (Bayley-III)*. San Antonio, TX: Pearson.

Bracken, B. A., & McCallum, R. S. (1998). *Universal Nonverbal Intelligence Test (UNIT)*. Rolling Meadows, IL: Riverside.

Brown, L., Sherbenou, R., & Johnsen, S. K. (2010). *Test of Non-Verbal Intelligence, Fourth Edition (TONI-4)*. San Antonio, TX: Pearson.

Chawarska, K., Klin, A., Paul, R., Macari, S., & Volkmar, F. (2009). A prospective study of toddlers with ASD: Short-term diagnostic and cognitive outcomes. *Journal of Child Psychology and Psychiatry, 50*(10), 1235–1245.

Conners, C. K. (2004). *Conners' Continuous Performance Test II Version 5 (CPT-II Version 5)*. San Antonio, TX: Pearson.

Delis, D. C., Edith, K., & Kramer, J. H. (2001). *Delis-Kaplan Executive Functioning System (D-KEFS)*. San Antonio, TX: Pearson.

Delis, D. C., Kramer, J. H., Kaplan, E., & Ober, B. A. (2000). *California Verbal Learning Test, Second Edition (CVLT-II)*. San Antonio, TX: Pearson.

Elliott, C. (2007). *Differential Ability Scales, Second Edition (DAS-II)*. San Antonio, TX: Pearson.

Gilotty, L., Kenworthy, L., Sirian, L., Black, D. O., & Wagner, A. E. (2002). Adaptive skills and executive function in autism spectrum disorders. *Child Neuropsychology, 8*(4), 241–248.

Gioia, G. A., Isquith, P. K., Guy, S. C., & Kenworthy, L. (2000). *Behavior Rating Inventory of Executive Functioning (BRIEF)*. Lutz, FL: Psychological Assessment Resources.

Heaton, R. K. (1981). *The Wisconsin Card Sorting Test Manual (WCST)*. Odessa, FL: Psychological Assessment Resources.

Joseph, R. M., Tager-Flusberg, H., & Lord, C. (2002). Cognitive profiles and social-communicative functioning in children with autism spectrum disorder. *Journal of Child Psychology and Psychiatry, 43*(6), 807–821.

Kaplan, E., Fein, D., Kramer, J., Delis, D., & Morris, R. (2004). *Wechsler Intelligence Scale for Children, Fourth Edition Integrated (WISC-IV Integrated)*. San Antonio, TX: Pearson.

Kaufman, A. S., & Kaufman, N. L. (1993). *Kaufman Adolescent and Adult Intelligence Test (KAIT)*. Circle Pines, MN: American Guidance Service.

Kaufman, A. S., & Kaufman, N. L. (2004). *Kaufman Assessment Battery for Children, Second Edition (KABC-II)*. Circle Pines, MN: American Guidance Service.

Klin, A., Saulnier, C., Chawarska, K., & Volkmar, F. R. (2008). Case studies of infants first evaluated in the second year of life. In K. Chawarska, A. Klin, & F. R. Volkmar (Eds.), *Autism spectrum disorders in infants and toddlers* (pp. 141–169). New York, NY: Guilford Press.

Klin, A., Volkmar, F., Sparrow, S. S., Cicchetti, D. V., & Rourke, B. P. (1995). Validity and neuropsychological characterization of Asperger syndrome: Convergence with Nonverbal Learning Disabilities Syndrome. *Journal of Child Psychology and Psychiatry, 36*(7), 1127–1140.

Korkman, M., Kirk, U., & Kemp, S. (2007). *NEPSY, Second Edition (NEPSY-II)*. San Antonio, TX: Pearson.

Mayes, S. D., & Calhoun, S. L. (2003). Ability profiles in children with autism: Influence of age and IQ. *Autism, 7*(1), 65–80.

McGrew, K. S. (2005). The Catell-Horn-Carroll theory of cognitive abilities: Past, present, and future. In D. P. Flanagan & P. L. Harrison (Eds.), *Contemporary intellectual assessment: Theories, tests, and issues.* New York, NY: Guilford Press.

Mullen, E. (1995). *Mullen Scales of Early Learning.* Circle Pines, MN: American Guidance Service.

Osterreith, P., & Rey, A. (1944). Le test de copie d'une figure complexe (The test of copying a complex figure). *Archives de Psychologie, 30,* 206–356.

Roid, G. (2003). *Stanford Binet Intelligence Scale, Fifth Edition.* Rolling Meadows, IL: Riverside.

Roid, G. H., & Miller, L. J. (1997). *Leiter International Performance Scale Revised (Leiter-R).* Wood Dale, IL: Stoelting.

Wechsler, D. (2002). *Wechsler Preschool and Primary Scale of Intelligence, Third Edition (WPPSI-III).* San Antonio, TX: Pearson.

Wechsler, D. (2003). *Wechsler Intelligence Scale for Children, Fourth Edition (WISC-IV).* San Antonio, TX: Psychological Corporation.

Wechsler, D. (2008). *Wechsler Adult Intelligence Scale, Fourth Edition (WAIS-IV).* San Antonio, TX: Pearson.

Woodcock, R. W., McGrew, K. S., & Mather, N. (2001). *Woodcock-Johnson III Tests of Cognitive Abilities (WJ-III).* Itasca, IL: Riverside.

🏹 TEST YOURSELF 🏹

1. **Fine and gross motor skills can be assessed on which of the following measures?**

   (a) Wechsler Intelligence Scale for Children, Fourth Edition

   (b) Behavior Rating Inventory of Executive Functioning

   (c) Mullen Scales of Early Learning

   (d) Leiter International Performance Scale, Revised

2. **If the verbal limitations of a child with ASD prohibit the use of a broad cognitive battery, then choosing a nonverbal measure of cognitive ability is sufficient for an assessment.**
   True or False?

3. **It is the norm rather than the exception to see a great deal of scatter among an individual with ASD's cognitive profile.**
   True or False?

4. **Common factors that impede an individual with ASD's test performance include which of the following?:**

    (a) Novel testing environment

    (b) Limited language skills

    (c) Lack of sleep

    (d) All of the above

5. **The Differential Ability Scales, Second Edition, yields an overall intelligence quotient.**
   True or False?

6. **Learning readiness skills include all of the following except?**

    (a) Vocalizing

    (b) Sitting

    (c) Attending

    (d) Imitation

7. **An example of an effective self-advocacy skill often absent in individuals with autism includes which of the following?**

    (a) Saying, "This is fun!"

    (b) Saying, "I don't know"

    (c) Tantruming

    (d) Complying with a task

8. **Qualitative observations are just as important to consider as standard scores when conceptualizing an individual with ASD's presentation.**
   True or False?

9. **Which of the following measures is parent report?**

    (a) Wisconsin Card Sorting Test

    (b) Leiter International Performance Scale, Revised

    (c) Mullen Scales of Early Learning

    (d) Behavior Rating Inventory of Executive Functioning

10. **Clinicians should avoid making diagnostic inferences based on cognitive profiles.**
   True or False?

Answers: 1. c; 2. False; 3. True; 4. d; 5. False; 6. a; 7. b; 8. True; 9. d; 10. True

Three

SPEECH, LANGUAGE, AND COMMUNICATION ASSESSMENT

Leah Booth, MA, CCC-SLP, Contributor

A s with developmental and cognitive profiles, communication skills vary tremendously across individuals with ASD. Age, level of functioning, and context need to be considered when evaluating speech, language, and communication skills; thus, careful attention must be given to selecting appropriate measures, as well as to the behavioral and qualitative aspects of an individual's presentation, in order to address specific areas of need accordingly. This includes obtaining information on prelinguistic, early linguistic, and advanced language abilities in standardized form, as well as in naturalistic contexts such as the home, community, and school environments (Paul, 2005).

With ASDs being detected increasingly earlier in development, the communication evaluation plays a critical role in the diagnostic differentiation of ASD from non-ASD conditions such as significant developmental delays and cognitive impairment, speech and language disorders, medical conditions that impact speech development, and language delays that might otherwise resolve in development. Thus, it becomes essential for clinicians to understand typical speech, language, and communication profiles and then thoroughly assess for the nuances of speech, language, and communication issues specific to

ASD. The atypicalities include, but are not limited to, atypical speech development such as echolalia; scripted speech; idiosyncratic and made-up speech (i.e., neologisms); pedantic or overly formal language; pronoun reversal; atypical prosody and intonation; limited gesture use and/or presence of hand-over-hand gestures; difficulty sustaining a conversational topic not of one's own designation; and difficulty developing narratives in order to share interpersonal experiences.

≡ *Rapid Reference 3.1*

Aspects of Speech, Language, and Communication Skills

Language Form
- Receptive language (comprehension and responsivity to language)
- Expressive language (vocabulary and language use)
- Syntax (morphology, grammar, sentence structure)
- Articulation (phonetics, intelligibility)
- Prosody (rate, volume, tone, inflection of speech)

Nonverbal Communication
- Facial expressions
- Gestures
- Joint attention
- Integration of eye gaze
- Shared affect

Social-Pragmatic Language
- Social use of language
- Imitation
- Using language to regulate behavior
- Requesting/protesting/choosing
- Perspective taking/theory of mind

Conversational Language
- Turn-taking
- Initiating, sustaining, and appropriately ending an exchange

- Topic recognition and maintenance
- Provisions/requests for background information
- Use/response to questions

Nonliteral Language
- Making inferences
- Understanding idioms/figures of speech/sarcasm
- Understanding metaphors and multiple meanings
- Understanding irony and humor

≡ *Rapid Reference 3.2*

....

Atypical Communicative Behaviors Observed in ASD

- **Echolalia** (immediate repetition of words/phrases/sentences)
- **Scripted speech/delayed echolalia** (reciting previously heard speech, videos, movies)
- **Neologisms** (made-up words)
- **Idiosyncratic speech** (using odd words)
- **Pedantic speech** (professorial speech; advanced for developmental/ mental age)
- **Pronoun reversal/confusion** (mixing up I/you; use of name in third person)
- **Atypical intonation/prosody** (sing-song, high-pitched, monotone, restricted voice)
- **Atypical fluency** (jerky and stammered speech, unusually rapid/slow speech)
- **Hand-over-hand gesture** (using another person's hand as a tool to do something; leading/guiding another person by the hand without integrated gaze)
- **One-sided conversational exchange** (talking "at" rather than "with" a conversational partner)
- **Topic control** (inability to converse or play on a topic not of one's own designation)

CAUTION

Many individuals with ASD can perform in the average range on standardized language measures but still have significant deficits in social communication.

DON'T FORGET

There is an important difference between being able to use and understand words and being able to use language as a tool for effectively communicating with others.

A comprehensive diagnostic evaluation for individuals with ASD is best conducted by a speech-language pathologist to assess communication skills. As is the case with any thorough language evaluation, a range of standardized and informal measures, coupled with observation and record review, are necessary components for evaluating the language of a person with ASD. It is important to note, however, that for the individual with ASD, the speech-language pathologist will need to place particular emphasis on evaluating the individual's social-communication skills for adaptive functioning in real-life contexts. Many people with ASDs perform in the average range or better for standardized language measures; nevertheless, these same individuals may have functional communication skills that are significantly impaired.

In approaching the comprehensive communication assessment for individuals with ASD, the speech-language pathologist will want to consider three primary areas:

1. Receptive language
2. Expressive language
3. Pragmatic language or social communication

RECEPTIVE LANGUAGE

In general terms, receptive language refers to one's ability to understand heard words, phrases, sentences, and conversational language. Evaluation of receptive language will include assessment of a person's abilities to attend to and accurately interpret language. For example, the *Clinical Evaluation of Language Fundamentals-4* (*CELF-4*) may be used to assess an understanding of grammar and word meaning in sentences, directions, and narrative paragraphs. Additionally,

> **CAUTION**
>
> Clinicians should be careful not to confuse strong rote expressive and receptive language skills with the ability to use and understand complex social and conversational language.

when assessing individuals with ASD, the speech-language pathologist must persistently consider the difference between "listening to" and truly "understanding" heard information. Many individuals on the autism spectrum present with echolalia, meaning they accurately repeat strings of heard language that are either drawn from the immediate conversation or are recalled from the past. This ability to "echo" language does not consistently reflect an equal ability to *understand* complex heard information. An individual with ASD may achieve solidly average standard scores for standardized measures of receptive language while simultaneously struggling to accurately interpret and respond to basic *conversational* language.

It is generally the norm that expressive language is stronger than receptive language in autism; that is, use of language tends to be stronger than comprehension of or attention to language. However, in some individuals with ASD, the ability to understand language can surpass the ability to produce words and sentences. Therefore, the speech-language pathologist will want to carefully consider all methods of expression demonstrated by the individual. Some children will speak to express understanding. Others may use sounds, gestures, eye contact, signs, pictures, or augmentative devices. Whatever the method of expression, it is important to document what the individual understands and how this understanding translates to functional social-communicative interactions with other people.

As mentioned previously, standardized language assessments play a role in the evaluation of individuals with ASD. Additionally, the speech-language pathologist will want to employ direct interaction

DON'T FORGET

For individuals with ASDs, the ability to "echo" or repeat long strings of heard information does not necessarily reflect an equal ability to understand conversational language.

and observation to assess what types of heard language the person understands and how this information supports social interactions in context. For example, how the individual responds to the following:

- Environmental sounds
- His or her name
- Greetings and farewells
- Rote social questions (e.g., "How are you?")
- Choices
- Contextual *one-* and *multi-*step directions
- Concrete and abstract yes/no questions
- Concrete and abstract *wh-* questions
- Conversational comments
- Abstract or figurative language

EXPRESSIVE LANGUAGE

Broadly speaking, expressive language refers to the ability to produce words and sentences in order to convey meaning to others. In addition to spoken language, expression may include use of nonverbal signals such as eye contact, body language, sign language, pictures, and augmentative devices. As is the case with receptive language, for individuals with ASD, evaluation of expressive language goes beyond administration of standardized measures. In addition to evaluating syntactic (i.e., grammar) and semantic (i.e., word meaning/vocabulary) skills, the speech-language pathologist will need to assess *contextual* and *social* language use. Included here is the ability to formulate meaningful narratives in order to share stories and ideas with others. Many individuals with ASD will achieve average and above-standard scores for structured tests measuring expressive grammar and vocabulary, but these same people will struggle to use language as a tool for effectively interacting with others.

Many individuals with ASDs produce echolalia or repeat language heard in either the immediate context or in the past. In addition to evaluating the use

of generative or novel language, the speech-language pathologist will want to assess if echoed speech serves a functional purpose for the person with ASD. In some instances, individuals will repeat the last words heard as a method for sustaining a conversation. For example, a child might say, "play outside" in response to the question, "Do you want to play outside?" Here, the repetition of the last words heard can serve as a functional means for getting wants and needs met. In other cases, verbal echolalia takes the form of a stream of ongoing verbal "scripting" that is without purposeful function. For example, a child who is overwhelmed by classroom expectations may continuously repeat all dialogue from a favorite cartoon in order to tune out confusing language, social interactions, and activities.

When assessing expressive language, the speech-language pathologist must keep *intent* at the forefront of his or her mind. That is, ask "Does this person use language to regulate others' behavior?" Fundamentally, words and sentences serve as tools for getting others to help us get what we want and need. Individuals with ASD may be able to "talk," while simultaneously struggling to effectively request, choose, inquire, decline, protest, and so forth.

It is worth noting that in the absence of an ability to effectively use spoken words, many children with ASD use behavior as a means to communicate. Rather than asking, "May I have a cookie, please?" a child on the spectrum might use an open-handed reaching gesture to indicate he wants the cookies on the top shelf. In more extreme examples, a child might grab, hit, dart, or tantrum to indicate his wants

DON'T FORGET

....

Behavior Is Communication:
Some individuals will use
unconventional methods of
expression (e.g., grab, reach, pull, lead,
hit, dart/run, avoidance, self-injury,
tantrum, etc.) to convey their wants
and needs. These methods may be
neither functional nor adaptive, but
they nevertheless are communicative.
Ask yourself: "What is this person
trying to tell us? How could I help this
person to express the same need in a
more adaptive way?"

and needs. While these physical methods of expression are not particularly adaptive or functional, they nevertheless serve as clear expressions of preference. In evaluating the individual with ASD, the speech-language pathologist needs to continuously recognize that *behavior is communication*. With this in mind, it will be possible to document what behaviors are used and the functions they serve, so that a plan can be developed for teaching the individual more functional methods for self-expression.

When assessing the expressive language of a person on the autism spectrum, the speech-language pathologist will want to identify and document any and all attempts made to convey wants and needs. In addition to spontaneous word production, look for the following:

- Nonspeech sounds (e.g., shrieks)
- Speech sounds
- Eye contact
- Facial expressions
- Body movement, position, location
- Sign language
- Conventional gestures (point, wave)
- Descriptive gestures (i.e., pantomime)
- Pictures
- Augmentative devices
- Echolalia—immediate, delayed, functional, nonfunctional
- Directed imitation
- Spontaneous phrases, sentences, narrative, conversation

PRAGMATIC LANGUAGE/SOCIAL COMMUNICATION

Individuals with ASD struggle with a primary social disability that, to varying degrees, can negatively impact meaningful reciprocal interactions with others. Many of these individuals are quite capable of producing and understanding concrete spoken language, but they struggle with the nuances that are essential components of social interactions. In particular, attention and response to nonverbal cues, such as eye contact, facial expressions, body language, and gestures, may be impaired. Also, interpretation of abstract or nonliteral language (e.g., slang, colloquialisms, metaphor, idioms, irony, humor) may be compromised. These individuals are often prone to difficulty using language as a tool for establishing shared meaning and interpersonal connections with others. They may "talk over" or "talk at" a conversational partner; offer too much information; inaccurately assume that a listener has background knowledge; or fail to respond to comments and questions. They also often experience difficulty using narrative language as a tool for conveying personal stories. Perspective-taking—or the idea that others' thoughts and feelings may be different from one's own—is difficult as well, resulting in misunderstanding and miscommunications.

While some standardized measures are available to help assess pragmatic and abstract language skills (see standardized measures), assessment of pragmatic language and social communication requires a skilled clinician who recognizes the need for direct, unstructured interaction with the client. When assessing very young, nonverbal, or low-functioning individuals, a play session involving motivating toys and/or gross motor activities will support assessment of contextual social-communication skills. Cause-effect toys (e.g., bubbles, balloons, pop-ups, wind-ups, ball towers, music toys, spinners/tops) and gross motor activities (e.g., swing, trampoline, slide, ball pit, scooter) are often very popular and may be used as tools to draw a child into an interaction.

In working with these individuals, it may be necessary to create an environment with pronounced external structure to help clarify

DON'T FORGET

In addition to standardized measures, assessment of pragmatic language and social-communication skills requires direct play and/or unstructured conversation with the client.

expectations. Pictures schedules, timers, designated seating, limited access to materials, timed intervals for activities, and the involvement of a second adult may be necessary to support the child's participation in assessment activities. Certainly, information regarding an individual's response to such structure is important and should be documented. Many individuals with ASD struggle to sustain social interactions without support; however, given external structure, their abilities to initiate and sustain social-communicative interactions increase and may expand. Documenting this information is crucial as it offers a solid starting point for intervention.

STAGES OF LANGUAGE DEVELOPMENT

Prelinguistic Stage

For infants and toddlers with or at risk for ASD, as well as for older individuals with ASD who have a very limited or absent language repertoire, prelinguistic skills can be evaluated. Again, both quantitative and qualitative information need to be gathered on the child's

≡ Rapid Reference 3.3

Prelinguistic Behaviors Predictive of Later Speech

- Joint attention
- Imitation (verbal and motor)
- Rate of language acquisition
- Responsivity to language
- Use of eye gaze to communicate
- Range of communicative gestures

means of communication (e.g., quality of vocalizations and nonverbal means), communicative functions, frequency of communication, symbolic behaviors, joint attention, reciprocity, and responsivity to language. Furthermore, behavioral observations can offer information about the child's learning-readiness skills (e.g., frustration tolerance, ability to follow adult-led instructions), which are important to address when making treatment recommendations following the assessment.

In observing the very young, nonverbal, or low-functioning individual, the speech-language pathologist will want to consider factors such as:

- How does the child interact with familiar adults?
- How does the child respond to new adults?
- Does the child attempt to regulate adults in his or her environment?
- Is the child able to accept new people and routines?
- Does the child imitate?
- Does the child respond to his or her name?
- Does the child follow basic directions?
- Does the child participate in reciprocal routines?
- Does the child follow a turn-taking routine?
- Does the child participate in activities not of his or her own designation?
- Does the child spontaneously use and imitate spoken words?
- Do structure and predictability have a positive impact on the child's ability to use new skills and expand on current skills?
- Does the child have "learn to learn" skills (e.g., hands back, sit, look, listen)?
- Does the child maintain shared attention?
- Does the child know how to wait?
- Does the child respond to visual information?

Linguistic Stage

For individuals with more advanced linguistic skills, comprehensive communication measures can be administered. Comprehensive batteries include subtests that evaluate language form, structure, syntax, nonverbal communication, responsivity to language, pragmatic language, prosody, conversational skills, and metalinguistic skills—all of which are important to assess in individuals with ASD (Klin, Sparrow, Marans, Carter, & Volkmar, 2000). Yet, just as higher-functioning individuals with ASD can produce adequate to advanced scores on cognitive measures, they can also perform well on communication assessments, including subtests assessing theory of mind (e.g., DELV, NEPSY-II). For this reason, qualitative observations, parent and teacher report, and measures of adaptive communication (e.g., Vineland Communication and Socialization subdomains—described in detail in Chapter 4) are just as important as standardized measures to the assessment process. Additionally, conversation regarding age-appropriate topics or topics of preferred interest will serve for assessment of these skills. For this population, the speech-language pathologist will want to document the presence and quality of skills such as the following:

- Reciprocity
- Eye gaze/eye contact
- Turn-taking
- Prosody, intonation, vocal intensity
- Response to nonverbal signals
- Use of nonverbal language to regulate others' behavior (e.g., to choose, request, decline, protest, etc.)
- Use of verbal language to regulate others' behavior
- Use of language to inquire and to comment
- Topic maintenance
- Provision of background information, clarification, details
- Topic shifting
- Integration of relevant facts, past information, new information
- Understanding of abstract/figurative language
- Perspective-taking
- Inferencing, predicting, drawing conclusions, problem-solving

≡ Rapid Reference 3.4

Measures of Prelinguistic and Basic Linguistic Skills
- *Bayley Scales of Infant Development, Third Edition* (Bayley-III; Bayley, 2005)
- *Clinical Evaluation of Language Fundamentals, Preschool, Second Edition* (CELF-P-2; Semel, Wiig, & Secord, 2004)
- *Communication and Symbolic Behavior Scales* (CSBS; Wetherby & Prizant, 2001)
- *Communication Development Inventory* (CDI; Fenson et al., 1993)
- *Mullen Scales of Early Learning* (Mullen, 1995)
- *Preschool Language Scale, Fifth Edition* (PLS-5; Zimmerman, Steiner, & Pond, 2011)
- *Reynell Developmental Language Scales* (RDLS; Reynell & Gruber, 1990)

Measures of Advanced Language Skills
- *Clinical Evaluation of Language Fundamentals, Fourth Edition* (CELF-4; Semel, Wiig, & Secord, 2003)
- *Comprehensive Assessment of Spoken Language* (CASL; Carrow-Woolfolk, 1999)

Measures of Metalinguistic Skills
- *Diagnostic Evaluation of Language Variation* (DELV; Seymour, Roeper, & Villiers, 2005)
- *Test of Language Competence* (TLC; Wiig & Secord, 1989)
- *Test of Narrative Language* (TNL; Gilliam & Pearson, 2004)
- *Comprehensive Assessment of Spoken Language* (CASL; Carrow-Woolfolk, 1999)

- Narrative construction to relay information, to share understanding, to build a conversation, to share and interpret ideas, perspectives, feelings

FORMULATION OF FINDINGS

The formulation of the speech, language, and communication test results becomes a critical aspect of the overall diagnostic formulation. First and foremost, there is the identification of specific language

Table 3.1. Standardized Measures to Assess Communication Skills in Persons with ASDs

Communication and Symbolic Behavior Scales (CSBS; Wetherby & Prizant, 2001)
- For functional communication between ages 6 months and 24 months
- Examines frequency, means, and range of communicative intent using toys and interactions to gain information regarding:
  - Emotion and eye gaze
  - Communication
  - Gestures
  - Sounds
  - Words
  - Understanding
  - Object use

Peabody Picture Vocabulary Test (PPVT-4; Dunn & Dunn, 2007)
- Normed for ages 2 years, 6 months through 90+ years
- Measures single-word receptive semantic (i.e., vocabulary) skills
- Closed field of four pictures; child has to find one in four that matches target word
- This score will not necessarily reflect the child's ability to interpret the meaning of integrated language.
- Children on the spectrum tend to have strong labeling skills, particularly for nouns (i.e., words to label "things") as "things" are concrete and thus predictable.

Clinical Evaluation of Language Fundamentals Preschool, 2nd edition (CELF Preschool-2; Semel, Wiig, & Secord, 2004)
- Normed for ages 3 to 6 years
- Overview of receptive syntactic and semantic skills
- Overview of expressive syntactic and semantic skills
- Keep in mind these tasks are closed-ended and many subtests include pictures. A child's performance on standardized testing will not necessarily reflect his or her abilities for integrated social conversations.
- A child on the spectrum may "talk" conversationally, but his or her language does not have true meaning.
- Useful to give specific information regarding amounts and types of information the child understands (i.e., abilities with words, word groups, word problems, phrases, sentences, heard narratives)
- Specific information regarding type of language the child is capable of using: single words, phrases, sentences

Table 3.1. Continued

- Offers specific information about syntactic usage (many children on the spectrum will struggle with pronouns or will be better with nouns than with verbs.)
- May use this to obtain discrepancy between receptive and expressive language.
- May use to identify areas of relative strength and weakness within receptive or expressive skills (i.e., he can answer factual questions regarding narratives, but has more trouble with inferencing).
- May use this to obtain age-equivalents in children who are chronologically beyond norms but for whom you want some qualitative information about level of understanding.

Clinical Evaluation of Language Fundamentals, 4th edition (CELF-4; Semel, Wiig, & Secord, 2003)

- Normed for ages 5 to 21 years
- Overview of receptive syntactic and semantic skills
- Overview of expressive syntactic and semantic skills
- Keep in mind these tasks are closed-ended and many subtests include pictures. A child's performance on standardized testing will not necessarily reflect his or her abilities for integrated social conversations.
- A child on the spectrum may "talk" conversationally, but his or her language does not have true meaning.
- Useful to give specific information regarding amounts and types of information the child understands (i.e., abilities with words, word groups, word problems, phrases, sentences, heard narratives)
- Specific information regarding type of language the child is capable of using: single words, phrases, sentences
- Offers specific information about syntactic usage (many children on the spectrum will struggle with pronouns or will be better with nouns than with verbs.)
- May use this to obtain discrepancy between receptive and expressive language.
- May use to identify areas of relative strength and weakness within receptive or expressive skills (i.e., he can answer factual questions regarding narratives, but has more trouble with inferencing).

Test of Narrative Language (TNL; Gilliam & Pearson, 2004)

- Normed for ages 5 years to 11 years, 11 months
- Offers standard scores for Narrative Comprehension and Oral Narration

(*continued*)

Table 3.1. Continued

- Narrative Comprehension subtests require individuals to attend to narrative sequences and short stories in order to answer both factual and inferential questions regarding characters and plot.
- Oral Narration subtests require individuals to retell heard sequences; to generate a narrative that would logically accompany a given five-picture sequence; and to generate a narrative in response to a single stimulus picture depicting a number of characters and events.

Comprehensive Assessment of Spoken Language (CASL; Carrow-Woolfolk, 1999)

- Normed for ages 3 to 21 years
- Comprehensive language battery assesses comprehension, expression, and retrieval of spoken language in the areas of Lexical/Semantic Tests, Syntactic Tests, Supralinguistic Tests, and Pragmatic Tests
- Specifically offers information regarding an individual's ability to:
  - Understand nonliteral spoken language, such as indirect questions, figurative language, and sarcasm
  - Infer meaning of an unknown word from an oral linguistic context
  - Infer meaning using world knowledge when the information needed for responding is not available in the oral text provided
  - Recognize ambiguity in spoken sentences and to verbalize the source of ambiguity
  - Express a specific communicative intent
  - Recognize appropriate topics for conversation
  - Select relevant information in order to give directions and make requests
  - Initiate conversations and describe the importance of turn-taking routines
  - Adjust the communication level to situational factors

Expressive Vocabulary Test (EVT; Williams, 2007)

- Normed for ages 2 years, 6 months to 90+ years
- Measures single-word expressive vocabulary skills
- Some children on the spectrum will be better at using nouns to label objects than they will be at using verbs to label actions
- Children on the spectrum may struggle to identify the whole rather than the parts (e.g., say "a horse" rather than "a herd")

Table 3.1. Continued

Test of Language Competence—Expanded Edition
(TLC-E; Wiig & Secord, 1989)

- Normed for ages 1 year, 5 months to 9 years, 11 months (Level 1) and 10 to 18 years (Level 2)
- Looks at abilities to make inferences and analyze figurative language in response to picture and auditory stimuli
- Offers a good tool for assessing underlying social-language weaknesses in a child whose "concrete" language skills are average and above
- Because this measure requires understanding of abstract and figurative language and multiple meanings, many children on the spectrum will struggle with it even after doing well on the *CELF-4*

impairments within the individual's profile apart from autism symptomatology (e.g., Receptive, Expressive, and Mixed Language Disorders; Developmental Apraxia; articulation and oral-motor impairments). Second, the evaluation outlines the social communication profile of the individual—what strengths and vulnerabilities exist above and beyond basic speech and language skills. Finally, there is the integration of these results with the other aspects of a diagnostic evaluation so as to determine if the social communication and language impairments evidenced are characteristic of ASD or the manifestation of a non-ASD developmental disorder.

SUMMARY

A comprehensive speech-language evaluation plays a critical role in autism assessment. As children are being referred for diagnostic evaluations at younger ages, the communication evaluation is often crucial for differential diagnosis. Additionally, individuals with ASD present with a multitude of unusual qualities to their language, such as profound deficits in receptive and expressive language, echolalia, scripted language, and syntactical errors. Some children with ASD also exhibit a highly unusual pattern of language development, where their expressive language skills surpass their receptive skills. This pattern can be problematic, as those interacting with the children often assume that the children are understanding at the same level that they are speaking, leading to confusion, noncompliance, and possibly other maladaptive behaviors.

In addition to the delays and deviancies in core receptive and expressive language development, by definition, individuals with ASD have deficits in pragmatic language, or the social use of language. Pragmatic skills include nonverbal communication (e.g., eye contact and gestures), body positioning, conversational topic maintenance, appreciation of one's listener's perspective, and prosody and intonation. Therefore, careful attention must be taken when assessing language and communication skills in ASD, and a comprehensive speech-language assessment is needed to obtain a full picture of an individual's skills. Common language batteries include the *Communication and Symbolic Behavior Scales* (CSBS; Wetherby & Prizant, 2001), the *Communication Development Inventory* (CDI; Fenson et al., 1993), the *Clinical Evaluation of Language Fundamentals, Fourth Edition* (CELF-4; Semel, Wiig, & Secord, 2003), and the *Comprehensive Assessment of Spoken Language* (CASL; Carrow-Woolfolk, 1999).

REFERENCES

Bayley, N. (2005). *Bayley Scales of Infant and Toddler Development, Third Edition (Bayley-III)*. San Antonio, TX: Pearson.

Carrow-Woolfolk, E. (1999). *Comprehensive Assessment of Spoken Language (CASL)*. Circle Pines, MN: American Guidance Services.

Dunn, L. M., & Dunn, D. M. (2007). *Peabody Picture Vocabulary Test, Fourth Edition (PPVT-4)*. San Antonio, TX: Pearson.

Fenson, L., Dale, P. S., Reznick, J. S., Thal, D., Bates, E., Hartung, J. P., Pethick, S., & Reilly, J. S. (1993). *The MacArthur Communicative Development Inventories: User's guide and technical manual (CDI)*. San Diego, CA: Singular.

Gilliam, R. B., & Pearson, N.A. (2004). *Test of Narrative Language*. Austin, TX: Pro-ed.

Klin, A., Sparrow, S. S., Marans, W. D., Carter, A., & Volkmar, F. R. (2000). Assessment issues in children and adolescents with Asperger syndrome. In A. Klin, F. R. Volkmar, & S. S. Sparrow (Eds.), *Asperger syndrome* (pp. 309–339). New York, NY: Guilford Press.

Mullen, E. (1995). *Mullen Scales of Early Learning*. Circle Pines, MN: American Guidance Service.

Paul, R. (2005). Assessing communication in autism spectrum disorders. In F. R. Volkmar, R. Paul, A. Klin, & D. Cohen (Eds.), *Handbook of autism and pervasive developmental disorders* (3rd ed., pp. 799–816). Hoboken, NJ: Wiley.

Reynell, J. K., & Gruber, C. P. (1990). *Reynell Developmental Language Scales (RDLS)*. Torrance, CA: Western Psychological Services.

Semel, E., Wiig, E., & Secord, W. A. (2003). *Clinical Evaluation of Language Fundamentals, Fourth Edition (CELF-4)*. San Antonio, TX: Pearson.

Semel, E., Wiig, E. H., & Secord, W. A. (2004). *Clinical Evaluation of Language Fundamentals, Preschool, Second Edition (CELF-Preschool 2)*. San Antonio, TX: Pearson.

Seymour, H. N., Roeper, T. W., & Villiers, J. (2005). *Diagnostic Evaluation of Language Variation (DELV)*. San Antonio, TX: Pearson.

Wetherby, A., & Prizant, B. (2001). *Communication and Symbolic Behavior Scales Developmental Profile, Preliminary Normed Edition (CSBS)*. Baltimore, MD: Paul H. Brookes.

Wiig, E. H., & Secord, W. (1989). *Test of Language Competence, Expanded Edition (TLC-Expanded)*. San Antonio, TX: Pearson.

Williams, K.T. (2007). *Expressive Vocabulary Test (EVT)*. San Antonio, TX: Pearson.

Zimmerman, I. L., Steiner, V. G., & Pond, R. E. (2011). *Preschool Language Scales, Fifth Edition (PLS-5)*. San Antonio, TX: Pearson.

🦎 TEST YOURSELF 🦎

1. **In ASD, individuals' core language skills are on par with their ability to effectively communicate with others. True or False?**

2. **What are the three areas a speech-language pathologist should consider in an autism assessment?**

3. **Define:**
   Receptive language
   Expressive language
   Pragmatic language

4. **Echolalia refers to:**
   (a) Social communication
   (b) Repeating previously heard information
   (c) Nonsensical sounds
   (d) Prosody

5. **What does the phrase "Behavior is communication" mean? How is it important in an autism assessment?**

6. **An expressive language assessment only measures an individual's spoken language.**
   True or False?

7. **Describe examples of ways the clinician can provide external structure to the assessment session in order to facilitate the child's participation and clarify expectations.**

8. **What are some pragmatic skills the clinician needs to consider when evaluating younger or low-functioning children?**

9. **What are some pragmatic skills the clinician needs to consider when evaluating older or high-functioning children?**

10. **Name four instruments appropriate for assessing language and communication skills in children on the autism spectrum.**

Answers: 1. False; 2. Receptive language, expressive language, pragmatic language; 3. Receptive language: the ability to understand heard words, phrases, sentences, and conversational language; Expressive language: the ability to produce words and sentences in order to convey meaning to others; Pragmatic language: social use of language, including nonverbal communication, conversational skills, taking the perspective of one's conversational partner, and nonliteral language.; 4. b; 5. Refer to p. 45–46; 6. False: Expressive language includes both spoken and nonverbal communication; 7. Pictures schedules, visual timers, designated seating, limited access to materials, timed intervals for activities. The assistance of a second adult may be helpful as well.; 8. Imitate words and actions, respond to language, initiate interactions, participate in social routines, maintain shared attention; participate in adult-led activities. Refer to p. 48–49 for additional examples.; 9. Turn-taking, eye contact, prosody, topic maintenance, topic shifting, perspective-taking, inferencing, nonliteral language. Refer to p. 50–51 for additional examples.; 10. Examples include: Communication and Symbolic Behavior Scales (CSBS); Peabody Picture Vocabulary Test (PPVT-4); Clinical Evaluation of Language Fundamentals Preschool, 2nd edition (CELF Preschool-2); Clinical Evaluation of Language Fundamentals, 4th edition (CELF-4); Test of Narrative Language (TNL); Comprehensive Assessment of Spoken Language (CASL); Expressive Vocabulary Test (EVT); and Test of Language Competence—Expanded Edition (TLC-E).

Four

ASSESSMENT OF BEHAVIORAL PROFILES

Understanding an individual's behavioral profile is just as important as determining developmental, language, and cognitive profiles. Many individuals with autism present with aberrant or maladaptive behaviors that although not specific to autism symptomatology, can negatively impact social, communication, and behavioral functioning, as well as mask an individual's true range of skills. These typically include externalizing behaviors (e.g., aggression, self-injury, impulsivity, hyperactivity, explosive behavior, tantruming), internalizing behaviors (e.g., anxiety, depression, passivity), and atypical behaviors. Additionally, an individual might be perfectly capable of performing tasks on a standardized assessment in a highly structured and supportive setting, but is incapable of demonstrating these skills in naturalistic contexts that can be extraordinarily overwhelming to an individual on the spectrum. This is defined as having deficits in adaptive behavior, or functional skill application. For this reason, clinicians need to identify and assess which behaviors are most problematic and subsequently recommend how to minimize, eliminate, and/or replace them.

The following chapter focuses on various measures to assess and analyze externalizing, internalizing, and adaptive *behaviors*, rather than comorbid conditions, per se. The latter are described in greater detail in Chapter 7.

≡ Rapid Reference 4.1

Behaviors That Negatively Impact Learning

- Anxiety
- Inattention/distractibility
- Hyperactivity
- Impulsivity
- Behavioral dysregulation
- Difficulty transitioning to novel environments/people
- Difficulty tolerating task demands
- Limited language comprehension for complex instructions
- Limited motivation to perform
- Compulsive behaviors and rigidities
- Stereotypical motor mannerisms
- Limited imitation skills

STANDARDIZED ASSESSMENTS OF BEHAVIOR

There are many standardized assessments of behavior, with a sampling of measures listed in Table 4.1. Most of these measures can be administered through clinician observation and/or by parent/caregiver report. As is the case with measures of autism symptomatology (outlined in Chapters 5 and 6), these assessments should not be considered diagnostic in nature; that is, they should be administered as a means for identifying problematic behaviors to address in intervention and for gathering information to contribute to the diagnostic formulation.

When assessing for problematic behaviors in ASD, it is helpful if the clinician bears in mind that, as emphasized in Chapter 3, behavior is often an individual's means of communicating in the face of limited language and communication skills. A behavior should never be interpreted in isolation (e.g., treated with extinction merely to eliminate the unwanted or inappropriate behavior). Rather, by understanding

Table 4.1. Sample Measures to Assess Aberrant Behavior

1. *Aberrant Behavior Checklist* (ABC; Aman, Singh, Stewart, & Field, 1985)
2. *Beck Anxiety Inventory* (BAI; Beck, 1993)
3. *Beck Depression Inventory, Second Edition* (BDI-II; Beck, Steer, & Brown, 1996)
4. *Behavior Assessment Scale for Children, Second Edition* (BASC-2; Reynolds & Kamphaus, 2003)
5. *Brown Attention-Deficit Disorder Scales* (Brown, 2001)
6. *Child Behavior Checklist* (CBCL; Achenbach, 2001)
7. *Children's Depression Inventory, Second Edition* (CDI 2; Kovacs, 2010)
8. *Children's Yale-Brown Obsessive Compulsive Scale for Pervasive Developmental Disorders* (CYBOCS-PDD); Scahill et al., 2006)
9. *Conners, Third Edition* (Conners 3; Conners, 2008)

what triggers the behavior in question, as well as what serves to sustain it over time, appropriate modifications can be set into place to not only eliminate or decrease the undesired behavior, but also to introduce a more appropriate and functional means of communicating. This process of analysis is called functional behavior assessment.

FUNCTIONAL BEHAVIOR ASSESSMENT

The purpose of a functional behavior assessment (FBA) is to determine specific behaviors that need to be changed because of their disruptive nature and to develop a plan for modifying the specified behaviors. The FBA focuses both on reducing maladaptive behaviors, while also building appropriate replacement or compensatory skills. An FBA is typically conducted by a behavioral specialist, such as a Board Certified Behavior Analyst (BCBA) or a clinician skilled in the techniques of applied behavior analysis.

For an FBA, the clinician obtains the necessary information by consulting with relevant adults in the child's life, including the parents and school personnel. The child may behave differently in various settings, so it is important for the clinician to talk with a range of individuals. The clinician should ask the individuals about the behaviors they view as most problematic and in need of modification. Gathering information about the perceived purpose of the behaviors, where they occur, and their impact both on the child as well as on others, such as peers or teachers, is also indicated. Most importantly, the clinician needs to observe the child in the setting where the problematic behaviors occur.

The first step of an FBA is to identify specific behaviors that need to be targeted for change. Examples of behaviors targeted using an FBA in a child with ASD include:

- Decreased noncompliance
- Increased use of verbal expression
- Decreased stereotyped mannerisms
- Decreased aggressive behaviors

As part of identifying the behaviors, the clinician needs to specifically define them for the given child. For example:

- *Noncompliance* could be defined as refusal to follow a distinct verbal cue delivered by staff within 10 seconds of the directive.
- *Aggression to objects* could be defined as kicking, slamming, or shoving inanimate objects with the intent to cause disruption.

Once the behaviors have been identified and defined by the school staff and parents, the clinician can then assess the behaviors and the factors that contribute to their function.

When assessing behaviors, the clinician needs to consider the function of the behavior, and to do so, needs to consider the *antecedent* and *consequence* of the behavior. The antecedent is the situation immediately preceding the behavior. It can be related to a myriad of factors, including demands placed on the individual (e.g., a teacher tells a child to sit at the table and begin working), the individual's internal states (e.g., frustration), the immediate external environment (e.g., noisy hallway), or a combination of such factors. At times, the antecedent is not readily apparent and takes a thorough evaluation of the individual's functioning to determine the true antecedent. For

≡ *Rapid Reference 4.2*

Functional Behavior Assessment: A-B-C

- **Antecedent:** What triggers the behavior?
- **Behavior:** What is the target behavior?
- **Consequence:** What happens as a result of the behavior?

individuals with ASD, particularly with regards to noncompliance, the antecedent often appears to be a demand placed on the person, when in fact, that is only part of the antecedent. A more careful review of the individual's functioning and behavior reveals that their language is significantly impaired, and it is not that the person is demonstrating noncompliant behavior per se, but that there is a limited understanding of the task instructions and the necessary language to request help.

The clinician also needs to assess the consequence of the behavior, meaning the function of the individual's behavior or that which is reinforcing it. To do so, the clinician needs to observe specifically when the behavior occurs and what happens following the event or targeted behavior. For example, the individual may engage in a targeted behavior (e.g., whining) as a means to escape from a low-preference activity or direction. As another example, the individual may engage in a targeted behavior (e.g., aggression to objects), which serves the function of attention. The individual may exhibit this behavior when he or she perceives an adult to be ignoring his or her requests.

Importantly, for individuals with ASD, the function of the behavior may not be readily apparent and may seem counter to what clinicians/ teachers working with him or her may initially perceive. Specifically, time out of the classroom is commonly used as a negative punishment for maladaptive behavior, but this negative punishment may actually serve as negative reinforcement for the individual with ASD, who could be using behavior to avoid social interactions and/or demands within the classroom. Even the behavioral clinician conducting the FBA may need some time to determine the function of a behavior, and different strategies for reinforcing the behavior may need to be attempted to determine the exact consequence or function.

Based on the results from the FBA, as described, the clinician can precisely identify problematic behaviors, as well as the triggers for and function of them. The clinician can then utilize this information to develop a behavioral plan that reduces the frequency of the maladaptive behaviors and increases the frequency of adaptive ones.

DON'T FORGET

Identify the A-B-Cs of a functional behavior assessment:

1. *Antecedent:* What triggers the behavior in question?
2. *Behavior:* What is the behavior in question?
3. *Consequence:* What response(s) to the behavior serve to sustain the behavior over time?

ASSESSMENT OF ADAPTIVE BEHAVIOR

One of the most critical aspects of the diagnostic evaluation for individuals with ASD is the assessment of adaptive functioning. Adaptive behavior is best defined as "the performance of daily activities required for personal and social sufficiency" (Sparrow, Cicchetti, & Balla, 2005). These are skills that individuals should be performing

≡ *Rapid Reference 4.3*

Vocabulary of Behavior Change

- **Positive Reinforcement:** Goal—increase targeted behavior; Means—add contingent (e.g., take trash out, receive praise)
- **Negative Reinforcement:** Goal—increase targeted behavior; Means—remove contingent (e.g., take trash out, stop reminders)
- **Positive Punishment:** Goal—decrease targeted behavior; Means—add contingent (e.g., whining, assigned additional chore)
- **Negative Punishment:** Goal—decrease targeted behavior; Means—remove contingent (e.g., whining, remove preferred toy)

independently in their daily lives based on their level of ability. That is, adaptive behavior is what an individual *does* perform, day to day, as opposed to what he or

she is *capable* of performing. For example, if an individual is capable of speaking in sentences, but does not spontaneously do so, this is a deficit in that individual's adaptive communication. Unlike cognitive skills that are thought to stabilize in typical development within the school-age years, adaptive skills can change over time and are quite sensitive to external or environmental factors. These include direct intervention, environmental changes (e.g., moving, divorce), trauma, or developmental maturity. This sensitivity to change makes adaptive behavior extremely important to consider when tracking intervention progress, as well as treatment outcome. Furthermore, adaptive assessments can be repeated with more frequency than other standardized measures, as there is no practice effect.

Adaptive behavior has historically been included in the definition of intellectual disability (ID) in that deficits in self-sufficiency beyond cognitive impairment are required for a diagnosis of ID. The current criteria set forth in the *DSM-IV-TR* (APA, 2000) require at least two areas of deficit in adaptive functioning for what is still categorized as Mental Retardation, and some variation of these criteria will likely be retained in the criteria for ID in the forthcoming *DSM-5*. The qualitative difference that is often observed in the profile of an individual with ASD and comorbid ID is that the adaptive deficits are likely to be above and beyond those that would be expected given the cognitive impairment alone.

There are several measures of adaptive behavior (see Table 4.2), including the *Vineland Adaptive Behavior Scales, Second Edition* (Vineland II; Sparrow, Cicchetti,

Table 4.2. Comparison of Measures of Adaptive Functioning

The Vineland Adaptive Behavior Scales, Second Edition
(Vineland II; Sparrow, Cicchetti, & Balla, 2005)
- Birth to 90 years
- Approximately 45 to 60 minutes to administer interview
- Survey and expanded interview
- Parent/caregiver rating form
- Teacher rating form
- Eleven areas of adaptive behavior
- Four areas of maladaptive behavior

Adaptive Behavior Assessment System, Second Edition
(ABAS-II; Harrison & Oakland, 2003)
- Birth to 89 years
- Approximately 15 to 20 minutes for respondents to complete a checklist
- Infant/preschool form
- Adult form
- Teacher/daycare provider form
- Ten areas of adaptive behavior

Scales of Independent Behavior, Revised
(SIB-R; Bruininks, Woodcock, Weatherman, & Hill, 1996)
- Infancy to 80 years
- Approximately 45 to 60 minutes to complete full-scale interview
- Fourteen areas of adaptive behavior
- Eight areas of problem behavior

& Balla, 2005); the *Adaptive Behavior Assessment System, Second Edition* (ABAS-II; Harrison & Oakland, 2003); and the *Scales of Independent Behavior, Revised* (SIB-R; Bruininks, Woodcock, Weatherman, & Hill, 1996). All three measures assess adaptive functioning from birth through late adulthood, although there are certainly more items relevant to early development and adolescence across adaptive domains than there are for geriatric years.

The Vineland and Vineland II are the most widely used and researched measures of adaptive functioning in the field of autism, and include normative data standardized on individuals with ASD that were published for the original edition (Carter et al., 1998). Furthermore, adaptive behavior profiles are evident based on Vineland domain and subdomain scores. For instance, Daily Living skills tend to be an area of relative strength, Socialization skills are often the greatest area of weakness, and Communication skills tend to fall in between (e.g., Volkmar, Sparrow, Goudreau, & Cicchetti, 1987; Carter et al., 1998). Within domains, Written Communication scores are often higher than Receptive and Expressive Communication scores, as items within this subdomain assess knowledge of numbers, letters, reading, and writing—often areas of relative strength in ASD regardless of cognitive functioning. To the contrary, Interpersonal Socialization skills tend to be the lowest subdomain score across domains, exemplifying deficits in social communication and interaction.

The Vineland was developed as a semistructured interview with a parent or caretaker in order to promote an open-ended discussion about an individual that emphasizes what the individual does rather than does not do. This conversational approach leads to obtaining richer clinical information than would otherwise be obtained by more directive questioning. This process sets the Vineland apart from other scales, including the widely used ABAS-II, which is a parent/caretaker questionnaire rather than interview. For the Vineland II Survey Interview, items are scored on a 3-point scale: A score of 2 indicates the skill is usually performed without help or reminders; a score of 1 indicates that the skill is sometimes or partially performed without physical help; and a score of 0 indicates the skill is rarely or never performed. In ASD, many individuals can perform a skill with prompting (i.e., physical, verbal, or visual). When this is the case, a score of 1 is typically provided.

In ASD, adaptive skills have been found to fall significantly below cognitive ability, particularly for individuals on the

CAUTION

If an individual requires prompting to engage in a behavior, this should not score more than a "1" on the Vineland Survey Interview. A score of "2" should be reserved for complete independence in performing the behavior.

spectrum who do not have cognitive impairment (Klin et al., 2007; Perry, Flanagan, Dunn, & Freeman, 2009; Kanne et al., 2010). The widest gap is often observed between adaptive socialization skills and IQ. That is, higher-functioning individuals with ASD have difficulty applying their repertoire of skills (particularly social communication skills) to daily contexts in

DON'T FORGET

The gap between IQ and adaptive functioning appears to widen with age, particularly for more cognitively able individuals, indicating that the acquisition of new adaptive skills is not keeping pace with the acquisition of cognitive skills. Moreover, cognition is assumed to be more stable than adaptive behavior, though certainly changes in IQ are evident in ASD.

the absence of external supports. Historically, cognitively able individuals with ASD have been less likely to receive the same intensity of interventions as those individuals with comorbid intellectual disability. Yet, current research is showing that higher-functioning individuals are not achieving levels of independence into adulthood, and that adaptive behavior is actually a stronger predictor of outcome than IQ alone (Farley et al., 2009; Howlin, Goode, Hutton, & Rutter, 2004).

Current research is also highlighting the different profiles in adaptive functioning observed between individuals with ASD both with and without cognitive impairment. For instance, recent studies have shown that Vineland standard scores fall above IQ scores for cognitively impaired individuals, suggesting that lower-functioning individuals with ASD are potentially able to apply their capacity of skills to daily contexts (e.g., Perry et al., 2009; Kanne et al., 2010)—perhaps a manifestation of treatment on teaching daily life skills to very impaired individuals. Nevertheless, the gap between IQ and adaptive functioning appears to widen with age regardless of cognitive ability, suggesting that as individuals grow older, they are less able to acquire new functional skills at the same pace as their conceptual development (Klin et al., 2007; Szatmari, Bryson, Boyle, Streiner, & Duku, 2003). This research highlights the need for repeated evaluation of adaptive skills over time to best inform intervention practices. It also emphasizes the utility of using the Vineland as a measure of intervention outcome, especially because it is so sensitive to change.

DON'T FORGET

Adaptive behavior is very sensitive to change and can be impacted by external factors (e.g., environment, intervention, trauma).

≡ Rapid Reference 4.4

Vineland Adaptive Behavior Scales, Second Edition (Sparrow, Cicchetti, & Balla, 2005)

Communication: Ages birth to 90 years
- Receptive
- Expressive
- Written

Daily Living Skills: Ages birth to 90 years
- Personal
- Domestic
- Community

Socialization: Ages birth to 90 years
- Interpersonal relationships
- Play and leisure time
- Coping skills

Motor Skills: Ages birth to 6 years; adults 50 to 90 years
- Gross
- Fine

Maladaptive Behavior: Ages 3 to 90 years
- Internalizing
- Externalizing
- Other
- Maladaptive critical items

SUMMARY

Behavioral assessments are of the utmost importance for individuals with ASD. Both children and adults with ASD often present with numerous problematic and maladaptive behaviors, ranging from self-stimulatory behaviors to noncompliance, aggression, and self-injury. When an individual exhibits particularly difficult behaviors or ones that impact functioning, a functional behavioral assessment (FBA) is completed. The purpose of an FBA is to identify the antecedents and consequences for the given behavior and then develop a behavioral plan to decrease the behavior and replace it with a more adaptive one. Examples of assessment measures of aberrant behavior include the *Aberrant Behavior Checklist* (ABC; Aman et al., 1985); the *Conners, Third Edition* (Conners 3; Conners, 2008); and the *Child Behavior Checklist* (CBCL; Achenbach, 2001).

The importance of an adaptive behavior assessment in ASD cannot be overstated. Individuals with ASD almost ubiquitously have impaired adaptive functioning; their ability to function within the context of their daily life is significantly impaired relative to their cognitive capacity. Even cognitively able individuals, those with average to above-average intellectual capacity, often have substantial delays in adaptive skills. Adaptive behavior is a strong predictor of outcome, and current research is showing that higher-functioning individuals are not achieving levels of independence into adulthood, largely because of impaired adaptive skills. Common measures for assessing adaptive functioning include the *Vineland Adaptive Behavior Scales, Second Edition* (Vineland II; Sparrow et al., 2005); *Adaptive Behavior Assessment System, Second Edition* (ABAS-II; Harrison & Oakland, 2003); *Scales of Independent Behavior, Revised* (SIB-R; Bruininks et al., 1996). These measures provide standardized scores, comparing the individual's functioning to that of his or her same-aged peers, but they can also provide caregivers and service providers with discrete behaviors and skills that the individual should be completing independently based on age and cognitive ability. These identified behaviors can then be incorporated into the individual's treatment plan.

REFERENCES

Achenbach, T. M. (2001). *Manual for the Child Behavior Checklist*. Burlington: University of Vermont, Department of Psychiatry.

Aman, M. G., Singh, N. N., Stewart, A. W., & Field, C. J. (1985). The Aberrant Behavior Checklist: A behavior rating scale for the assessment of treatment effects. *American Journal of Mental Deficiency, 89*(5), 485–491.

American Psychiatric Association. (2000). *Diagnostic and statistical manual of mental disorders* (4th ed., text rev.). Washington, DC: Author.

Beck, A. T. (1993). *Beck Anxiety Inventory*. San Antonio, TX: Pearson.

Beck, A. T., Steer, R. A., & Brown, G. K. (1996). *Beck Depression Inventory, Second Edition*. San Antonio, TX: Psychological Corporation.

Brown, T. E. (2001). *Attention-Deficit Disorder Scales*. San Antonio, TX: Pearson.

Bruininks, R. H., Woodcock, R. W., Weatherman, R. F., & Hill, B. K. (1996). *Scales of Independent Behavior, Revised*. Rolling Meadows, IL: Riverside.

Carter, A. S., Volkmar, F. R., Sparrow, S. S., Wang, J., Lord, C., Dawson, G., . . . & Schopler, E. (1998). The Vineland Adaptive Behavior Scales: Supplementary norms for individuals with autism. *Journal of Autism and Developmental Disorders, 28*(4), 287–302.

Conners, C. K. (2008). *Conners Third Edition*. Torrance, CA: Western Psychological Services.

Farley, M. A., McMahon, W. M., Fombonne, E., Jenson, W. R., Miller, J., Gardner, M., & Coon, H. (2009). Twenty-year outcome for individuals with autism and average or near-average cognitive abilities. *Autism Research, 2*(2), 109–118.

Harrison, P., & Oakland, T. (2003). *Adaptive Behavior Assessment System, Second Edition*. San Antonio, TX: Pearson.

Howlin, P., Goode, S., Hutton, J., & Rutter, M. (2004). Adult outcome for children with autism. *Journal of Child Psychology and Psychiatry, 45*(2), 212–229.

Kanne, S. M., Gerber, A. J., Quirmbach, L. M., Sparrow, S. S., Cicchetti, D. V., & Saulnier, C. A. (2010). The role of adaptive behavior in autism spectrum disorders: Implications for functional outcome. *Journal of Autism and Developmental Disorders, 41*(8), 1007–1018.

Klin, A., Saulnier, C. A., Sparrow, S. S., Cicchetti, D. V., Volkmar, F. R., & Lord, C. (2007). Social and communication abilities and disabilities in higher functioning individuals with autism spectrum disorders: The Vineland and the ADOS. *Journal of Autism and Developmental Disorders, 37*(4), 748–759.

Kovacs, M. (2010). *Children's Depression Inventory, Second Edition*. North Tonawanda, NY: MHS.

Perry, A., Flanagan, H. E., Dunn, G., & Freeman, N. L. (2009). Brief report: The Vineland Adaptive Behavior Scales in young children with autism spectrum disorders at different cognitive levels. *Journal of Autism and Developmental Disorders, 39*(7), 1066–1078.

Reynolds, C. R., & Kamphaus, R. W. (2003). *Behavior assessment system for children, Second Edition*. San Antonio, TX: Pearson.

Scahill, L., McDougle, C. J., Williams, S. K., Dimitropoulos, A., Aman, M. G., McCracken, J. T., . . . & Vitiello, B. (2006). Children's Yale-Brown Obsessive Compulsive Scale Modified for Pervasive Developmental Disorders (CYBOCS-PDD). *Journal of American Academy of Child and Adolescent Psychiatry*, *45*(9), 1114–1123.

Sparrow, S. S., Cicchetti, D. V., & Balla, D. A. (2005). *Vineland Adaptive Behavior Scales, Second Edition*. San Antonio, TX: Pearson.

Szatmari, P., Bryson, S. E., Boyle, M. H., Streiner, D. L., & Duku, E. E. (2003). Predictors of outcome among high functioning children with autism and Asperger syndrome. *Journal of Child Psychology and Psychiatry*, *44*(4), 520–528.

Volkmar, F. R., Sparrow, S. S., Goudreau, D., & Cicchetti, D. V. (1987). Social deficits in autism: An operational approach using the Vineland Adaptive Behavior Scales. *Journal of the American Academy of Child & Adolescent Psychiatry*, *26*(2), 156–161.

🐦 TEST YOURSELF 🐦

I. A behavioral assessment is important because:

(a) Problematic behaviors negatively impact social communication functioning.

(b) Problematic behaviors negatively impact one's ability to function in the community.

(c) Behavioral functioning as a preschooler is related to adult outcome.

(d) Both A and B

2. Adaptive behavior is defined as:

3. Internalizing behaviors include _____ and _____, among others.

4. Externalizing behaviors include _____ and _____, among others.

5. A Functional Behavioral Assessment (FBA) is:

6. An FBA is typically conducted by:

(a) Teacher

(b) Parent

(c) BCBA

(d) Speech and language pathologist

7. In a behavioral assessment, A-B-C stands for: _____.

8. **Why is an FBA often an important component to an autism assessment?**

9. **Define:**

   positive reinforcement

   negative reinforcement

   positive punishment

   negative punishment

10. **Adaptive behaviors are skills an individual is capable of doing. True or False?**

11. **Why is an assessment of adaptive skills essential in autism assessment?**

12. **To meet criteria for a classification of intellectual disability, an individual needs to demonstrate significant deficits in what two areas?**

13. **Which is a stronger predictor of outcome in individuals with ASD? Cognitive ability or adaptive skills.**

14. **As an individual grows older, he or she is less likely to acquire functional skills at the pace of cognitive development. True or False?**

15. **Adaptive behavior is a static construct. True or False?**

16. **Name two measures of adaptive functioning.**

Answers: 1. d; 2. The performance of daily activities required for personal and social sufficiency; 3. Anxiety, sadness, withdrawal; 4. Aggression, self-injury, impulsivity, tantrums; 5. An FBA is a behavioral assessment used to determine specific behaviors that need to be changed due to their disruptive nature and to develop a plan for modifying the specified behaviors. The FBA focuses both on reducing maladaptive behaviors, while also building appropriate replacement or compensatory skills.; 6. c; 7. Antecedent-Behavior-Consequence; 8. Refer to p. 61–64; 9. Positive Reinforcement: Goal—increase targeted behavior; Means—add contingent   Negative Reinforcement: Goal—increase targeted behavior; Means—remove contingent   Positive Punishment: Goal—decrease targeted behavior; Means—add contingent   Negative Punishment: Goal—decrease targeted behavior; Means—add contingent; 10. False; 11. Refer to p. 64–68; 12. Cognition and adaptive skills; 13. Adaptive skills; 14. True; 15. False; 16. *Vineland Adaptive Behavior Scales, Second Edition* (Vineland II; Sparrow, Cicchetti, & Balla, 2005); *Scales of Independent Behavior, Revised* (SIB-R; Bruininks, Woodcock, Weatherman, & Hill, 1996); and *Adaptive Behavior Assessment System, Second Edition* (ABAS-II: Harrison & Oakland, 2003)

Five

CLINICAL INTERVIEW AND RECORD REVIEW

The assessment of autism symptomatology is multifaceted. It involves direct observations of and interactions with the individual who has or is at risk for ASD, as well as gathering extensive information from parents, caregivers, and outside providers/clinicians. It should be emphasized here that both the clinical assessment and the report from others (e.g., parents, caregivers, service providers, physicians, teachers) are equally valued and essential sources of information. In fact, it is necessary to integrate information from all of these sources in order to fully understand an individual's diagnostic profile. Thus, the assessment components described in the following two chapters should contribute equally to the diagnostic formulation.

The focus of this chapter is on obtaining detailed information on the individual's current presentation and early developmental history through a clinical interview with a parent or caregiver, record review of the child's assessment in educational settings and other clinical evaluations, and observation of the child in naturalistic settings, if possible. Note that clinicians from various disciplines can gather this information, given that they are

DON'T FORGET

Understanding the diagnostic picture of any individual involves the collection of information from multiple sources, including parents/caregivers, school providers, intervention providers, physicians, and so forth, in addition to the direct assessment of the individual.

knowledgeable of and have experience with developmental profiles of autism and related conditions.

CLINICAL INTERVIEW

Given that the majority of clinicians obtain historical information from a parent, the term "parent" will be used throughout this chapter, though representing any informant who takes on the role of primary caregiver (e.g., parent, family member, guardian) and who knows the individual well.

When conducting a clinical interview with a parent, open-ended questions work best because they allow the parent to provide the clinician with detailed descriptions of the child's behavior. This also helps to establish rapport. However, closed-ended questions can be helpful in getting more specific details, as needed.

A comprehensive diagnostic interview entails gathering the following information:

1. Presenting concerns
2. Developmental history
3. Medical history
4. Family history
5. Education and intervention history
6. Social and play development
7. Behavioral presentation

Presenting Concerns

Interviews typically begin with obtaining information regarding the presenting concerns of the individual. This information is generally at the forefront of parents' minds and the reason for seeking an evaluation. This often includes information directly relating to autism symptomatology, such as speech, language, and communication delays; atypical behaviors; restricted interests; and maladaptive social development. However, present-ing concerns can often be un-related to the diagnostic criteria and involve issues of safety, atyp-ical feeding or sleep patterns, academic problems, behavioral aggression or self-injury, or delays/deviance in daily living skills. These behaviors often mask autism symptomatology in that they can be more debilitating to the individual and the family's daily life. Clinicians need to be cognizant of this so as to avoid misdiagnoses such as disruptive behavior disorders, mood instability, or learning disabilities, where more often these behaviors are the result of the underlying social disability (refer to Chapter 4 for a discussion of conducting FBAs to assess functions of behavior).

When gathering information on presenting concerns, it is also important to inquire about the various contexts in which the concerning behaviors are noted (e.g., home, school, community) and to what extent these behaviors interfere with the child and family's ability to function on a daily basis. Individuals with ASD can present quite differently across contexts depending upon familiarity, structure, environmental stimuli, and complexity of demands. This emphasizes the need to collect information from a variety of informants across contexts.

Developmental History

The next step entails gathering information regarding the indi-vidual's early developmental history. Particular attention should be paid to ages when

CAUTION

Presenting concerns often include behavioral problems that are not indicative of autism diagnostic criteria on face value (e.g., sleep and eating disturbances; aggression; self-injury; and lack of safety awareness). Clinicians need to be cognizant of the fact that these behaviors can mask autism symptomatology and therefore should not be misinterpreted as, for example, disruptive behavior disorders in isolation of ASD.

DON'T FORGET

When inquiring about presenting concerns, ask about the contexts in which concerning behaviors are notable and to what extent they interfere with daily routines.

early developmental milestones were met (motor, language, social, and behavioral), such as when the child rolled over, sat without support, crawled, walked independently, babbled, spoke single words, and spoke in two-word phrases and simple sentences (see Rapid Reference 5.1). Information about the child's early social development includes pointing, social smiling, eye contact, and playing simple reciprocal games, such as peek-a-boo, as these skills are often delayed, inconsistent, or absent in young children with ASD. Information about the child's behavioral patterns includes toileting, sleep patterns, feeding patterns (including bottle/breast feeding), and behavioral regulation (e.g., aggressing, self-injury, tantruming/meltdowns).

As previously noted, a small percentage of children with ASD experience a plateau or regression in their development; that is, their skill acquisition appears to slow down and/or they actually lose previously acquired skills. This plateau or regression is often reported to occur between 12 and 24 months of age, when the emergence of autism symptomatology is most prominent. Therefore, clinicians need to inquire about any periods of time during which a change in presentation is reported to have occurred. Clinicians should also be knowledgeable of current research on the lack of associations between environmental factors and ASD (e.g., vaccines, mercury, or thimerisol) so as to assuage parental fears of causal relationships that are unfounded (e.g., Keelan & Wilson, 2011; Gupta, 2010; Offit, 2008, and Institute of Medicine Immunization Safety Review Committee, 2004).

CAUTION

Worldwide studies have shown no association between autism spectrum disorders and vaccines, mercury, or thimerisol. Clinicians need to be knowledgeable of this research base so as to best inform parents and assuage any fears of unfounded causal relationships between known environmental agents and ASD.

After gathering information about the developmental history, ask the parents when the first concerns about the child were raised and by whom (e.g., by the parents, pediatrician, daycare provider). Identify what

≡ Rapid Reference 5.1

Developmental Milestones

Motor Skills
- Rolling over
- Sitting without support
- Purposeful hand movements
- Walking independently

Language Skills
- Cooing
- Babbling
- First words
- Phrase speech
- Full-sentence speech

Socialization Skills
- Social smile
- Eye contact
- Joint attention
- Pointing to indicate interest
- Playing reciprocal games

Behavioral
- Feeding
- Sleep patterns
- Toileting
- Aggression
- Self-injury
- Tantruming/meltdowns

developmental factors the earliest concerns were in regards to, as well as what action was taken when concerns were raised. This can be a sensitive topic for parents, as there is often a gap between when the first concerns were raised and when the child was actually diagnosed and treated. Furthermore, many first-time parents have no normative reference with which to compare their child's development and, consequently, might not be aware of expected developmental milestones that were unmet. Therefore, be cognizant of these factors and empathic toward parents when discussing the topic of first concerns.

Medical History

In addition to developmental milestones, the clinician needs to collect information about any medical problems that may be related to the child's current presentation and could be informative with regards to differential or comorbid diagnoses. This includes asking about the mother's pregnancy, labor and delivery, any pre-, peri-, or postnatal complications, APGAR scores, oxygen deprivation at birth, jaundice, and if any postnatal procedures were conducted (e.g., oxygen, incubation, phototherapy). When a child is at risk for autism, it is also standard practice to inquire if the child has undergone any formal genetic testing, hearing testing, and if there has been any concern regarding seizure activity in the child, including staring spells.

When a child presents with delayed language skills, as many children with ASD do, clinicians should inquire about any history of otitis media with effusion (i.e., ear infections) that may account for, at least in part, the child's delayed language development. If the child's only hearing test was the one conducted at birth, it is standard practice to recommend a more current audiological assessment. If the child is unable to tolerate a behavioral hearing test, then an audiological brainstem response test may be indicted, which could require sedation.

CAUTION

Every child with language delays should have an audiological assessment to rule out potential hearing loss. If a child with ASD cannot tolerate a behavioral test, then an audiological brainstem response test may be indicated, which could require sedation.

Family History

Given the genetic risk factors in ASD, gathering information on family history is important. This begins with inquiring about any first, second, or third degree relatives that have been diagnosed with or suspected to have ASD or associated features (e.g., social vulnerabilities, social anxiety, speech delays, stereotypical behaviors, compulsions, tics, etc.). In addition, clinicians should gather information on other clinical conditions, such as developmental and cognitive delays, mood disorders, schizophrenia, or any known genetic syndromes. It can be helpful to conduct a formal pedigree as a platform for gathering this information.

Keep in mind that sensitive information collected about family history is not always appropriate to include in a written report, but can be extremely useful to the clinicians when formulating their diagnostic impressions, as well as when making recommendations for family support services. For instance, if a mother discloses having a mood disorder for which she is medicated and functioning well, there is no need to highlight this in the report. However, if the mother discloses that her depression prevents her from adequately caring for her child, this information can be relayed in the form of a recommendation for parent support services without stigmatizing the mother. Family history can also be included in the report without directly identifying a particular family member. For instance, statements can be broad (e.g., "Family history is significant for depression on the maternal side") rather than specific (e.g., " Family history is significant for autism in the

CAUTION

Sensitive information gathered during the family history does not necessarily need to be included in the written report unless there is a direct impact on the well being of the individual being evaluated. Even then, clinicians can avoid stigmatizing particular family members by including broad rather than specific statements about family history.

- **Good Example:** "Johnny's family history is significant for a sibling with autism and depression on the maternal side."
- **Bad Example:** "Johnny's **6-year-old** sister, Lisa, has autism and his mother, Jennifer, has Major Depressive Disorder and is treated with Zoloft."

older sister, Lisa, age 6"). Refer to Chapter 8 for samples of how historical information is provided in comprehensive written reports.

Education and Intervention History

History of education and/or intervention is also essential. Begin inquiring about any early intervention services, even if the individual is older, and whether the services were public, private, or both. Common services to inquire about include speech and language therapy, occupational therapy, physical therapy, developmental/play therapy, and behavioral interventions. For school-age children, in addition to the aforementioned services, inquire about any social skills interventions, such as groups, individualized services (e.g., one-on-one therapy; designated paraprofessional; consultation services). Also ask about any complementary and alternative methods of intervention, such as diets, animal therapy, medical procedures, supplements, and so forth, and to what degree the parents feel these interventions have been effective.

With regards to academics, the clinician needs information about the child's performance in each subject, especially any subjects that are particularly challenging or come more easily for the child, both presently and historically. Gathering as much information as possible on the child's strengths is just as informative as assessing the child's areas of weakness or vulnerability because areas of strength can be used to build upon more vulnerable skills. In ASD, challenging academic subjects tend to be those that require conceptualizing abstract information (e.g., mathematics, time concepts) and sequencing narratives and themes either verbally or in written form (i.e., reading comprehension, writing book reports, reporting on events). It is often

DON'T FORGET

Inquire about the child's areas of strengths and weaknesses in school. Topics of strength can often be used to build upon more vulnerable areas. Significant gaps between strengths and weaknesses should also be assessed.

≡ *Rapid Reference 5.2*

Areas of Academic Performance to Inquire About

- Understanding of time and math concepts
- Reading decoding versus reading comprehension skills
- Comprehending narratives, themes, and sequences of events
- Ability to make inferences and judgments from social and narrative contexts
- Ability to engage in a topic not of one's designation

the case that reading decoding skills far outweigh reading comprehension skills; that is, the child with ASD is better able to recognize letters and words compared to their ability to comprehend the meaning of what is read. As this discrepancy increases, the child is at risk for learning difficulties (see Chapter 7).

In addition to gathering this information from parent report, it is helpful to request a copy of the child's Individualized Education Program or Individualized Family Service Plan (i.e., IEP or IFSP), which contains the types and amounts of intervention services that the child is currently receiving, as well as the goals and objectives that are currently being worked on. Furthermore, IEPs and IFSPs provide an indication of progress made on each objective. If the clinician has these documents ahead of the interview, they can aid in the collection and clarification of information regarding educational programming (see the discussion later in this chapter).

Social and Play Development

Typically developing children, even beginning at less than

DON'T FORGET

Asking for a child's current and prior Individualized Education Program or Individualized Family Service Plan (IEP or IFSP) can be a helpful way of obtaining information about special education services.

one year of age, often enjoy watching other people, especially other children. This interest only intensifies as the child develops. Children with ASD are less likely to watch and observe others and are less interested in the behavior of others. However, it is important to keep in mind that there are wide and normal variations in temperament, with some children being outgoing and gregarious from a young age and others being more reserved and tentative, particularly in new situations.

After gathering information about the individual's early developmental history, it is necessary to probe for information on current social behavior. For toddlers and young children, the clinician can inquire about how the child interacts with familiar adults (e.g., family, caregivers, daycare providers), as well as other same-aged children (e.g., in daycare, parent-child groups, at birthday parties). Inquire about whether the child is interested and engages in reciprocal games, plays appropriately with toys, and tolerates other children in close proximity. Many children with ASD are more interested in the sensory aspects that toys can provide, such as spinning the wheels of cars, examining objects through peripheral vision, and lining up toys/objects, as opposed to playing functionally with the toys. Also, the capacity for abstract play begins in the second year of life, often around the child's second birthday. Typically developing children will feed dolls, pretend to make food, push cars along pretend roads, and so on, whereas children who have or are at risk for ASD tend to have delays in their capacity for symbolic and pretend play. Therefore, clinicians want to specifically ask about the quality of the child's play, with an emphasis on any emerging creative elements.

For school-age children, clinicians can inquire about the child's interest in peers, number of reciprocal friendships, opportunities for playdates and social outings, involvement in group/ recreational activities including

DON'T FORGET

There are wide and normal variations in temperament, with some children being outgoing and gregarious from a young age and other children being more reserved and tentative, particularly in new situations.

sports, and the nature of the child's particular hobbies or interests. When gathering this information, it can be helpful to inquire about the child's level of awareness of social challenges, if any. Also inquire about the child's social motivation—if the

DON'T FORGET
....
Individuals with ASD are often victims of bullying. Ask parents and the individual directly about any bullying, hurtful teasing, and/or victimization. Many states have anti-bullying laws.

child is motivated to engage with others or prefers to be alone. Some children with ASD are motivated to engage but do not know how to initiate or sustain an interaction, and other children show less interest in others. The degree of social motivation varies in ASD, as it does in typical development.

It is important to gain information about how a child engages as well. For example, does the child need a high level of structure from an adult to maintain an appropriate interaction with peers? Are there certain situations where the child does best in terms of engaging with peers? Does the child engage with others around only a limited range of topics? All of this is important information both for the diagnostic assessment as well as for informing intervention. It is also essential to ask the parent if the child has been teased or bullied at school, because bullying can be devastating to a child's sense of self and self-concept. Many states have anti-bullying laws to prevent bullying and protect victims. These resources should be made available to parents and school providers.

Behavioral Presentation

When conducting a parent interview, it is necessary to ask about any atypical and/or problematic behaviors that negatively impact the child and family's life. Beginning with the diagnostic criteria, it is important to inquire about both past and current behaviors that include the following: restricted interests; repetitive and perseverative behaviors (i.e., getting stuck on something and/or engaging in a behavior

DON'T FORGET

Don't forget to inquire about how much an individual with ASD's atypical behaviors interfere with a family's ability to function, and to what lengths family members must go in order to accommodate such behaviors. Parents can be especially forgiving of their child's behavior and, as a result, may not be as aware of the significant accommodations that they are, in fact, making.

repeatedly); sensory-oriented behaviors (e.g., seeking out sensory input, avoiding sensory input, visual peering out of peripheral vision); circumscribed interests (i.e., extreme topics of interest that become fixations); and stereotypical motor mannerisms (e.g., hand flapping, finger posturing, body rocking). The clinician should also ask about whether any of these behaviors interfere with the individual or family member's ability to function within an environment (e.g., Does the family go to great lengths to avoid potential meltdowns in order to accommodate the behavior?).

Many individuals with ASD have difficulty with flexibility and tend to be quite rigid in their thinking and behavior. Therefore, ask about any rituals, compulsive tendencies, or scripted patterns of behavior. For example, if the individual insists on saying phrases certain ways or insists that others say statements in the same way; insists on performing certain behaviors and actions in a routinized fashion and becomes upset if unable to do so; and if the individual has difficulties with changes in routine. Keep in mind that typically developing children, particularly toddlers, can have certain routines that they find comforting and, thus, can exhibit some ritualized behavior. These routines and rituals, however, are not to the extent that they interfere with their functioning.

Inquiring about aggressive and self-injurious behavior is also important. Children with ASD, particularly those without well-developed communication strategies, communicate with their behavior. This can escalate to aggression, most often directed toward family, teachers, and caregivers. Similarly, children with ASD can have strong reactions to seemingly minor events and can then present with episodes of behavioral dyscontrol or prolonged and extreme tantrums. When discussing tantrums, meltdowns, and behavioral dysregulation (including self-injury and aggression), inquire about how often these behaviors occur, to what extent they are distressing to both the individual and others in the environment, and what factors might trigger and alleviate them from occurring. As out-

> **DON'T FORGET**
> ....
> When assessing school-age children, adolescents, and adults with ASD, obtain information about mood—in particular, feelings of anxiety, sadness, hopelessness, and helplessness.

lined in Chapter 4, conducting Functional Behavior Assessments for behaviors in question can be extremely informative in this regard.

For school-age children, adolescents, and adults, it is essential to inquire about mood—in particular, feelings of anxiety, sadness, hopelessness, and helplessness. Even individuals with ASD who have limited language skills can experience symptoms of anxiety and depression—often in the form of behavioral dysregulation, irritability, or changes in patterns of behavior (e.g., sleeping and eating patterns). Therefore, clinicians need to be thorough in assessing for potential mood disorders. More information on this topic is provided in Chapter 7.

METHODS OF COLLECTING INFORMATION ON CURRENT AND HISTORICAL PRESENTATION

Clinical Interview

Within the field of autism, there is a semistructured interview that is considered to be the gold standard or best practice in obtaining information regarding diagnostic presentation from a caregiver: the *Autism Diagnostic Interview, Revised* (ADI-R; Rutter, LeCouteur, and Lord, 2003). This measure requires extensive training in order to both administer and score the instrument. Questions are keyed directly to the *DSM-IV-TR* criteria for Pervasive Developmental Disorders and therefore probe for behaviors that are specifically related to ASDs. A diagnostic algorithm is then obtained based on critical scores that indicate whether the individual's scores meet the criteria for autism, autism spectrum, or nonspectrum. However, *these scores should never*

CAUTION

....

Algorithm scores from the ADI-R should never be used in isolation when determining a diagnosis. These scores—more importantly, the behaviors that contributed to them—should be interpreted in the broader context of results from the entire evaluation.

be used in isolation to determine a diagnosis; the information gathered should be integrated and interpreted with all results from the comprehensive evaluation.

The ADI-R takes about three hours to administer and covers the three primary diagnostic domains of socialization, communication, and repetitive behaviors/restricted interests. It includes very specific questions about the child's early history as well as current presentation in these three areas. The ADI-R also has a section on loss of skills to assess for potential regression or plateaus in skill development. It is used predominantly in research settings for obtaining standardized parent-report information regarding a child's symptoms of ASD; however, the information gathered can be extremely useful when used clinically, as well.

Screening Measures

Several screening measures are available that are designed to detect very young children who are at risk for ASD in the general population. Screening measures are typically based on parent-reported information, but some also include clinician observations. The items generally relate to common risk factors for autism, such as limited observations of the following behaviors: eye contact, social smile, joint attention, imitation skills, interest in others, pointing to indicate interest, and pretend play. Importantly, these screening measures are intended as such: *to screen for the risk of ASD*. They are by no means diagnostic in nature, nor should they be used in place of a diagnostic evaluation.

The most commonly used screeners include the following:

- *The Checklist for Autism in Toddlers* (CHAT; Baron-Cohen et al., 2000)

≡ Rapid Reference 5.3

At-Risk Behaviors That Are Often Detected by Screeners

- Limited responsivity to name
- Limited eye contact
- Limited joint attention
- Limited imitation skills
- Lack of social smile

- *The Modified Checklist for Autism in Toddlers* (M-CHAT; Robins, Fein, Barton, & Green, 2001)
- *The Communication and Symbolic Behavior Scales, Developmental Profile: Infant-Toddler Checklist* (Wetherby & Prizant, 2002)
- *The Screening Tool for Autism in Two-Year-Olds* (STAT; Stone, Coonrod, & Ousley, 2000)

Many screening tests are created so that they can be conducted in the most efficient manner with a parent. For instance, both the CSBS-DP Infant Toddler Checklist and the M-CHAT take about 5 minutes to complete. Pediatricians or clinicians who are concerned about at-risk behaviors can administer one of these screening tests quite easily. The CSBS-DP Infant Toddler Checklist is a broadband screener and is useful for detecting at-risk behaviors for general developmental delays in children between the ages of 6 and 24 months, whereas the M-CHAT is an autism-specific screener that is more useful between the ages of 16 and 30 months. Although the ranges of sensitivity and specificity for each measure vary depending on the age and how many follow-up questions are provided, screening tests are exceptionally useful for

DON'T FORGET

Screening measures are intended to screen for the risk of ASD. *They should not be used to determine diagnosis* and they do not replace a developmental, language, or diagnostic evaluation.

raising red flags in behavior that signify that a child's developmental profile should be examined more closely. The behaviors that best discriminate risk factors for ASD include a child's limited responsivity to his or her name, limited eye contact, limited joint attention, limited imitation skills, and lack of a social smile (e.g., Robins et al., 2001). Thus, screening tests typically instigate the referrals for diagnostic evaluations.

Rating Scales

In addition to comprehensive interviews, rating scales can be used to assess a child's social skills and behaviors associated with ASD. These rating scales typically have parent, self, and teacher-report versions, so the clinician can obtain information from a variety of sources, as the child's behavior may vary depending on the situation. As with screening instruments, these measures are extremely useful in gathering information, but caution is given to using any rating scale in isolation when formulating a diagnosis; that is, if an individual's score on a measure falls within the "autism range," this information alone is insufficient to determine whether that individual truly has the disorder. Nevertheless, the specific symptoms identified on these measures are not only informative for the diagnostic formulation but for informing intervention programming as well.

The most commonly used rating scales include the following:

- *The Social Responsiveness Scale* (SRS; Constantino & Gruber, 2005)
- *The Social Communication Questionnaire* (SCQ; Rutter, Bailey, & Lord, 2003)
- *The Childhood Autism Rating Scale, Second Edition* (CARS-2; Schopler, Van Bourgondien, Wellman, & Love, 2010)
- *The Gilliam Autism Rating Scale, Second Edition* (GARS-2; Gilliam, 2006) and *Gilliam Asperger Disorder Scale* (GADS; Gilliam, 2002)
- *The Autism Behavior Checklist* (Krug, Arick, & Almond, 1980)

A Note About Sensory Processing Behaviors

Sensory processing impairments are often reported to be prevalent in individuals with ASD across the life span, despite the equivocal evidence of specific interventions to address them. These symptoms can present as overreactivity or underreactivity to sensory stimuli, or the direct seeking of sensory input. For example, some individuals present with hypersensitivity to sound (e.g., covering the ears with hands) or tactile input (e.g., having an aversion to tags inside clothing); some individuals may be unresponsive to pain or touch, which can place them at great risk for injury; and some individuals may seek out sensory input, such as visually examining objects out of their peripheral vision or by dangling objects in front of the eyes. Though highly prevalent in ASD, these behaviors are not specific to autism and, therefore, have not historically been considered part of the diagnostic criteria. Nonetheless, the criteria set forth in the *DSM-5* do account for these behaviors in the subcategory of restricted interests and repetitive behaviors. The most widely used measure for assessing sensory processing impairments across disorders is the Sensory Profile, which has a version for Infants and Toddlers (Dunn, 2002), school-age children (Dunn, 1999) and adolescents/adults (Brown & Dunn, 2002), as well as a version for school-based clinicians (Dunn, 2006).

Record Review

In order to obtain a full appreciation of an individual's diagnostic presentation, clinicians need to conduct a comprehensive review of records, including reports from prior specialty evaluations and any educational/treatment records. Specialty evaluations are often conducted before the diagnostic evaluation, when particular areas of vulnerability or concern were flagged before the question of an ASD. Conversely, the diagnostic evaluation may unveil areas of concern that merit further exploration. Nonetheless, the following records are often reviewed as part of the diagnostic evaluation:

1. Review of educational/intervention programming
   a. The Individualized Education Plan (IEP) or Individualized Family Service Plan (IFSP)
   b. Teacher evaluations and progress reports
2. Review of specialty assessments
   a. Academic and/or private specialty assessments (speech, language, and communication; cognitive/achievement testing; behavioral assessments)
   b. Motor assessments (physical therapy, occupational therapy, oral-motor)
   c. Medical (genetics, neurology, audiology, gastrointestinal, developmental pediatrics)
   d. Psychiatric

Review of Educational/Intervention Programming

In most states, the Department of Education takes on the responsibility of evaluating and treating children with special needs between 3 and 21 years of age. Children are provided with an educational classification or label that deems them eligible for special educational services. However, school systems are not always equipped with the clinical specialization that is required to fully evaluate and diagnose autism spectrum disorders. Therefore, the school system often conducts a developmental/cognitive assessment and/or achievement testing and then refers the family to outside providers for diagnostic testing. Obtaining school records (and early intervention records for children under the age of 3) is an essential component to the diagnostic process in that it provides a holistic picture of the individual's historic presentation. Specific records to request include the following:

- The Individualized Education Program (IEP) or Individualized Family Service Plan (IFSP)
- Academic testing reports
- Clinician and teacher observations

The IEP is a document that contains the educational classification for the individual, as well as the goals and objectives for intervention that are developed by the educational team. These goals and objectives are created to measure educational progress; thus, the document should provide a comprehensive overview of current strengths and weaknesses. Specific areas of interest for informing the diagnostic evaluation would include:

- Educational classification
- Specialty services (e.g., speech therapy, occupational/physical therapy, social skills groups)
- Hours of intervention (e.g., two 45-minute speech sessions per week)
- Individualized versus group implementation of services

It is important for all clinicians who make recommendations based on the results of their evaluations to be knowledgeable about how IEPs are structured for the child in question, so that the recommendations made can be implemented directly into the child's programming. The most useful recommendations are those that are explicit and include time-limited and measurable objectives that any service provider could read and successfully implement. For instance, if testing results reveal that a child is unable to make basic social initiations, then an appropriate recommendation could be as follows: "Johnny will approach a peer and say 'Hello' 3 times per day, 5 days per week." This objective is explicit, time-limited, and measurable for determining progress.

Review of Specialty Evaluation Reports

Many school systems have clinicians who conduct direct observations and assessment of skills, including school psychologists, speech pathologists, and

> **DON'T FORGET**
> ....
> Recommendations can be written as objectives that can be implemented directly within an individual's IEP. Such objectives should be explicit, time-limited, and measurable. For example, instead of the broad objective, "Johnny will improve his social skills," a more explicit, measurable, and time-limited objective would be "Johnny will approach a peer and say 'Hello' 3 times per day, 5 days per week."

occupational and physical therapists. The results of these assessments are extremely useful to the diagnostic evaluation, as they provide an overview of the individual's academic profile, as well as developmental strengths and weaknesses. As outlined in Chapters 2 and 3, the behavioral observations of the professionals interacting with the individual in natural environments, such as a school setting, are just as informative as standardized scores on testing in regards to an individual's presentation. Therefore, if no formal testing reports are available for review, it is often useful to request progress reports or behavioral observations from the teachers and service providers who work directly with the individual within the school setting.

Given that educational professionals are typically not providing diagnostic evaluations, when the question of an autism spectrum disorder is raised, individuals are often referred for private specialty evaluations (i.e., unless the school system is equipped with trained clinicians who can make diagnoses of autism for educational classification purposes). Referrals for specialty evaluations can similarly include speech and motor assessments, cognitive, academic, and/or neuropsychological assessments, as well as medical evaluations. Common medical evaluations include genetic testing (e.g., to rule out Fragile X syndrome or other associated genetic disorders), neurological assessments (e.g., to assess for seizures), audiological assessments (to rule out hearing loss), gastrointestinal procedures, nutritional assessments for feeding difficulties, and psychiatric/psychological assessments for mood, anxiety, and psychopathology. These results help inform the diagnostic formulation, particularly in instances of comorbidity or diagnostic differentiation of complex medical conditions, speech, language, and communication disorders, motor and developmental delays, and learning disabilities. Refer to Chapter 7 for more detailed descriptions of specific disorders to consider.

SUMMARY

The clinical interview and history taking of an individual with ASD is just as critical to the diagnostic formulation as direct diagnostic assessment. Part of the diagnostic criteria for autism in the *DSM-IV-TR* (APA, 2000) requires delays in early development; thus clinicians need to have a comprehensive understanding of early developmental milestones to effectively differentiate not only between ASDs and other conditions, but currently between ASD subtypes as well (e.g., PDD-NOS vs. autism vs. Asperger syndrome). Clinicians can obtain historical information in various ways, including obtaining and reviewing records from previous evaluations, communicating with service providers, and conducting a direct interview with a parent or caregiver.

It is essential to gain information on early social, language, communication, motor, and behavioral development. It is not uncommon for older, even higher-functioning individuals to lack early developmental milestones, such as joint attention, social smiling, eye contact, imitation, and social initiation skills. One cannot merely assume that these skills exist because the individual possesses higher-order, "splinter" skills that can mask the true level of functioning. Furthermore, by obtaining information from parents on current concerns, a clinician is able to determine what factors most significantly impact the individual with ASD and the family. The behaviors that are most disruptive and that interfere with functional life are often not the symptoms of autism, but include limited safety awareness, behavioral dysregulation, aggression, self-injury, and sleep and feeding disturbances.

Detection of ASD certainly begins with screening for symptoms as early as possible, although it needs to be emphasized that screening measures do not diagnose ASD. The most commonly used screeners include the *Communication and Symbolic Behavior Scales, Developmental Profile Infant Toddler Checklist* (Wetherby & Prizant, 2002), which identifies broad developmental delays between the ages of 6 and 24 months, and the *Modified Checklist for Autism in Toddlers* (Robins et al., 2001), which detects red flags for ASD between the ages of 15 and 30 months. Rating scales for ASD can also offer information on current and past autism symptomatology, with common measures including the *Social Responsiveness Scale* (Constantino & Gruber, 2005), the *Social Communication Questionnaire* (Rutter, Bailey, & Lord, 2003), the *Childhood Autism*

Rating Scale, Second Edition (Schopler et al., 2010), and the *Gilliam Rating Scales* (Gilliam, 2002, 2006). However, the gold standard interview that assesses for comprehensive autism symptomatology from early development through current presentation is the *Autism Diagnostic Interview, Revised* (Rutter, LeCouteur, & Lord, 2003). Nevertheless, clinicians are cautioned from using any results of rating scales and interviews in isolation when making a diagnostic formulation.

REFERENCES

American Psychiatric Association. (2000). *Diagnostic and statistical manual of mental disorders* (4th ed., text rev.). Washington, DC: Author.

Baron-Cohen, S., Wheelwright, S., Cox, A., Baird, G., Charman, T., Swettenham, J., Drew, A., & Doehring, P. (2000). Early identification of autism by the Checklist for Autism in Toddlers (CHAT). *Journal of the Royal Society of Medicine, 93*(10), 521–525.

Brown, C. & Dunn, W. (2002). *The Adolescent/Adult Sensory Profile*. San Antonio, TX: Pearson.

Constantino, J. N., & Gruber, C. P. (2005). *Social Responsiveness Scale*. Torrance, CA: Western Psychological Services.

Dunn, W. (1999). *The Sensory Profile*. San Antonio, TX: Pearson.

Dunn, W. (2002). *The Infant/Toddler Sensory Profile*. San Antonio, TX: Pearson.

Dunn, W. (2006). *The Sensory Profile School Companion*. San Antonio, TX: Pearson.

Gilliam, J. E. (2002). *Gilliam Asperger's Disorder Scale*. San Antonio, TX: Pearson.

Gilliam, J. E. (2006). *Gilliam Autism Rating Scale, Second Edition (GARS-2)*. San Antonio, TX: Pearson.

Gupta, V. B. (2010). Communicating with parents of children with autism about vaccines and complementary and alternative approaches. *Journal of Developmental Behavioral Pediatrics, 31*(4), 343–345.

Institute of Medicine (US) Immunization Safety Review Committee (2004). Immunization safety review: vaccines and autism. Washington, DC: National Academies Press.

Keelan, J. & Wilson, K. (2011). Balancing vaccine science and national policy objectives: lessons from the National Vaccine Injury Compensation Program Omnibus Autism Proceedings. *American Journal of Public Health, 101*(11), 2016–2021.

Krug, D. A., Arick, J., & Almond, P. (1980). Behavior checklist for identifying severely handicapped individuals with high levels of autistic behavior. *Journal of Child Psychology and Psychiatry, 21*(3), 221–229.

Offit, P.A. (2008). *Autism's false prophets: bad science, risky medicine, and the search for a cure*. New York, NY: Columbia University Press.

Robins, D. L., Fein, D., Barton, M. L., & Green, J. A. (2001). The Modified Checklist for Autism in Toddlers: An initial study investigating the early detection of autism and pervasive developmental disorders. *Journal of Autism and Developmental Disorders, 31*(2), 131–144.

Rutter, M., Bailey, A., & Lord, C. (2003). *SCQ: Social Communication Questionnaire.* Torrance, CA: Western Psychological Services.

Rutter, M., LeCouteur, A., & Lord, C. (2003). *Autism Diagnostic Interview, Revised (ADI-R).* Torrance, CA: Western Psychological Services.

Schopler, E., Van Bourgondien, M. E., Wellman, G. J., & Love, S. R. (2010). *Childhood Autism Rating Scale, Second Edition (CARS-2).* San Antonio, TX: Pearson.

Stone, W. L., Coonrod, E. E., & Ousley, O. Y. (2000). Screening Tool for Autism Two-Year-Olds (STAT): Development and preliminary data. *Journal of Autism and Developmental Disorders, 30*(6), 607–612.

Wetherby, A. M., & Prizant, B. M. (2002). *CSBS DP Infant Toddler Checklist.* Baltimore, MD: Brookes.

⚓ TEST YOURSELF ⚓

1. **Direct assessment of a child is more important than obtaining information from parents and other service providers. True or False?**

2. **A comprehensive diagnostic interview entails gathering which of the following pieces of information?**

   (a) Medical history

   (b) Family history

   (c) Behavioral presentation

   (d) All of the above

3. **When obtaining information regarding an individual with ASD's behavior, only focus on the symptoms related specifically to autism spectrum disorders. True or False?**

4. **Early language milestones to inquire about when gathering historical information include all of the following except:**

   (a) Social smile

   (b) Cooing

   (c) Jabbering

   (d) Phrase speech

5. **Due to vulnerabilities in social awareness, individuals with ASD are often not the victims of bullying.**
   True or False?

6. **Gathering information on an individual's personal strengths is just as important as collecting information on areas of weakness.**
   True or False?

7. **Important factors to consider in regards to academic performance include all of the following except:**

   (a) Conceptualization of abstract concepts (e.g., math, time)

   (b) Reading decoding versus reading comprehension skills

   (c) Fixation on numbers and letters

   (d) Ability to follow a narrative

8. **If parent report on the ADI-R yields an algorithm of ASD, then this is sufficient for confirming a diagnosis.**
   True or False?

9. **Which of the following is a screening measure for young children who are at risk for ASD?**

   (a) *The Modified Checklist for Autism in Toddlers*

   (b) *The Childhood Autism Rating Scale, Second Edition*

   (c) *The Gilliam Autism Rating Scale, Second Edition*

   (d) *The Autism Behavior Checklist*

10. **A sufficient IEP objective for an individual with ASD is to "Improve upon social skills."**
    True or False?

Answers: 1. False; 2. d; 3. False; 4. a; 5. False; 6. True; 7. c; 8. False; 9. a; 10. False

Six

DIRECT DIAGNOSTIC ASSESSMENT

The purpose of the diagnostic assessment is for the clinician to observe and evaluate first-hand the presentation of autism symptomatology. The primary areas to consider are social communication, play and interaction skills, and atypical behaviors or interests through both observation and direct interaction. Observations of the individual in natural settings, such as home or school, are ideal, if these can be accommodated as part of the evaluation. If not, then requesting videos of the individual in these contexts is recommended in addition to the teacher or therapist reports and record review described in Chapter 5.

DIRECT OBSERVATION

If it is possible to conduct a direct observation of an individual in an academic or home setting after standardized testing scores have been obtained, then the clinician is able to assess the individual's level of functioning as it compares to the expectations placed on the individual in the respective setting. For instance, when conducting a classroom observation, the clinician can assess whether verbal instructions are at or above the individual's comprehension level, if instructional materials are appropriate to the individual's developmental level and to what degree the level of social demands impacts functioning. Additionally, it is just as important to document observations of successes in the

CAUTION

School observations should not merely consist of reporting what events transpired during the observation. Clinicians need to illustrate the contexts in which the individual's strengths and vulnerabilities are observed, as well as opportunities for teaching moments.

environment as it is to identify problem areas. A similar process can be applied to viewing videotapes.

When conducting an observation of an individual in a school setting, the observer should have clear objectives in mind that will generate a productive report of recommendations for potential change. The observation should not merely consist of a transcription of events that transpired. Objectives to consider during an observation include the following:

1. What are the presenting concerns of the parents and teachers?
2. How is the individual able to communicate his or her needs to others?
3. What is the level of the individual's social communication skills?
4. How does the individual respond to direct instruction versus group instruction?
5. What atypical behaviors, if any, are present, and what appears to trigger them?
6. What is the frequency and intensity of aberrant behaviors?
7. What are effective/ineffective strategies that impact the individual's behavior and performance?
8. What are the opportunities for teaching moments observed throughout the time period and contexts?

DIAGNOSTIC ASSESSMENT

For the direct diagnostic assessment, the goal is to create as naturalistic a context as can be provided through play and interaction. The content and format of the session will vary depending on the age and functioning level of the individual. Play-based assessments are usually conducted on infants, toddlers, and preschool-aged children. Verbal school-aged children can typically do some play-based activities, as well as some interview-based questions and discussion, and verbal adolescents and adults can typically tolerate a clinical interview. Diagnostic assessments can be tricky with nonverbal or verbally impaired children, adolescents, and adults, where activities need to be catered to the individual's developmental level, thus highlighting the need for the cognitive and language assessments *before* the diagnostic session.

Given that the age and level of functioning of an individual impacts the nature and course of the diagnostic assessment, this chapter outlines strategies based on the following age levels:

1. Young children
2. School-aged children
3. Adolescents and adults

Direct Diagnostic Assessment With Young Children

Although there is a wide range of normative language development, typically developing children usually speak in single-word utterances from about 12 to 18 months and begin combining words between 18 and 24 months. Most toddlers with ASD, however, have delayed development of speech, and these delays are typically the impetus for referral. It should be noted that young children with Asperger syndrome do not typically exhibit delayed speech and, in fact, are often described as precocious and verbose talkers. As such, they are often not referred for an evaluation until later into their preschool or school-age years when vulnerabilities in social communication and interaction become more apparent. Given the varied language level of this age group, the direct assessment is often primarily play-based. Additionally,

DON'T FORGET

When conducting assessments with young children, it is recommended that a parent or familiar adult be present in the room. This allows for a more accurate sampling of the child's naturalistic social communication and play behaviors that might not otherwise be observed in absence of some familiarity.

play skills are an essential component to both language and social development and therefore are, in and of themselves, pivotal skills to assess.

For children in this age group, it is recommended that parents accompany the child into the testing room. Children are often anxious about separating from their parents, particularly in unfamiliar settings. In addition, young children are more comfortable interacting with their parents and, therefore, are likely to present more naturalistic behaviors in their parents' presence. This affords the clinician a more accurate assessment of the child's skills.

Suggestions for Structuring the Diagnostic Assessment

When assessing children, the clinician can "test the limits" of the child's skills. For example, begin with providing minimal support or structure to the interaction by sitting quietly and observing how the child approaches toys and people in the room. The clinician can then see how the child reacts to a higher level of support, such as a semi-structured game (e.g., rolling a ball back and forth) or setting up a play sequence (e.g., putting a baby to bed, making food). The clinician can further increase support by modeling an action, directly instructing the child to perform an action (e.g., "Now feed the baby"), or by providing physical prompting (e.g., guiding the child's hand to throw a ball).

Clinicians can follow a similar hierarchy for observing language. Initially, the clinician can sit quietly and wait for the child to comment on or spontaneously request items. Then, the clinician can structure an interaction where the child needs to make a communicative attempt to receive an object or continue an activity. For example, the clinician can perform a motivating activity, pause, and then wait for the child to spontaneously request the activity to continue. If the child does not respond, the clinician can ask the child, "Do you want more?" or model the appropriate language. The clinician can also direct the child's speech: "Say 'more.'" Visual supports can be helpful for some children as well; for example, the clinician can use basic sign language or a simple communicative gesture and then determine if the child can either produce spoken language or use the alternative communication strategy to request more of the activity.

> **DON'T FORGET**
> ....
> Clinicians should begin the diagnostic session by observing the child's behavior in the absence of direct instruction, prompting, or support. This allows for the assessment of spontaneous social communication and play behaviors. Only after these observations are made should the clinician then probe for responsivity and reaction to the introduction of a hierarchy of supports (e.g., expectant waiting; offering a choice; providing a verbal or gestural prompt, etc.).

For a child who is already using basic language, a similar approach can be used to determine if the child can speak in longer or more complex utterances. Instead of responding to single words or two-word phrases, the clinician can use the hierarchical approach described previously by using expectant waiting, modeling, or direct requests for longer utterances, such as "I want more ___."

Context is another important consideration for children with ASD. They often have highly variable performances and have difficulty demonstrating their skills across contexts, which can be frustrating to parents, because they know that their child can perform the skill in more familiar settings. Therefore, it is important for the clinician to consider generalizability of skills when assessing these children, as well as parent report of whether the

> **DON'T FORGET**
> ....
> Don't forget to ask the parents if their child's behavior is consistent with their general presentation in other contexts. If there are inconsistencies, inquire about potential reasons for the observed discrepancies. Comparing this information with measures of parent report (e.g., measures of adaptive functioning described in Chapter 4 and parent report measures of symptomatology described in Chapter 5) can also be quite useful.

≡ Rapid Reference 6.1

....

Strategies for Structuring the Diagnostic Assessment for Young Children

- Initially provide minimal structure and direction—observe the spontaneous behavior of the child
- Use expectant waiting by presenting an object of interest and then holding it out of reach to elicit a communicative act
- Provide a prompt or model that the child can build upon
- Play with a motivating toy to elicit interest and interaction
- Initiate a simple interactive game to elicit reciprocity
- Ask the parent if the child's presentation is consistent with behavior in other contexts

observed behaviors are consistent with expectations. It is also essential to attend to what may be motivating the child. For example, some children will ignore others unless they are offered a preferred activity, or some children will only spontaneously use language when requesting food. It is also necessary to consider the level of supports the child needs in order to demonstrate the skill.

Developmental Areas to Assess

Specific behaviors to probe for and observe during the diagnostic assessment are outlined as follows in the areas of verbal communication, social initiation/responsivity/conversation, play, and behavior:

Verbal Communication

- What is the child's repertoire of words/phrases/speech?
- How does the child use speech—to label, comment, request, interact, and for what purpose (i.e., to access preferred activities/topics or to interact socially)?
- For children with limited language skills, what communicative means, if any, do they use to compensate for lack of speech (e.g., vocalizations, gestures, eye contact, facial expressions, behavior)?

- Are there any atypical speech patterns (e.g., echolalia, scripted speech, pronoun reversal/confusion, neologisms)?

Nonverbal Communication
- How does the child use eye contact, facial expressions, gestures?
- How does the child understand and respond to the use of gaze, facial expressions, and gestures of others?
- How well are the child's nonverbal skills integrated with speech, if at all?
- Does the child require a visual cue, such as a gesture (e.g., point or open-hand reach) to comprehend a verbal bid?

Social Initiation
- Does the child comment on objects of interest?
- Does the child bring objects to another person to "show"?
- Does the child spontaneously share toys and food?
- Does the child make independent requests?
- Does the child give objects for the purpose of gaining help or for sharing?
- Does the child point to or look at objects of interest and then to another adult for the purpose of shared attention?
- Does the child use eye contact to "check in" with an adult (e.g., if unsure of an activity or to gauge a response)?

Social Responsivity
- Does the child respond to his or her name?
- Does the child respond to familiar words and phrases? To a parent's name (e.g., "Where's Mommy?")?

DON'T FORGET

Children *without* ASD who have limited, emerging, or impaired language will often compensate for their lack of speech with compensatory strategies that are very communicative in nature (e.g., gesturing, eye contact, facial expressions, affect regulation), whereas children who have or are at risk for ASD will often lack these compensatory strategies.

- Does the child respond to a social smile or endearing phrase by smiling back at another person?
- Does the child respond to direct requests?
- Does the child respond to open-ended verbal requests?
- Does the child follow the attention of another person using shared eye contact?
- Does the child respond to the gestures of others (e.g., shrugging shoulders; head nodding/shaking; pointing to objects in the distance)?
- Does the child respond to social games such as peek-a-boo, tickling games, or chasing games (e.g., "I'm going to get you!")?
- How does the child react to bids for interaction (e.g., unresponsive; escape/avoidant; with distress)?

Conversational Skills (for verbal children)
- Does the child respond to open-ended questions?
- Can the child sustain a topic of conversation by adding comments and follow-up questions?
- Can the child respond to a bid for conversation by inquiring about a topic?
- Can the child initiate a conversation by asking the clinician about his or her experiences or interests?
- Can the child tolerate shifts in topic?

CAUTION

When conversing with children, adults can often be "forgiving" and inadvertently repair conversational breakdowns and/or rapid topic shifts. Therefore, it can be helpful to transcribe and/or record exactly what is said during the interaction to better evaluate the child's true capabilities in the absence of external support.

Play Skills Play skills serve a significant role in speech, language, and social development. For this reason, assessing a child's level of play is fundamental to the diagnostic assessment. In typical development, plays skills tend to progress in the following sequence:

1. *Sensorimotor/Exploratory Play:* Exploring the sensory aspects of toys and

objects (e.g., manipulating, mouthing, dropping, throwing objects)

2. *Cause-and-Effect Play*: Pressing buttons to create an effect (e.g., musical toys, pop-up toys, Jack-in-the-Box)
3. *Functional Play*: Using a toy for its intended purpose (e.g., rolling a train on a track; putting a toy telephone to an ear; flying a toy airplane)
4. *Symbolic Play*: Using toys to represent other objects (e.g., "cooking" with utensils; feeding dolls; pretending a banana is a phone)
5. *Complex Imaginative Play*: Developing creative themes in play (e.g., creating a sequence of a family going on a picnic; having characters enact a story)

Children with ASD tend to exhibit atypical play patterns. They will engage in sensorimotor and exploratory play, but they might get stuck on the physical attributes of an object, resulting in perseverative play. Similarly, children can gravitate to cause-and-effect toys, yet get caught up in repeatedly pressing buttons.

Additionally, children with ASD tend to show impairments in functional play in that they generally prefer to explore the sensory properties of the toys, as opposed to using them for their intended purpose. For example, children with ASD may rub the surfaces of toys, spin the wheels on cars, line up objects, or visually examine parts of objects, as opposed to playing with them in a more functional manner. In ASD, symbolic and imaginary skills are often absent or significantly impaired. Thus, teaching functional and symbolic play skills becomes essential to the intervention process for young children.

Unusual/Repetitive Behaviors Young children with ASD can display unusual and repetitive behaviors, although they may not be of high

≡ *Rapid Reference 6.2*

Stages of Play Development

1. Sensorimotor/Exploratory Play: Exploring the sensory aspects of toys and objects
2. Cause-and-Effect Play: Pressing buttons to create an effect
3. Functional Play: Using a toy for its intended purpose
4. Symbolic Play: Using toys to represent other objects
5. Complex Imaginative Play: Developing creative themes in play

enough frequency to observe directly within the assessment. This is why gathering parent report and outside information is necessary (refer to Chapters 4 and 5). Common behaviors include atypical sensory responses, such as sensory sensitivities (e.g., covering ears to block noise) or seeking out sensory input (e.g., throwing one's body into things, licking objects). Restricted and repetitive behaviors can include hand-flapping, odd posturing of hands/fingers, repetitive jumping/spinning, and body rocking. These types of behaviors often occur during times of heightened affect, when the child is upset or excited; during unstructured times when the child is not able to structure his or her activities independently; and when not actively engaged in an activity. In order to fully appreciate the factors that trigger and sustain these behaviors, a functional behavior assessment is needed, as described in Chapter 4.

CAUTION

Stereotypical behaviors and restricted interests/routines are not high frequency behaviors and therefore may not be observed during the direct diagnostic assessment. This reiterates the need for obtaining parent report of stereotypical behaviors and for inquiring about contexts in which they tend to occur most often.

A Note About Levels of Functioning
All of the procedures listed earlier pertain to toddlers and preschool-aged children. The same assessments and techniques can

≡ Rapid Reference 6.3

Sample Activities for Diagnostic Assessment

- Free play with a variety of toys, allowing for a variety of play skills from sensory exploration to pretend play (e.g., cars, dolls, miniature figurines, pretend food, cause-and-effect toys)
- Social routines: Interactive songs or patty-cake
- Reciprocal games: Tickle games, rolling a ball
- Highly motivating adult-led activities: Bubbles

also be appropriate for older individuals who have mental ages at the toddler/preschool level. Clinicians can be wary of introducing "baby toys" to an adolescent who is low-functioning. However, for some older individuals with ASD, toys designed for younger children are interesting and motivating, as they are appropriate for the individual's developmental level. Otherwise, clinicians can assess the same skills and behaviors needed for the evaluation but utilize modified materials. For instance, instead of presenting a low-functioning adolescent with a baby doll, the clinician can assess the individual's capacity for abstraction using action figures. Clinicians need to utilize their judgment as to what would be the most appropriate materials for any given child, with both the child and parents' perspective in mind. Refer to Chapter 2 for more specific information about assessment strategies for individuals with cognitive impairment.

Direct Diagnostic Assessment With School-Aged Children

Direct diagnostic assessments with school-aged children can involve primarily a clinical interview as well as some interactive activities designed to assess the

CAUTION

Toys and activities that are designed for young children can often be interesting and motivating to older individuals with ASD who have cognitive impairment because they are appropriate for the individual's developmental level.

child's capacity for abstraction or representational thought. During the assessment, the clinician is required to keep a multitude of factors in mind, particularly potential behaviors to monitor and skills to assess. The clinician needs to observe the child's skills and behaviors while simultaneously conceptualizing the information gathered into a framework of a social disability. As such, it takes a high level of training, experience, and clinical skills to conduct diagnostic assessments for ASD. When clinicians are beginning their training, it can be helpful to videotape sessions that can be reviewed with a supervisor before formulating a diagnosis. Diagnostic evaluations for this age group focus on social communication and interaction skills, insight and awareness into social and emotional experiences, and restricted and repetitive interests and behaviors.

Social Communication and Interaction Skills
- Requesting and commenting
- Asking for information/clarification
- Offering information about oneself or personal experiences
- Providing background information/clarification for communicative partner
- Ability to monitor a conversational partner for interest and understanding
- Ability to initiate, sustain, and appropriately end a conversation
- Ability to engage in a conversational topic not of one's own designation
- Ability to take another's perspective
- Ability to use a range of gestures and facial expressions
- Ability to respond appropriately to the gestures and facial expressions of others
- Ability to follow a narrative sequence
- Ability to report on events, both familiar and novel

In comparison to diagnostic assessments with toddler- and preschool-aged children, major areas to target in school-aged assessments are the more subtle and nuanced elements of social interaction.

The clinician needs to attend to how the child interacts with an unfamiliar adult, both in terms of content and quality of the interaction.

With regards to topics of interest, the clinician can be mindful of the following:

- What are the child's topics of interest?
- Are topics of interest inappropriate to a given situation?
- Are topics of interest generally appropriate for the child's age group? Many children with ASD have unusual interests (e.g., interests in street signs, trains, politics, toilets, or exotic animals). Some of these interests are atypical for any age group (e.g., street signs) or merely atypical for the child's age group (e.g., an 8-year-old with a strong interests in local politics). However, circumscribed interests can also be age appropriate (e.g., an 8-year-old with a strong interest in baseball teams). Therefore, when evaluating topics of interest, the clinician needs to keep typical stages of development in mind.

With regard to the child's interactive style:

- Does the child speak in an overly formal or too casual manner?
- Does the child make statements or ask questions that may be appropriate with some people, such as close family members and friends, but not appropriate for unfamiliar adults? For instance, some children with ASD are highly interested in dates and numbers; asking a parent or friend their age or birthday is appropriate, but such a question is less appropriate for a stranger.
- Does the child engage in behaviors that are inconsistent with the context (e.g., laughing when another person is injured)?

Insight and Awareness Into Social and Emotional Experiences

With school-aged children, the social dynamics with peers increase in complexity. Therefore, it is important to evaluate the child's understanding of their social relationships and experiences. The clinician can gain information about how a child views and understands the social world by asking the child about friendships. For instance:

- Does the child have friends?
- What is the nature of these relationships?
- Are the friendships reciprocal? (e.g., Does the child see the friend outside of school? Outside of arranged playdates?)
- What is the age range of friends? (Some children with ASD will provide names and descriptions of "friends" who are, in reality, older adults (e.g., service providers, teachers, babysitters.)

It is also critical to inquire about potential bullying/victimization:

- Has the child ever been teased or bullied?
- What was the nature of the teasing?
- What actions did the child take, if any?
- What role does the child's own behavior play in the interaction? (e.g., Did the child engage in any behavior to provoke, annoy, or irritate a peer?)

In addition to gaining a sense of the child's understanding, the clinician needs to obtain information about the child's emotional experiences and presentation:

- Can the child give descriptions of his or her affective and emotional experiences?
- Does the child have an understanding of the meaning of these emotional experiences?
- Does the child have strategies to regulate emotional experiences?
- Does the child seem anxious or apprehensive in the face of social demands?
- Does the child appear sad, tearful, or distressed when discussing social or emotional experiences?
- Is the child aware of his or her areas of vulnerability? How these behaviors impact oneself and others?

Capacity for Abstraction

Although play skills do not play as central of a role in school-aged assessments as they do in toddler and preschool-aged assessments, delays in imaginative play skills and capacity for abstraction remain important areas to assess. To assess capacity for abstraction in a school-aged child, the clinician can still base the evaluation largely on play, but it is important to provide the child with age-appropriate toys, such as action figures/figurines/puzzles. It can be helpful to introduce the activity as a creative game rather than "play," per se. Particular attention should be paid to the levels of creativity, complexity, and fluidity in developing and following through with play schemas:

- Does the child have the figurines act as independent agents?
- Does the child use the objects purely on the basis of their physical properties or in a more creative manner (e.g., having a box serve as a television)?
- Does the child organize a comprehensive narrative or sequence to play or is the schema random?
- Do circumscribed interests pervade play?
- Is the child able to build on a theme not of one's own designation (e.g., follow a theme introduced by the examiner that does not involve a topic of interest)?

Unusual Behaviors/Interests

Overt, obvious repetitive behaviors often attenuate with age; however, some children continue to engage in the classic repetitive behaviors, such as hand-flapping, body rocking, or finger fanning/posturing. With intervention, many children can learn to control and/or minimize these behaviors as well. As mentioned, parents may still report these as problematic even if the behaviors are not directly observed by the clinician.

Children with ASD are at greater risk for developing obsessive, compulsive, and tic behaviors, and these tend to manifest later in the school-age years. Therefore, clinicians should assess for the development and/or increased intensity of rigid, compulsive behaviors both through direct observation and parent report.

Direct Diagnostic Assessment With Adolescents and Adults

Direct diagnostic assessments with older adolescents and adults are similar in many ways to the assessments with school-aged children. However, as discussed, expectations and demands will increase with age and skill acquisition. For more sophisticated individuals with ASD, the clinician's job is to assess the nuances and subtleties of social behavior, including the following:

- Does the individual recognize and understand humor? Sarcasm? Figures of speech? Colloquialisms?
- Does the individual recognize if/when they are being taken advantage of or stigmatized?
- Can the individual repair or recover from breakdowns in conversational exchanges?

It is also critical to evaluate the individual's level of independence and ability to self-manage, as these skills are imperative to successful outcomes into adulthood. The clinician needs to inquire about the individual's sense of responsibility for their daily life and future. For example:

- What are the individual's future aspirations, career interests, and personal goals?
- Does the individual understand the necessary steps involved to obtain these goals?
- Is an adolescent planning to go to college? If so, does he or she have the organizational skills to navigate the academic demands of college coursework? The social skills necessary to navigate campus life?
- Does an adult live at home? In a supported living arrangement? Independently?

- Can the adult manage his or her own finances, or is some level of assistance required?
- Can the individual independently take care of daily living needs, such as completing household chores, finances, shopping, etc.?
- What community supports are available and set into place (e.g., job coaches, life coaches, physicians, therapists)?
- What financial assistance is set up, if any (e.g., social security, guardianship, housing, health care)?

It should be emphasized that many older adolescents and adults struggle in college and vocational settings because of the demands of navigating the social and organizational aspects of the setting and *not* because of lack of skill to successfully complete the coursework or job. For this reason, clinicians should have explicit discussions with individuals with ASD and their family members as to what supports can be set into place within an academic or vocational setting to ensure success.

Another area that is often salient to older adolescents and adults is romantic relationships and marriage. Some individuals with a social disability have limited interest in seeking a romantic partner, whereas others are highly motivated but do not possess the skills needed to do so effectively. In some instances, individuals can create troubling situations by making repeated bids to those who they perceive to be potential romantic partners without recognizing the other person's cues and rebuttals. Therefore, the clinician should gain information about the individual's level of insight and understanding of romantic relationships and what their interests and intentions are (e.g., seeking companionship versus sexual relationships). Clinicians can ask about the person's understanding of the constructs of both marriage and sex and how

> **DON'T FORGET**
>
> Many adolescents and adults struggle in college and vocational settings because the demands of navigating the social and organizational aspects of the campus or job become overwhelming and *not* because they lack the necessary skills to complete the coursework or job.

≡ *Rapid Reference 6.4*

···

Specific Areas to Assess With Adolescents and Adults

- Verbal and nonverbal communication
- Social initiations
- Social responses
- Peer relationships
- Insight and awareness into social experiences
- Insight and awareness into emotional experiences
- Career aspirations and future goals
- Levels of independence and self-management
- Levels of daily living skills
- Creativity and capability for abstract thought
- Presence of unusual, restricted, and/or repetitive behaviors and interests

one may know when another person is or is not reciprocating the interest. The clinician can also ask about ways the person may be able to meet or form relationships with a potential partner, again as a means of assessing insight and realistic understanding.

SEMISTRUCTURED MEASURES FOR DIAGNOSTIC ASSESSMENT

Autism Diagnostic Observation Schedule

Similar to the ADI-R, the gold-standard diagnostic assessment measure in the field is the *Autism Diagnostic Observation Schedule, Generic* (ADOS; Lord, Rutter, DiLavore, & Risi, 1999). The ADOS is a semistructured measure that involves direct clinical assessment. Like the ADI-R, this measure requires extensive training in order to both administer and score the instrument, and scores generate an algorithm for autism, autism spectrum, or nonspectrum conditions. The administrator of the ADOS probes for behavioral symptomatology through play and interview-based activities. There are four published Modules of the ADOS that are based on language and age level, and a Toddler Module for use with children under the age of 30 months is in development for publication (Luyster, Gotham, Guthrie, et al., 2009).

Module 1 of the ADOS is administered to children with little to no language. The activities are predominantly play based, using motivating activities such as bubble and balloon play to elicit communicative attempts. Module 1 can be modified for older individuals with limited to no language, but as noted earlier, toys and activities that are exciting to very young children can also be enticing to older individuals whose level of developmental functioning is like that of a much younger child.

Module 2 of the ADOS is administered to children who have spontaneous phrase speech, and it also consists of the activities described earlier. However, the demands for social communication are greater in that children are probed for conversational reciprocity and the ability to interpret themes in pictures and books.

Module 3 is designed for school-aged individuals with complex spontaneous speech; that is, speech that includes the use of multiple clauses (e.g., and, but, or). Although there are play-based activities similar to Modules 1 and 2, there are also interview-based activities that elicit information regarding insight and awareness into social and emotional experiences. Additionally, the demands for social communication and interaction are much greater. For this reason, caution should be taken when using Module 3 on young children (e.g., 3- to 5-year-olds with complex speech) because although they may have advanced speech skills, they will not have the level of insight and awareness into social and emotional experiences expected of an older child.

Module 4 is designed for adolescents and adults with full speech. The measure is predominantly interview based, and it assesses insight and awareness into social and emotional experiences, and also probes for information regarding an individual's future goals, plans for obtaining them, and vocational interests.

The Toddler Module of the ADOS is soon to be published along with Modules 1 through 4, and it is catered to young children between

≣ *Rapid Reference 6.5*

....

The Five Modules of the Autism Diagnostic Observation Schedule

- Toddler Module is appropriate for walking toddlers between 12 and 30 months who have a nonverbal mental age 12 months or above
- Module 1 is appropriate for children over the age of 24 months who are nonverbal or have single-word speech
- Module 2 is appropriate for children over the age of 24 months who have spontaneous phrase speech
- Module 3 is appropriate for school-age children who have spontaneous speech that includes multiple clauses
- Module 4 is appropriate for adolescents and adults with spontaneous full speech

the ages of 12 and 30 months. However, this module is not appropriate for toddlers within this age range who have a nonverbal mental age below 12 months and/or toddlers who are not yet walking. The activities are similar to those in Module 1, but the coding criteria and behavioral probes are more specific, generating different algorithms.

CAUTION

....

Similar to the ADI-R, the ADOS generates algorithms for autism, autism spectrum, and non-spectrum diagnoses. Clinicians are cautioned against using these scores in isolation when determining an individual's diagnosis. That is, scores and the behaviors that were observed in generating them should be interpreted in the broader context of all information gathered during the diagnostic evaluation.

As with the ADI-R, the ADOS was designed primarily for research purposes, but it is now becoming more widely used by clinicians as a means to inform diagnostic assessments. In fact, any practitioner can obtain clinical training on the ADOS either by attending a two-day training course or by ordering training materials from the publisher (Western Psychological Services). However, the clinical course does not provide training on coding items to standards of research reliability, which is offered in the additional three-day research training course. Regardless of how the ADOS is being used, as cautioned with the ADI-R, the ADOS algorithms should never be used in isolation to determine a diagnosis.

Autism Observation Scale for Infants

The *Autism Observation Scale for Infants* (AOSI; Bryson et al., 2008) is a more recently developed diagnostic instrument. Like the ADOS, the AOSI is primarily used for research purposes, although as research continues on the measure, it will likely be used more widely in clinical settings as well. It is designed to detect and monitor early signs of autism in infants between the ages of 6 and 18 months. The AOSI is an observational measure, similar to the ADOS, and it also requires a high level of training to administer. It consists of a set of semistructured activities that provide the clinician opportunities to engage with the infant while conducting a series of "presses" to elicit specific targeted behaviors. Examples of social and behavioral presses include peek-a-boo, rolling a ball back and forth, and looking at a picture book. Examples of skills measured include orientation to name, imitation, eye contact, and social smile. The child's responses and behaviors are then numerically coded based on operationalized definitions. The individual scores are combined into a composite total score, which reflects the infant's risk for ASD.

SUMMARY

The diagnostic assessment involves both direct observation of and interaction with the individual suspected of having ASD. The direct observations can be conducted in the school, home, or community settings, during which the clinician should be observing for contextual information that both aids and impedes successful functioning within that context. If direct observations in naturalistic contexts are not possible, it is often beneficial to request videos of the individual within these settings. The direct diagnostic assessment is often conducted within a lab or clinic setting, resulting in the clinician having to set up a quasi-natural social and play-based environment so that naturalistic social and communicative behaviors can be elicited and observed. The nature of the diagnostic session depends on the age and level of functioning of the individual, with play-based activities and presses indicated for younger and lower-functioning individuals and more interview-based interactions for older and more verbal individuals. Regardless of context, the clinician is observing and probing for the behavioral characteristics of ASD, including vulnerabilities in social communication, interaction, and rigid, repetitive, and stereotypical behavior.

Current semistructured instruments in use for diagnostic evaluation include the *Autism Diagnostic Observation Schedule* (Lord et al., 1999) and the *Autism Observation Scale for Infants* (Bryson et al., 2008). However, it cannot be stressed enough that results from one instrument alone do not diagnosis ASD. Diagnoses of ASD require integration of information from multiple sources and assessments from clinicians who are knowledgeable about social communication and behavioral development.

REFERENCES

Bryson, S. E., Zwaigenbaum, L., McDermott, C., Rombough, V., & Brian, J. (2008). The Autism Observation Scale for Infants: Scale development and reliability data. *Journal of Autism and Developmental Disorders, 38*(4), 731–738.

Lord, C., Rutter, M., DiLavore, P., & Risi, S. (1999). *Autism Diagnostic Observation Schedule (ADOS)*. Los Angeles, CA: Western Psychological Services.

Luyster, R., Gotham, K., Guthrie, W., Coffing, M., Petrak, R., Pierce, K., Bishop, S., Esler, A., Hus, V., Oti, R., Richler, J., Risi, S., & Lord, C. (2009). The Autism Diagnostic Observation Schedule—Toddler Module: A new module of a standardized diagnostic measure for autism spectrum disorders. *Journal of Autism and Developmental Disorders, 39*(9), 1305–20.

🐟 TEST YOURSELF 🐟

1. **Which of the following behaviors would be considered most relevant when conducting a school observation?**

(a) When the child ate a snack

(b) How the child responded to an instruction within a group activity

(c) That the child wrote his or her name on a worksheet

(d) When the bell for recess rang

2. **During the diagnostic assessment, it is important to give as many prompts and supports as needed to obtain optimal levels of performance.**
   True or False?

3. **Which of the following areas are least relevant to the diagnostic assessment?**

   (a) Social communication

   (b) Play and interaction

   (c) Reading decoding

   (d) Stereotypical motor mannerisms

4. **If a child can speak in long, complex sentences and sustain a conversational volley on a topic of interest, then there are no concerns regarding communication.**
   True or False?

5. **Which of the following are nonverbal communication behaviors to assess in ASD?**

   (a) Eye contact

   (b) Descriptive gestures

   (c) Facial expressions

   (d) All of the above

6. **Children with ASD will often compensate for their limited speech with a wide range of communicative gestures.**
   True or False?

7. **All of the following are examples of reciprocal social interaction skills to assess for in ASD except:**

   (a) Talking about topics of interest

   (b) Responding to name

   (c) Initiating a game of peek-a-boo

   (d) Asking for information about another person

8. **Which of the following is a functional play skill?**

   (a) Playing with a pop-up toy

(b) Squishing Play-Doh

(c) Rolling a train on a train track

(d) Pressing buttons on a toy phone

9. **It is not uncommon for typically developing children to develop topics of strong interest at certain ages.**
   True or False?

10. **If an adult with ASD gets fired from his or her job, it's likely that the adult lacks the capacity to perform the skills necessary for that job.**
    True or False?

Answers: 1. b; 2. False; 3. c; 4. False; 5. d; 6. False; 7. a; 8. c; 9. True; 10. False

Seven

DIAGNOSTIC DIFFERENTIALS AND COMORBIDITY

W hen the question of an autism spectrum disorder is raised, many diagnostic differentials need to be considered during the evaluation, with age, level of functioning, and certainly symptomatology coming into play. Several disorders can easily be mistaken for an ASD because they may involve atypical patterns of communication, social difficulties, or odd or perserverative behaviors. In this regard, individuals who have non-ASD conditions may have symptoms that appear to fit the *DSM-IV-TR* criteria for ASD. Moreover, many individuals with ASD suffer from symptoms either unrelated to or as a result of their social disability. Thus, comorbidity—or having the presence of more than one co-occurring disability—can be quite common as well. It is therefore critical that diagnosticians have training in how the features of ASD manifest, so that they are able to appropriately interpret the DSM criteria for related conditions.

The following chapter outlines the common differentials and comorbidities that arise during a diagnostic evaluation for autism and related conditions, with a focus on the following:

1. Intellectual disability
2. Learning profiles
3. Specific language impairment
4. Attention deficit hyperactivity disorder
5. Anxiety and tic disorders

6. Mood disorders
7. Psychiatric conditions and comorbidity in adulthood

INTELLECTUAL DISABILITY

Individuals with ASD are often described in terms of their level of functioning, such as "high-functioning" or "low-functioning." These terms tend to refer to the individual's cognitive or intellectual ability as opposed to degree of social impairment or symptomatology. For this differential, people often use the cutoff of an overall IQ score of 70, where scores falling below 70 delineate intellectual disability (ID) or Mental Retardation (MR) in the *DSM-IV-TR* (APA, 2000). As with ASD, there will be forthcoming changes in the *DSM-5*, with ID falling under the umbrella of Neurodevelopmental Disorders and being categorized as Intellectual Developmental Disorder (IDD; APA, 2000). Yet, the diagnostic criteria will still be similar to the *DSM-IV-TR*, requiring a Full Scale IQ to fall at least 2 standard deviations below the mean; significant impairment in adaptive functioning; and onset in the developmental years. Nevertheless, caution should be taken when using the terms "high and low functioning" with individuals with ASD, as they tend to overgeneralize an individual's presentation. Many individuals with ASD who do not have ID (i.e., those deemed as "high-functioning") may have areas of cognitive deficit and can struggle tremendously throughout life despite their cognitive prowess. This is particularly the case when Full Scale IQ scores fall

DON'T FORGET

If an individual with ASD's Full Scale IQ falls below 70 and there are corresponding deficits in adaptive functioning, a comorbid diagnosis of Intellectual Disability is warranted. Remember that many individuals with ASD will have areas of cognitive impairment, while their overall IQ falls within the Borderline range (i.e., Full Scale IQ 70–80) or higher. For these individuals, clinicians may need to place extra emphasis on areas of impairment so that intervention services do not inadvertently overshoot the individual's true level of functioning.

within the Borderline range of impairment (i.e., scores between 70 and 80), for which extra advocacy may be indicated so that intervention strategies do not inadvertently overshoot the individual's true level of func-

DON'T FORGET

The terms "high-functioning" and "low-functioning" tend to refer to an individual's level of cognitive ability, as opposed to level of social disability.

tioning. Profiles of adaptive behavior are also extremely important to compare with IQ in ASD, as it is often the case that functional skills fall far below cognition (see Chapter 4).

Historically, research has shown that the majority of individuals with ASD also have cognitive impairment or ID. However, current studies are showing less of an overlap between these conditions, ranging from 20% to 70% depending on the study (e.g., Fombonne, 2005), with lower rates likely contributable to both the impact of early and intensive intervention as well as better detection of higher-functioning ASDs. Nonetheless, determining either the comorbidity or diagnostic differential of ID and ASD becomes a standard component of every diagnostic evaluation.

The diagnostic differential between individuals with ID and individuals with ID in addition to ASD is a challenging one. This complexity is most pronounced in very young children, where distinguishing social communication vulnerabilities above and beyond significant global developmental delays can be quite nuanced. Additionally, in older individuals with severe and profound intellectual disability (i.e., IQ scores falling below 40), there can be substantial overlap in

CAUTION

Many individuals with ASD who do not have comorbid intellectual disability still can struggle tremendously throughout life because their adaptive skills are limited and because they may have areas of cognitive deficit despite an overall IQ falling above 70. Therefore, avoid making global generalizations about level of functioning based on cognitive ability alone, particularly if these interpretations will misinform intervention practices.

autistic symptomatology, particularly in the presence of repetitive motor behaviors and significant social communication deficits, which makes parsing out the autism complicated.

Common Features

Individuals with ID and those with both ID and ASD share many common features. In addition to cognitive delays, both groups have significantly impaired language skills. The most impaired individuals are often nonverbal or have limited expressive language (e.g., a few single words).

Additionally, and likely related to their cognitive impairments, these individuals can have great difficulty regulating their behavior and, consequently, end up presenting with extreme dysregulation, aggression, and/or self-injurious behaviors. Because the neurocognitive processes of these individuals are delayed globally, their capacity for sustained attention and ability to engage in a sustained interaction are also limited, making it challenging to engage them in structured tasks for any length of time. As a result, many clinicians fail to obtain valid test scores on standardized measures of cognitive and language functioning. This, in turn, can result in a discrepancy between the individual's true level of ability and where intervention is pitched—often with the latter being higher than the former, which breeds frustration and behavioral dysregulation. Moreover, this negatively impacts learning in that expectations and demands become unobtainable.

CAUTION

When an accurate assessment of an individual with ASD's cognitive functioning is unable to be obtained, providers can erroneously pitch goals and objectives too high, resulting in a great deal of frustration on the individual's behalf due to failure to meet unrealistic expectations and demands. This, in turn, can negatively impact learning, stressing the importance for obtaining estimates of mental age even if standard scores are unable to be obtained.

Distinctions

Although there are many similarities between individuals with ID and individuals with ID and ASD, some key distinctions can be helpful in making the differential diagnosis (see Table 7.1). It is stressed, however, that none of these characteristics should be considered in isolation. Furthermore, these characteristics are not observed in all individuals, as both ID and ASD are heterogeneous conditions with widely varying presentations. Therefore, the clinician needs to consider the child's profile as a whole when making a differential diagnosis.

Table 7.1. Distinctions Between Intellectual Disability With and Without Autism

	Intellectual Disability	Autism and Intellectual Disability
Cognitive Profiles	Relatively even distribution of skills	Scatter among skills, often with areas of significant strength and weakness
	Relatively even verbal and nonverbal skills	Nonverbal skills tend to be higher, overall, than verbal skills
Language Skills	Tend to be delayed but not atypical	Tend to be atypical (e.g., echolalia, pronoun reversal)
Communication Skills	Tend to compensate for verbal impairments through gestures, facial expressions, and eye contact	Limited compensatory strategies for functional communication
Social Skills	Tend to be on par with mental age	Tend to be lower than what would be expected based on mental age
Adaptive Skills	Tend to be on par or even above mental age in some cases	Tend to be lower than mental age, particularly in adaptive socialization scores

DON'T FORGET

Any report of a regression or plateau in the development of skills should trigger concern and the consideration for an ASD diagnosis as well as referrals to medical specialists.

Early history can also be quite informative for the differential diagnosis. Parents of both groups of children often describe their first concerns as delayed language (e.g., limited speech) or motor (e.g., delayed sitting, crawling, walking) skills. Parents of children with ASD and ID also often describe social concerns, even within the first year of life, such as poor eye contact, difficulty engaging, or limited social smiling. Children with ID, even in the first year of life, generally make appropriate eye contact, smile reciprocally, and play basic reciprocal social games with adults. Additionally, a minority of children with ASD (current estimates of about 10%) experiences a regression or plateau in skill development, most notably in language and level of social engagement. As mentioned previously, this regression or stalled development is typically reported within the second year of life; the child develops apparently normally but then is reported to lose previously acquired skills and/or fail to progress in development. A report that includes a regression before the child's second birthday should definitely trigger the clinician to consider a diagnosis of ASD. Also of note, if a parent reports a regression or loss of skills, the clinician should also consider a referral for a specialty evaluation, such as neurology, to rule out the presence of any potential underlying medical condition that may account for changes in development.

Associated Medical Conditions

Many medical conditions, such as seizure disorders and genetic syndromes, can complicate the diagnostic differential with ASD, particularly in individuals with intellectual disability. Seizures occur in about 25% of ASD cases (Filipek, 2005) and often are not a good prognostic indicator; that is, they tend to occur in individuals on the spectrum who also have intellectual disability. Seizures can develop either before the age of three or later in development, often around puberty or adolescence. Given the comorbidity rates, it is essential that clinicians assess for and inquire about any potential seizure activity, including staring spells, especially during these developmental stages.

Autism spectrum disorders have also been associated with more than 20 genetic syndromes, with the most common being Fragile X syndrome and tuberous sclerosis complex (Filipek, 2005; Harris, 2010). In addition to the inherited mutation on the FMR1 gene on chromosome Xq27-3, Fragile X syndrome is marked by mild to severe intellectual disability, vulnerabilities in executive functioning, social and communication impairments, and limited eye contact (Harris, 2010). Tuberous sclerosis complex is caused by mutations in either the TSC1 gene on chromosome 9q34 or the TCS2 gene on chromosome 16p13.3, resulting in a host of physiological and neurological sequelae, including intellectual disability (Filipek, 2005). Associated features with ASD include stereotypical behaviors, social impairments, and deficits in speech. Given the overlapping symptomatology across these conditions, there are variable views regarding the question of comorbidity versus mere associated symptoms. For example, studies have estimated the prevalence rates of ASD in Fragile X syndrome to range between 15% and 30%, although some argue that true comorbidity is likely lower (Harris, 2010).

The prevalence of Down syndrome, which is the most common chromosomal cause of intellectual disability, in ASD is also questionable, with rates as low as 0% to as high as 16% (Filipek, 2005). Despite the equivocal findings regarding

DON'T FORGET

Given the high rate of both intellectual disability and genetic abnormalities associated with ASD, it is standard practice that every individual identified with an ASD be referred for genetic testing, at the very least to rule out associated genetic conditions and for family planning.

DON'T FORGET

ID and ASD are heterogeneous conditions, so the individuals within these groups can have widely differing presentations.

comorbidity, identification of these conditions can be confirmed through genetic testing and neuroimaging (i.e., in the case of tuberous sclerosis complex, tubers can be identified in the brain through neuroimaging tests).

Given the high rate of both intellectual disability and genetic abnormalities associated with ASD, it is standard practice that every individual identified with an ASD be referred for genetic testing. Clinicians are encouraged to have these difficult discussions with families upon diagnosis. The test results may not alter recommendations for interventions for autism, but they certainly can be informative for family planning (not only for parents of individuals with ASD, but biological siblings as well) and potential medical treatments for conditions such as tuberous sclerosis and even, potentially, Fragile X.

LEARNING PROFILES

Nonverbal Learning Disability (NLD)

NLD is a learning disability characterized by a specific pattern of neuropsychological strengths and weaknesses. The NLD profile is commonly seen in individuals with Asperger's syndrome (AS), and Dr. Byron Rourke, who was at the forefront of NLD research, suggested that virtually all individuals with AS exhibit at least some features of NLD (Rourke, 1989).

The assessment of NLD requires a comprehensive neuropsychological evaluation, including cognitive and achievement testing as well as assessments of tactile perception, motor functioning, attention, and memory. Individuals with NLD have strengths in some neuropsychological processes, including simple motor tasks, auditory perception, verbal attention and memory, and phonological

Table 7.2.
Selected Features of NLD

Strengths	Weaknesses
Simple motor	Tactile perception
Auditory perception	Complex motor
Verbal attention	Visual perception
Verbal memory	Visual attention
Phonological processing	Visual memory
Rote academics	Problem solving
	Pragmatic language
	Mathematics
	Reading comprehension
	Social competency
	Emotion regulation

processing (see Table 7.2). These strengths translate into relatively strong rote academic skills, particularly reading decoding and spelling. Individuals with NLD have deficits in visual and tactile perception, complex motor tasks, visual attention and memory, problem solving, and social aspects of language, such as prosody and pragmatics. These weaknesses translate into difficulties in a variety of academic areas, including reading comprehension and mathematics. Additionally, individuals with NLD have vulnerabilities in social competency, including social perception, judgment, and interactions, adapting to change, and often exhibit trouble with emotion regulation (Rourke, 1989).

As described previously, individuals with NLD have deficits in social interaction skills, and some individuals with a social disability, namely AS, also evidence an NLD profile based on neuropsychological assessment; however, not all individuals with NLD have a primary social disability (i.e., AS or ASD). Instead, their social deficits are a function of their learning profile. Specifically, social interactions require an appreciation for the gestalt and require attention to the visual and verbal aspects of communication, which given the individuals' nonverbal deficits, are difficult. Furthermore, not only do the difficulties appreciating the gestalt interfere directly with social functioning, but they also can affect one's view of oneself; an individual may view oneself in a fragmented and noncohesive fashion, which impacts the ability to relate appropriately with others.

The mood and emotional dysregulation seen in individuals with NLD also likely impact social functioning, as they can interfere with the ability to create and sustain interpersonal relationships. Some individuals with NLD can also have deficits in critical judgment, as a function of deficient problem-solving skills and emotional dysregulation. Furthermore, given the poor perceptual abilities and fragmented and detail-focused processing, the individuals have difficulty integrating various pieces of information or thinking through all of the consequences, leading to potentially impulsive and poor decision making. Lastly, although individuals with NLD have these similar deficits in social interaction, insight, and judgment seen in individuals with AS, they do not exhibit the intense circumscribed interests or exhibit the precocious verbal abilities seen in individuals with AS.

Hyperlexia

Hyperlexia is defined as having word recognition and identification skills far above reading comprehension and cognitive skills (Grigorenko, Klin, & Volkmar, 2003). The deficits in reading comprehension occur both at the level of single words and connected text. The prevalence of hyperlexia in individuals with ASD is estimated to be about 5% to 10% (Burd & Kerbeshian, 1985).

Individuals with hyperlexia not only have high levels of reading decoding skills relative to their other cognitive abilities, but they are early readers as well. It is common for parents of children later classified as having hyperlexia to report that their child read single words at the age of 2 years or younger. This precocious reading is often exciting for parents and professionals; however, those working with the individual need to recognize that although individuals with hyperlexia have exceptional decoding skills, their reading comprehension skills

> **CAUTION**
>
> When recommending intervention strategies for individuals with ASD who also have hyperlexia, emphasize the importance of differentiated instruction; specifically that instruction for reading decoding can be pitched at a higher level than instruction for reading comprehension, while still focusing on closing the gap between the two.

are not as strong. As such, a precocious reader can be quite misleading for professionals, as those working with the individual need to understand that although the individual is seemingly reading, he or she is not necessarily understanding the text. Therefore, it is important to differentiate the instruction for these cases. For example, when the goal of the task is reading comprehension, the text will need to be at a much lower level than when the goal is reading decoding skills.

Also of importance, individuals with ASD and hyperlexia are often described as "obsessive readers" and are quite drawn to letters and numbers from an early age. This tendency can be problematic, as the propensity is to attend to the letters at the exclusion of more salient or socially relevant information. For example, when reading a picture book with a child with ASD, the child may solely attend to the page numbers at the bottom of the pages and miss the narrative storyline. As another example, in a classroom, a student may be so interested in the letters on the bulletin board that he or she does not attend appropriately to the teacher. Therefore, when assessing individuals with ASD and potential hyperlexia, it is important to consider strengths in reading decoding and the discrepancies between decoding skills and other cognitive processes.

Formal assessment of hyperlexia requires a standardized reading battery in addition to cognitive testing. Subtests for reading decoding

DON'T FORGET

Individuals with hyperlexia do not comprehend the text at the level at which they can decode.

and comprehension are commonly part of achievement batteries, such as the *Wechsler Independent Achievement Test, Third Edition* (WIAT-III; Wechsler, 2009), the *Kaufman Test of Educational Achievement, Second Edition* (KTEA-II; Kaufman & Kaufman, 2004), and the *Wide Range Achievement Test, Fourth Edition* (Wilkinson & Robertson, 2006). However, comprehensive reading batteries also exist, such as the *Gray Oral Reading Test, Fourth Edition* (GORT-4; Wiederholt & Bryant, 2001) and the *Early Reading Diagnostic Assessment, Second Edition* (ERDA; Psychological Corporation, 2003).

SPECIFIC LANGUAGE IMPAIRMENT

A primary feature of ASD is communication impairment, which often includes reduced abilities to use and understand grammar and vocabulary in spoken language. Specifically, these individuals may struggle with expressive formulation (i.e., production of words, phrases, sentences, and conversational language) and receptive understanding (i.e., accurate interpretation of heard information such as sentences, directions, narratives, or conversation). Additionally, and perhaps more significantly, individuals with ASD struggle to use both spoken and nonverbal language as a social tool (i.e., to effectively connect and interact with other people).

Rapid Reference 7.1

Hyperlexia is a condition in which an individual exhibits a significantly higher level of word-decoding skills relative to other cognitive processes and skills. Individuals with ASD and hyperlexia tend to be early readers, often identifying sight words before their second birthday.

With regard to diagnosis, it is important for the speech-language pathologist to differentiate between Specific Language Impairment (SLI) and communication weaknesses associated with ASDs. SLI refers to markedly delayed receptive and expressive language skills in the absence of additional developmental issues (i.e., cognitive

> **DON'T FORGET**
> ....
> Individuals with SLI will attempt to compensate for poor expressive formulation skills with nonverbal means of communication. This is in stark contrast to individuals with ASD who will also have impaired nonverbal communication and, thus, will lack these compensatory strategies.

impairment, hearing loss). Individuals with SLI will struggle to use and understand spoken language, but they will *not* demonstrate the primary deficits in social communication that are characteristic of individuals with ASD.

As highlighted in previous chapters, there is a fundamental difference between talking/listening and using language as a bridge for establishing shared meaning and interpersonal connection with others. Individuals with SLI will struggle to formulate language while having an *intact* understanding of the social world. These individuals will seek to compensate for poor expressive formulation skills through nonverbal means (e.g., joint referencing, gestures, facial expressions, eye contact) that enable relatively successful social interactions. By contrast, in addition to weak receptive and expressive language skills, those with ASD will lack an intuitive sense of the social world. These individuals often misinterpret or entirely overlook nonverbal aspects of social communication. Thus, unlike individuals with SLI, those with ASD will struggle to read and respond to nonverbal and verbal signals of social partners.

ATTENTION DEFICIT HYPERACTIVITY DISORDER

One of the most controversial topics of comorbidity with ASD is that of attention deficit hyperactivity disorder (ADHD). The *DSM-IV-TR*

CAUTION

Do not misconstrue overfocused attention for inattention. Individuals with ASD may not attend to external direction because they are fixated on their own object/topic of interest, *not* because they are *inattentive*.

rules against dual diagnoses of pervasive developmental disorders and ADHD (APA, 2000); however, there is a great deal of research to suggest that symptoms of hyperactivity, inattention, and impulsivity are present in more than 50% of individuals with ASD, meriting the comorbid diagnosis in many cases (e.g., Gadow, DeVincent, & Pomeroy, 2006).

When assessing symptoms of inattention, hyperactivity, and impulsivity in individuals with ASD, it is important to evaluate more than just the symptom expression at face value. For instance, what appears to be inattention in ASD is often the individual's failure to respond to an external direction because of an *overfocused* attention on a topic or object of interest. In this situation, the individual is so focused that he or she is unable to disengage and attend to what is requested. This is qualitatively different from an inability to focus, which is more often the case in ADHD.

Impulsivity can similarly be misinterpreted in ASD. When individuals with ASD make impulsive comments or act impulsively in a way that is inappropriate to the context, they often do not lack impulse control, per se, but they lack the necessary social cues to comprehend the underlying inappropriateness of their behavior. Without fully understanding the nature of these behaviors, they could be mistreated (e.g., pharmacological treatment would be ineffective for overfocused attention and/or inappropriate social behavior).

CAUTION

Do not misconstrue inappropriate social behaviors as lack of impulse control. Individuals with ASD often say or do things that are inappropriate because they lack the necessary social cues to comprehend the underlying inappropriateness of their behavior and *not* because they are *impulsive*.

To the contrary, when individuals with ASD suffer from comorbid inattention, hyperactivity, and/or impulse control, then traditional interventions for ADHD can be quite helpful on top of those proposed for ASD. For this reason, thorough evaluation of the overlapping symptoms is necessitated.

ANXIETY AND TIC DISORDERS

Anxiety Disorders

Anxiety is the most common condition to co-occur in individuals with ASD, with studies projecting comorbid anxiety to be as high as 80% (e.g., Muris et al., 1998). Research on specific anxiety disorders experienced in ASD are more variable, with one study showing that 30% of individuals with ASD met criteria for generalized anxiety disorder (Shtayermann, 2007), while panic disorder/agoraphobia, separation anxiety, and obsessive-compulsive disorder are also not uncommon. Adults with comorbid ASD and intellectual disability have been shown to have higher levels of anxiety than do adults with intellectual disability alone (Gillott & Standen, 2007). Fear and anticipation of change, an inability to comprehend the social demands of the environment, and reactivity to sensory stimuli all contribute to the stress experienced by individuals with ASD. Anxiety may be further exacerbated because many individuals with ASD lack the social support that would be effective for coping. Aggressive and self-injurious behaviors may subsequently function, in part, as maladaptive strategies for coping with anxiety. Although teaching effective coping and compensatory communication strategies can alleviate symptoms of anxiety, additional treatment to directly address the anxiety is often indicated (e.g., medication, cognitive-behavioral therapy, behavioral strategies).

CAUTION

In ASD, behavioral symptoms such as aggression and self-injurious behaviors can function as maladaptive strategies for coping with unbearable levels of anxiety and stress.

CAUTION

Symptoms of anxiety can mimic social vulnerabilities. Thus, clinicians need to evaluate whether symptoms of social withdrawal, passivity, and limited social initiations are due to *deficits* in social competencies or merely the manifestation of significant anxiety.

Although anxiety is often co-morbid with ASD, anxiety alone may account for features of an individual's presentation that suggest a social disability. For example, social phobia, general-ized anxiety, separation anxiety, and agoraphobia can all impact an individual's social functioning in the absence of a primary social disability. In differentiating between anxiety disorders and ASD, the clinician needs to evaluate whether the social vulnerabilities (i.e., avoidance, withdrawal, limited initiations) are due to *deficits* in skills or whether they are the manifestation of anxiety. Individuals with ASD present with deficits or extreme delays in social skills that account for their behavioral presentation (e.g., lack of social awareness or knowledge, or failure to make appropriate use of social skills). Individuals with anxiety, on the other hand, have the repertoire of social skills (i.e., social capability), but their anxiety prevents them from engaging with others. Thus, the apparent social vulnerabilities, such as avoidance, withdrawal, distress in the presence of groups, are the result of fear and anxiety. Nevertheless, intervention strategies could be similar depending upon the level of functioning of the individual (e.g., preteaching social scripts/skills; gradual exposure and practice; social modeling; etc.).

DON'T FORGET

It tends to be the norm rather than the exception that individuals with ASD will also suffer from symptoms of anxiety. When evaluating individuals of any age, clinicians should be assessing for levels of anxiety, as well as outlining specific strategies for minimizing anxiety when providing recommendations for services.

Common measures to assess symptoms of anxiety in ASD include the *Beck Anxiety Inventory* (BAI; Beck & Steer, 1993), the *Child Behavior Checklist* (CBCL; Achenbach & Rescorla,

2000), and the *Behavior Assessment Scale for Children, Second Edition* (BASC-2; Reynolds & Kamphaus, 2003).

Obsessive-Compulsive Disorder (OCD)

There are a host of obsessive-compulsive behaviors that, on face value, appear to be shared

> ## CAUTION
> ....
> Obsessive thoughts observed in OCD and circumscribed interests observed in ASD could both be described as recurrent and intrusive; however, obsessive thoughts cause significant distress for the individual with OCD, whereas circumscribed interests are often not distressing to the individual with ASD.

features of both ASD and obsessive-compulsive disorder (OCD). The features of OCD and ASD that are often the most challenging to differentiate include obsessive thoughts versus circumscribed interests, and compulsive behaviors versus restricted and repetitive behaviors. In OCD, obsessive thoughts are defined as recurrent and intrusive, and by nature cause anxiety or distress to the individual experiencing them. In contrast, circumscribed interests in ASD (as observed in Asperger syndrome), though also possibly recurrent and intrusive, are not typically distressing to the individual and, in fact, might alleviate anxiety. Moreover, the individual with ASD is less likely to be aware of the intrusive nature of the circumscribed interest as a person with OCD is, by definition (APA, 2000).

With regard to restricted and repetitive behaviors, compulsive behaviors in OCD are most often tied to a particular anxiety, worry, or intrusive thought (e.g., repeated hand-washing related to a fear of germs; repeated locking a door related to a fear of accidentally forgetting to lock the door). In ASD, the restricted behaviors (e.g., adherence to routines, lining up objects) are not as readily coupled with a specific worry or fear. As with circumscribed interests, the behaviors tend to be the individual's means of creating structure within a confusing, unstructured social world.

A common measure used to assess symptoms of OCD is the *Yale-Brown Obsessive Compulsive Scale* (Y-BOCS; Goodman et al., 1989). The

DON'T FORGET

ASD and OCD can share common features that are not necessarily indicative of comorbidity, such as restricted interests, repetitive behaviors, and rigidities. Parsing out this differential has important implications for intervention in that specific pharmacological treatments that are indicated for OCD (e.g., SSRI medications for compulsions) may not be as effective for the associated behavior in ASD (e.g., restricted and repetitive behaviors).

Children's Yale-Brown Obsessive Compulsive Scale for Pervasive Developmental Disorders (CYBOCS-PDD; Scahill et al., 2006) is a modified version of the Y-BOCS that was created to specifically define repetitive and ritualistic behaviors as associated with either OCD or ASD.

Although diagnostic differentials and establishing comorbidity are important factors to consider, clinicians need to be aware of the natural overlap in symptomatology between ASD and these conditions and that, although certain behaviors might be indicative of anxiety disorders or OCD, in many cases they are the manifestation of ASD symptomatology. This point is reiterated because specific treatments that are, for example, beneficial for obsessions and compulsions (e.g., pharmacological interventions, such as SSRIs) may not be effective for ASD symptomatology in isolation.

Tic Disorders

Tic disorders include the presence of motor or vocal tics, with Tourette's disorder containing features of both. The diagnostic criteria stipulate that the tics occur frequently throughout the day and persist longer than one year, and that there is no tic-free period longer than three consecutive months (APA, 2000). The overlap in ASD symptomatology typically lies in the differentiation between stereotypical motor mannerisms and motor tics. Research in ASD continues to be equivocal on the proposed causes of stereotypical motor mannerisms or "stereotypies." Clinical observations suggest that they are more prevalent when an individual is overstimulated, excited, or overwhelmed, or in the absence of structure (i.e., when the individual is left to his or her own devices). Motor stereotypies also tend to be under the individual's control in that direct instruction to, for example, "put hands down" or stop the behavior can be effective. To the contrary, literature on motor and vocal tics suggests that these behaviors are involuntary, although they still can be triggered or exacerbated by anxiety, as can stereotypies. Similar to what is studied in OCD, individuals with ASD are suspected to be at greater risk than the general population for developing tic disorders, with recent studies estimating as high as 11% of children with ASD also meeting criteria for Tourette's disorder (Canitano & Vivanti, 2007). For this reason, it is important to monitor school-aged children with overlapping symptomatology for the possible development of comorbid tic disorders and/or OCD.

MOOD DISORDERS

Rates of depression in individuals with ASD have been estimated to range between 20% (Shtayermann, 2007) and 33% (Howlin, 2000). Given the social challenges observed in ASD, it is expected that repeated failed or negative social experiences can result in feelings of helplessness and/or hopelessness. Furthermore, as a result of the perseverative behaviors that are characteristic of ASD, some individuals may tend to fixate on past negative experiences they have had, which can contribute to and/or exacerbate depressed mood.

Although depressed mood is common in more cognitively able individuals who have a higher degree of awareness and insight into their social and adaptive difficulties, lower-functioning individuals with ASD are certainly not immune to symptoms of depression. As

DON'T FORGET

Individuals with ASD who have endured repeated negative social experiences are at great risk for feelings of helplessness, hopelessness, and potential depression.

CAUTION

Although depressed mood is common in more cognitively able individuals who have a higher degree of awareness and insight into their social and adaptive difficulties, individuals with ASD and cognitive impairment are certainly not immune to symptoms of depression. In the absence of verbal expression, these symptoms may manifest in the form of mood lability, irritability, changes in appetite and sleep, and decreased interest in preferred activities.

in depression in individuals without ASD, symptoms in less verbal individuals can often manifest in the form of irritability, mood lability, changes in appetite and sleep, and decreased interest in previously preferred activities.

Depression can also contribute to secondary social impairments that can lead to a referral for possible ASD. For example, the lack of energy and lethargy associated with depressed mood can lead to a failure to take initiative, including in the social realm. Thus, individuals with depression often stay home and express no desire to socialize. However, this is entirely secondary to their depressed mood and not caused by a primary social disability. Therefore, it is critical for diagnosticians to determine whether the social difficulties can be accounted for by the depression, including examining an individual's history to determine whether the social isolation had an onset that coincided with the onset of the depression.

≡ Rapid Reference 7.2

Symptoms of depression to assess in individuals with ASD with limited cognitive/language functioning:
- Irritability
- Emotional lability
- Changes in appetite
- Changes in sleep patterns
- Decreased interest in preferred activities

Common measures to assess depressive symptoms in ASD are the same measures that would be used to assess general symptoms of depression, including the *Beck Depression Inventory, Second Edition* (BDI-II; Beck, Steer, & Brown, 1996) and the *Children's Depression Inventory, Second Edition* (CDI-2; Kovacs, 2010).

PSYCHIATRIC CONDITIONS IN ADULTHOOD

A diagnostic evaluation of adults with confirmed or suspected ASD presents special challenges and considerations. Adult referrals are often more complicated than child referrals for several reasons. Adults with ASD may develop secondary psychiatric conditions as a result of living with an autism spectrum disorder; for example, many years of social isolation or other struggles related to their ASD can contribute to an individual developing depression or other mood concerns by adulthood. Thus, evaluations of adults with ASD may require the clinician to tease apart the influences of multiple comorbid conditions.

It is not uncommon that an adult will present for a diagnostic evaluation with no prior ASD diagnosis. These individuals tend to have particularly complex presentations. For instance, they can have a mild ASD presentation with other comorbid conditions that masked the ASD earlier in development; or they might not have ASD but have other psychiatric conditions that have resulted in impaired social functioning characteristic of ASD. The identified rates of psychiatric comorbidities in ASD have varied widely across research studies, ranging from 9% to 89% (Howlin, 2000; Engstrom, Ekstrom, & Emilsson, 2003).

Schizophrenia and Psychotic Features

Individuals with schizophrenia or other psychotic disorders may share some characteristics with individuals with ASD. For example, psychosis can lead to socially inappropriate behaviors, as well as a lack of personal and social insight and awareness. In addition, individuals with thought disorders may use nonsensical or atypical language, be socially withdrawn or isolated, and have a monotone quality to their speech. In making the differential between a psychotic condition and an ASD, it is critical to obtain a detailed history in order to determine onset. While ASD symptoms must be present in early development (i.e., before age 3), the onset of psychotic disorders is typically in late adolescence or early adulthood. Although forms of childhood schizophrenia do exist, albeit rarely, individuals with an adolescent- or adult-onset psychosis may show some prodromal signs during childhood. In addition, the presence of positive symptoms such as hallucinations and delusions would be suggestive of a psychotic condition rather than an ASD.

When determining the diagnostic differential, the evaluation should also carefully assess the individual's grounding in reality. With regard to speech patterns, it is easy to mistake scripted language for non-reality-based language if the evaluator is not familiar with the source from which the individual is scripting. For example, an individual with ASD may make an off-topic, tangential, or fantastical comment that may appear disconnected from reality, when in fact the comment was a quoted line from a favorite movie or television program. It is helpful to transcribe samples of the individual's language and then investigate whether speech may have been scripted. Speaking with parents or siblings can be helpful, as they are often familiar with the individual's favorite television programs and movies and can identify scripted phrases that the individual frequently uses. In some cases, an Internet search with the phrasing in quotations may also identify the source from which the individual was repeating lines. If the individual seems to be making frequent

CAUTION

Scripted speech in ASD can present as tangential and not reality-based when in fact, it is extremely concrete and typically associated with a topic of interest. When observed or reported, clinicians should ask the individual or parent/caregiver where the phrase speech might have come from (e.g., a movie or video script).

nonsensical comments that cannot be tied to an identifiable source, then this may be more suggestive of a thought disorder. Some speech patterns (e.g., tangential or circumstantial speech, neologisms) may be common in both conditions. However, some patterns of speech (e.g., "word salad" in which the individual jumbles words together with no apparent meaning) are more specific to schizophrenia.

Personality Disorders

Several personality disorders share features with ASD, including avoidant, schizoid, schizotypal, and obsessive compulsive personality disorders. In differentiating between ASD and personality disorders, a detailed history to determine onset is critical, as ASDs must be present in early development, whereas personality disorders have an onset in late adolescence or adulthood.

Individuals with avoidant personality disorder may have reduced participation in social activities or lack friendships. However, this is attributable to an active avoidance of social situations because of anxiety (e.g., about being evaluated), rather than to limited social skill as would be more characteristic of ASD. In addition, individuals with avoidant personality disorder would not be expected to exhibit communication impairments or stereotyped behaviors.

Individuals with schizoid personality disorder show a pervasive pattern of detachment from social relationships, a lack of friendships, and flattened affect. The defining feature of schizoid personality disorder is a *disinterest* in social relationships. Although some individuals with ASD express a disinterest in social relationships, the majority of individuals often express a strong

DON'T FORGET

Autism spectrum disorders, by definition, are present from early childhood, whereas personality disorders have an onset in late adolescence or adulthood. Thus, when this particular diagnostic differential arises, it is imperative to collect information on the individual's early developmental history.

desire to form relationships, but they lack the knowledge or skills to do so. Thus, an assessment of social motivation is critical in differentiating these two conditions. In addition, individuals with schizoid personality disorder would not demonstrate stereotyped and repetitive behaviors of the sort observed in ASD.

One of the more difficult personality disorders to differentiate from adult ASD is schizotypal personality disorder. This disorder shares in common with ASD preoccupations, odd patterns of thinking or speech, atypical patterns of behavior, flattened affect, and a lack of peer relationships. However, individuals with ASD tend to show a greater degree of social impairment than is typically observed in schizotypal personality disorder, as well as stereotyped patterns of behavior that would not be observed in schizotypal personality disorder. Furthermore, individuals with schizotypal personality disorder may show behaviors that are more related to the psychotic spectrum (e.g., ideas of reference, magical thinking, unusual perceptual experiences, and paranoid ideation) than to the autism spectrum.

Obsessive-compulsive personality disorder (OCPD) shares some features with ASD, particularly with regard to the stereotyped and repetitive behavior domain of ASD. Like many individuals with ASD, those with OCPD may exhibit a preoccupation with details, a need for predictability, an inflexibility about rules and moral standards, and rigidity of thought and behavior. However, in individuals with OCPD, these behaviors occur in the absence of any core social or language impairments. If social difficulties are present, they are likely to be secondary to anxiety or to the individual's maladaptively rigid and inflexible behaviors.

SUMMARY

When an individual is referred for an autism evaluation, many diagnostic differentials need to be considered. Several disorders can easily be mistaken for ASD because they share clinical features. The diagnostic differential between individuals with intellectual disability (ID) and individuals with ID in addition to ASD is a challenging one, particularly in young children. No one feature can be used to make this differential, but instead the clinician needs to conceptualize the child's profile and history. Some key differences, however, are that individuals with ID tend to have evenly developed skills, whereas individuals with ASD and ID commonly have significantly discrepant cognitive profiles. Similarly, individuals with ID have delayed but not atypical language development, and individuals with ASD and ID often have atypical qualities to their language.

Nonverbal learning disability (NLD) is another common differential. NLD is defined by a particular cognitive profile, namely strengths in rote verbal tasks and weaknesses in perceptual reasoning. Many individuals with Asperger's syndrome (AS) exhibit an NLD profile, but not all individuals with NLD have comorbid AS.

Attention deficit hyperactivity disorder (ADHD) is likely the most controversial differential, as the *DSM-IV-TR* rules against dual diagnoses of pervasive developmental disorders and ADHD, because symptoms of hyperactivity and impulsivity are subsumed under the diagnosis of ASD. Nonetheless, some individuals present with such significant and impairing symptoms that a dual diagnosis is warranted.

Many individuals with ASD suffer from symptoms either unrelated to or as a result of their social disability, particularly internalizing symptoms, such as depression and anxiety. Studies project comorbid anxiety to be as high as 80% in individuals with ASD, and rates of depression range from about 20% to 33%. These mood disorders are likely related to the stress experienced by individuals with ASD as a result of fearing change, sensitivity to sensory stimulation, and inability to comprehend social demands, in addition to recurrent negative social experiences. Measures to assess these symptoms and comorbid disorders include the *Beck Anxiety Inventory* (BAI; Beck & Steer, 1993), *Beck Depression Inventory, Second Edition* (BDI-II; Beck, Steer, & Brown, 1996), and *Children's Depression Inventory, Second Edition* (CDI-2; Kovacs, 2010).

Lastly, adults present with unique challenges to differential diagnosis. Adult referrals are often more complicated than child referrals; adults with ASD may develop secondary psychiatric conditions as a result of living with an autism spectrum disorder, or adults presenting for evaluation may not have an inherent social disability but instead complex psychiatric conditions, including personality disorders and psychosis. As with any differential, clinicians need to consider the person's entire profile and history. Onset of difficulties is particularly relevant to adult differentials, as symptoms of ASD present within the first years of life, and individuals who later develop psychotic conditions or personality disorders may have prodromal symptoms in childhood but do not evidence full symptom expression until adolescence or early adulthood.

REFERENCES

Achenbach, T. M., & Rescorla, L. A. (2001). *Manual for the ASEBA School-Age Forms & Profiles*. Burlington: University of Vermont, Research Center for Children, Youth, & Families.

American Psychiatric Association. (2000). *Diagnostic and statistical manual of mental disorders* (4th ed., text rev.). Washington, DC: Author.

American Psychiatric Association. (2010). *DSM-5 development: Autism spectrum disorder*. Retrieved September 28, 2011 from http://www.dsm5.org/ProposedRevision/Pages/proposedrevision.aspx?rid=94

Beck, A. T., & Steer, R. A. (1993). *Beck Anxiety Inventory Manual*. San Antonio, TX: Psychological Corporation.

Beck, A. T., Steer, R. A., & Brown, G. K. (1996). *Beck Depression Inventory, Second Edition*. San Antonio, TX: Psychological Corporation.

Burd, L., & Kerbeshian, J. (1985). Hyperlexia and a variant of hypergraphia. *Perceptual and Motor Skills, 60*(3), 940–942.

Canitano, R., & Vivanti, G. (2007). Tics and Tourette syndrome in autism spectrum disorders. *Autism, 11*(1), 19–28.

Engstrom, I., Ekstrom, L., and Emilsson, B. (2003). Psychosocial functioning in a group of Swedish adults with Asperger syndrome or high-functioning autism. *Autism, 7*(1), 99–110.

Filipek, P.A. (2005). Medical aspects of autism. In F. R. Volkmar, R. Paul, A. Klin, & D. Cohen (Eds.), *Handbook of autism and pervasive developmental disorders* (pp. 534–581). Hoboken, NJ: Wiley.

Fombonne, E. (2005). Epidemiological studies of pervasive developmental disorders. In F. R. Volkmar, R. Paul, A. Klin, & D. Cohen (Eds.), *Handbook of autism and pervasive developmental disorders* (pp. 42–69). Hoboken, NJ: Wiley.

Gadow, K. D., DeVincent, C. J., & Pomeroy, J. (2006). ADHD symptom subtypes in children with pervasive developmental disorder. *Journal of Autism and Developmental Disorders, 36,* 271–283.

Gillott, A., & Standen, P. J. (2007). Levels of anxiety and sources of stress in adults with autism. *Journal of Intellectual Disabilities, 11*(4), 359–370.

Goodman, W. K., Price, L. H., Rasmussen, S. A., Mazure, C., Fleischmann, R. L., Hill, C. L., Heninger, D. R., & Charney, D. S. (1989). The Yale-Brown Obsessive Compulsive Scale: I. Development, use, and reliability. *Archives of General Psychiatry, 46*(11), 1006–1011.

Grigorenko, E. L., Klin, A., & Volkmar, F. (2003). Annotation: Hyperlexia: Disability or superability? *Journal of Child Psychology and Psychiatry, 44*(8), 1079–1091.

Harris, J. C. (2010). Autism spectrum diagnoses in neurogenetic syndromes. In E. Hollander, A. Kolevzon, & J. T. Coyle (Eds.), *Textbook of autism spectrum disorders* (pp. 223–237). Washington, DC: American Psychiatric Publishing.

Howlin, P. (2000). Outcome in adult life for more able individuals with autism or Asperger syndrome. *Autism, 4*(1), 63–83.

Kaufman, A. S., & Kaufman, N. L. (2004). *Kaufman Test of Educational Achievement: Second Edition, Comprehensive Form.* Circle Pines, MN: American Guidance Service.

Kovacs, M. (2010). *Children's Depression Inventory, Second Edition (CDI-2).* North Tonawanda, NY: MHS.

Muris, P., Steerneman, P., Merckelbach, H., Holdrinet, I., & Meesters, C. (1998). Comorbid anxiety symptoms in children with pervasive developmental disorders. *Journal of Anxiety Disorders, 12,* 387–393.

Psychological Corporation. (2003). *Early Reading Diagnostic Assessment, Second Edition: Technical manual.* San Antonio, TX: Author.

Reynolds, C. R., & Kamphaus, R. W. (2003). *Behavior Assessment System for Children, Second Edition (BASC-2).* San Antonio, TX: Pearson.

Rourke, B. P. (1989). *Nonverbal learning disabilities: The syndrome and the model.* New York, NY: Guilford Press.

Scahill, L., McDougle, C. J., Williams, S. K., Dimitropoulos, A., Aman, A. G., McCracken, J. T., & Vitiello, B. (2006). The Children's Yale-Brown Obsessive Compulsive Scales modified for pervasive developmental disorders. *Journal of the American Academy of Child and Adolescent Psychiatry, 45*(9), 1114–1123.

Shtayermann, O. (2007). Peer victimization in adolescents and young adults diagnosed with Asperger Syndrome: A link to depressive symptomatology, anxiety symptomatology, and suicidal ideation. *Issues in Comprehensive Pediatric Nursing, 30,* 87–107.

Wechsler, D. (2009). *Wechsler Individual Achievement Test, Third Edition (WIAT-III)*. San Antonio, TX: Pearson.

Wiederholt, J. L., & Bryant, B. R. (2001). *Gray Oral Reading Test-IV (GORT-4)*. Austin, TX: Pro-Ed.

Wilkinson, G. S., & Robertson, G. J. (2006). *Wide Range Achievement Test, Fourth Edition (WRAT-4)*. Lutz, FL: Psychological Assessment Resources.

🐊 TEST YOURSELF 🐊

1. True/False: High functioning means that the individual has only a mild social impairment.

2. John is a 4-year-old boy who presents with global delays in his development. His language, socialization, and nonverbal cognitive skills are about two years behind his chronological age. His developmental skills are fairly easily distributed, and his adaptive skills are slightly higher than his language and nonverbal skills, as measured by direct standardized testing. What would be important differential diagnoses to consider? Why? Based on this information, what is the most likely diagnosis?

3. For a differential diagnosis of ASD, which of the following most strongly triggers a concern specific to ASD?

    (a) Delayed language skills

    (b) Delayed motor skills

    (c) Regression or loss of language skills

    (d) Delayed nonverbal cognitive skills

4. Individuals with nonverbal learning disability have highly discrepant profiles of abilities.

    Common areas of strength include:

    Common areas of deficit include:

5. Children with hyperlexia read with equally high levels of decoding and understanding.
    True or False?

6. Children with Specific Language Impairment have deficits in _____ and _____ but intact _____.

7. Ann is a 3-year-old girl who was referred for an assessment. Her nonverbal cognitive and motor skills are within the level expected for her age. Her language skills, however, are delayed; she speaks

in some single words, although she is not yet using phrase speech. She responds to basic commands but not any multiple-step directions. She benefits from others' use of nonverbal communication, such as pointing, body positioning, and gestures, to augment her understanding. Similarly, she communicates her needs by using gestures, eye contact, and facial expressions, but when others cannot understand her, she will have tantrums. She does enjoy nonverbal reciprocal social games with peers and her caregivers. Based on this information, what diagnosis is the most likely and why?

8. Anxiety disorders are the most common comorbid psychiatric disorders in individuals with ASD.
   True or False?

9. Explain some possible reasons for the prevalence of anxiety in individuals with ASD.

10. Explain the difference between an obsession seen in OCD and a circumscribed interest.

11. Lower-functioning individuals with ASD do not experience symptoms of depression, given their delays in cognition and language.
    True or False?

12. List two measures that can assess for symptoms of anxiety and two that can assess symptoms of depression.

13. Henry is a 20-year-old man who presented to the clinic for an autism assessment. He came with his parents because of their concerns about his social isolation, unusual language, and odd behavioral presentation. His parents reported that although he has never had as many friends as some of his peers, they first became considered about him about six months prior, as he exhibited a marked decline in his functioning and began using nonsensical and tangential speech. What differential diagnosis should the clinician consider? Why?

14. The differential diagnosis between ASD and personality disorders can be difficult because they both have onsets in early childhood.
    True or False?

Answers: 1. False; 2. Global Developmental Delay, ASD, Specific Language Impairment; child presents with delays in a broad range of skills. Equally delayed nonverbal cognition, language, and socialization as well as a strength in adaptive skills points most likely to a global developmental delay. Refer to p. 126–127; 3. c; 4. Selected strengths: simple motor; auditory perception; visual attention; visual memory; phonological processing; rote academics. Selected weaknesses: tactile perception; complex motor; visual perception; visual attention; visual memory; problem-solving; pragmatic language; mathematics; reading comprehension; social competency; emotional regulation; 5. False; 6. Expressive language; receptive language; pragmatic language/social communication; 7. Specific language impairment; delays in language but intact nonverbal cognition, motor, and socialization skills. Also, strong nonverbal communication, including the use and understanding of gestures and directed facial expressions.; 8. True; 9. Fear and anticipation of change, inability to comprehend social demands of the environment, reactivity to sensory stimuli, and lack of social support that could be effective coping strategy; 10. Obsessions are recurrent, intrusive, and cause anxiety/distress; circumscribed interests are less likely to be distressing, and the individual is not generally aware that they are intrusive.; 11. False; 12. *Beck Anxiety Inventory* (BAI; Beck & Steer, 1993), the *Child Behavior Checklist* (CBCL; Achenbach & Rescorla, 2001), and the *Behavior Assessment Scale for Children, Second Edition* (BASC-2; Reynolds & Kamphaus, 2003). *Beck Depression Inventory, Second Edition* (BDI-II; Beck, Steer, & Brown, 1996) and the *Children's Depression Inventory, Second Edition* (CDI-2; Kovacs, 2010); 13. ASD and psychosis; limited socialization, unusual behaviors, odd language. Psychosis is more likely, however, as the onset was in early adulthood, although there may have been some prodromal symptoms in childhood due to limited social relations; individual has nonsensical and tangential speech, again beginning in adulthood, as opposed to early childhood as seen in ASD.; 14. False

Eight

CASE CONCEPTUALIZATION AND INTEGRATED REPORT WRITING

THE PARENT CONFERENCE

The presentation of results of the comprehensive diagnostic evaluation is two-fold: it begins with a parent/caregiver conference that allows for dissemination and discussion of findings, and it ends with a written report. Many clinicians choose to withhold having a parent conference until the report is written. However, it is our experience, particularly when conducting the initial diagnostic evaluation where parents are understandably extremely anxious about what their child's diagnosis might be, that providing immediate feedback is not only beneficial but also necessary. This allows for discussion of the child's presentation throughout the evaluation when observations are still fresh in everyone's minds and when parents' presenting concerns can be readily addressed.

Upon initial diagnosis, parents are left with a near infinite amount of resources to sift through in order to determine the best course of action for treating their child. Therefore, the parent conference offers the opportunity for clinicians to provide immediate recommendations for how to start services before even receiving the written report. The parent conference also allows for discussions about evidence-based practices and how best to seek out, evaluate, and make informed decisions about the treatment and intervention approaches that, although readily available, may not be the most appropriate given

DON'T FORGET

The parent conference provides the opportunity for clinicians to disseminate results of the comprehensive evaluation and provide a cohesive and integrated diagnostic formulation. This is often best served directly following the evaluation when observations of the individual's behavior are still fresh in the minds of both the clinicians and parents. This also allows for families to have their questions and concerns immediately addressed, as delays in days or even weeks can result in undue anxiety and stress. In addition, parents can leave the evaluation with enough information regarding their child's diagnosis to begin seeking appropriate services without delay.

the specific needs of their child. It is extremely beneficial to have a case manager or social worker as part of the evaluation process so that advocacy and support can begin within the parent conference. This clinician can then act as the liaison between the parents and the community to help set up the appropriate supports.

THE WRITTEN REPORT

In addition to the parent conference, the written report is going to serve as the individual's vehicle for receiving appropriate treatment and intervention services. When conducted by a multidisciplinary team, the report should be integrated so that results from all respective disciplines are provided within the same document, with one cohesive diagnostic formulation provided that best encapsulates the individual's presenting condition—even if this entails describing multiple comorbid conditions. Although recommendations might be discipline specific, it is helpful for these to be consolidated as well, so as to best illustrate the individual needs. Recommendations should be prioritized so that intervention providers are better able to effectively implement change.

While discussion about long-term goals and objectives can take place during the parent conference, it is often more helpful to focus on the individual's immediate needs; that is, recommendations for the upcoming year that can be modified and amended as needed with behavior change. Exceptions would be recommendations for vocational training and adaptive skills interventions that need to be planned out and implemented several years, at least, before exiting the school system. In fact, we recommend that transitional planning begin as early as middle school. Yet, in younger children, including every recommendation from the point of assessment to adulthood does not benefit the individual or the service providers in any way. Thus, it is better to focus on seminal skills that need to be immediately acquired so that future progress is obtainable.

CAUTION

Recommendations provided in the written report should be streamlined and focused on intervention strategies that can be implemented during the coming year. It is useful to provide recommendations in a hierarchical order based on current and immediate needs, highlighting teaching seminal skills that need to be acquired for functional success, as well as addressing behaviors that negatively impact safety and learning.

The components of a comprehensive written report for the multidisciplinary assessments outlined in this book include the following:

1. Reason for referral
2. Developmental, medical, family, and educational history
3. Review of previous evaluations
4. Cognitive or developmental testing results
5. Results of adaptive behavior assessments
6. Communication testing results
7. Results of diagnostic play or interview session
8. Summary, interpretations, and diagnostic formulation(s)
9. Recommendations for services and intervention
10. Recommended resources for parents and professionals

CASE SAMPLES

The following case samples are provided to exemplify how test results can be interpreted and disseminated within a comprehensive written report. These reports exemplify the comprehensive developmental approach to assessment where all findings are consolidated into the same written document, by all contributing clinicians, with one cohesive diagnostic formulation provided that best represents the individual's current presentation. Sample recommendation strategies are provided for each case based on age and level of functioning of the cases; however, clinicians should bear in mind that recommendations are the most individualized and specialized component of any evaluation; thus no one model, per se, would fit every child. For this reason, suggested topics for recommendations are provided here, but certainly not a comprehensive list of strategies that would typically be provided in an individualized report.

The two case samples provided in this chapter represent the more commonly observed profiles in ASD diagnostic evaluations:

1. An initial diagnostic assessment of a child under the age of 3
2. A school-age child with average intellectual abilities but a complex social, communication, and behavior profile

CASE SAMPLE: INITIAL DIAGNOSIS—TODDLER

Reason for Referral

Johnny is an 18-month-old boy who received a multidisciplinary evaluation at the request of his pediatrician, who noted concerns regarding Johnny's delays in speech and social development. The evaluation included assessments of Johnny's developmental, language, and behavioral skills; extensive review of his prior records; and interviews with his parents. The evaluation took place over the course of two consecutive days.

DON'T FORGET

Start the report with the referral concerns to establish a context for the reader.

History

Johnny's mother provided the following information regarding her son's developmental history.

≡ Rapid Reference 8.1

The History section provides information about:
- Developmental milestones
- Social development
- Play and interaction skills
- Behavioral concerns
- Medical history
- Family history
- Treatment/educational history
- Current presentation

Early Developmental History

Johnny's mother reported that her pregnancy course was complicated by contractions starting in the seventh month, requiring bed rest until delivery. Active labor began naturally and Johnny was born vaginally at 39 weeks and 6 days' gestation, in vertex position. He weighed 8 pounds and 7 ounces, and Apgar scores at 1 and 5 minutes were 8 and 9, respectively. There were no complications following delivery, and Johnny was bottle-fed formula until he was 12 months old.

Johnny met his early developmental milestones as follows: He smiled at 1 month, sat without support at 6 months, crawled at 9 months, walked alone at 13 months, and began babbling at 6 months ("mama," "dada"). He currently has about five words ("mama," "dada," "bubba" for bottle, "ya" for yes, and "no"), which he uses inconsistently.

Johnny's mother attends a Mommy and Me group one afternoon, weekly, for one hour. During these play sessions, Johnny does not appear to show interest in the other children in the group, preferring instead to sit on the periphery with his preferred toys (e.g., a truck from the movie *Cars*).

Medical History

Johnny had one febrile seizure at the age of 12 months. His parents were recommended to monitor his behavior closely, and no reported seizure activity has been observed since. Johnny is otherwise a healthy baby.

Family History
Johnny's family history is significant for social anxiety on his father's side and an autism spectrum disorder in a first cousin on his mother's side.

Current Concerns and Behaviors
Johnny's pediatrician, Dr. Smith, raised concerns regarding Johnny's development during his most recent well child visit. Dr. Smith was concerned about Johnny's limited use of words, inconsistent eye contact, and limited motor and speech imitation skills. Johnny's parents were then referred to this clinic for a diagnostic evaluation.

Developmental Assessment

Tests Administered
Mullen Scales of Early Learning (Mullen Scales)
The Vineland Adaptive Behavior Scales, Second Edition, Survey Form (Vineland-II)

Behavioral Observations
Johnny came to the evaluation with his parents. When greeted in the waiting area, he was playing with toys and had a difficult time transitioning into the testing room. However, with encouragement

≡ Rapid Reference 8.2

Behavioral Observation section includes:
- Response to greeting
- Effort/attention/compliance/approach
- Speech and language skills
- Behavioral presentation (e.g., unusual behaviors, fidgety)
- Any particular testing accommodations, such as use of a visual schedule, reinforcers, sign language, etc.

from his mother, he eventually accompanied the examiner into the room and engaged in structured tasks at a small table. His mother was then able to transition into another room to be interviewed, while Johnny's father remained in the testing room for the duration of the assessment.

With continued encouragement and reinforcement, Johnny engaged in most tasks presented. He fared better on tasks that involved manipulatives (e.g., objects that he could hold, sort, or match) as opposed to those that were purely verbal or involved looking at pictures in a book. Johnny's language consisted of a few vocalizations and some babbling. He used a limited range of gestures to accompany his speech (e.g., one proximal point and a sign for "more"), and his eye contact was inconsistent. Thus, it was often difficult to discern what Johnny wanted when making requests, as he did not appear to have persistent means of indicating his needs to another person.

Johnny's father, who observed the entire assessment, indicated that Johnny's presentation was consistent with his behavior in the home environment. Therefore, the results of this assessment are judged to be an accurate representation of Johnny's developmental abilities at this time.

Developmental Testing

Johnny's developmental level was assessed using the *Mullen Scales of Early Learning*. The *Mullen Scales* measure a child's developmental abilities in five domains: (1) Visual Reception (nonverbal problem-solving skills), (2) Receptive Language (ability to understand language), (3) Expressive Language (ability to use language

> # CAUTION
> ....
> Validity statements are essential, as the clinician needs to make a determination as to the validity of the findings. If the parents reported that the child's behavior or skills demonstrated were not consistent with expected performance, or if the child had significant difficulty with the testing because of unexpected circumstances, then the clinician needs to include a qualifying statement that the obtained results may be an under- or overestimate of the child's true ability.

Table 8.1. Mullen Scores

Domain	Standard Score	Age Equivalent	Percentile	Descriptive Category
Visual Reception	49	18	46	Average
Fine Motor	38	14	12	Below Average
Receptive Language	20	9	1	Very Low
Expressive Language	21	8	1	Very Low
Gross Motor	43	16	24	Average

to communicate), (4) Fine Motor, and (5) Gross Motor. Standard scores in each domain have a mean of 50 and standard deviation of 10. Johnny's standard scores on the Mullen are provided in Table 8.1, along with age-equivalent and percentile scores.

Johnny's performance on the *Mullen Scales* revealed a variable developmental profile. Johnny's visual reasoning and gross motor skills fell within age expectations, whereas he exhibited significant developmental delays in both expressive and receptive language. His fine motor abilities fell below average for his age.

CAUTION

Remember to discuss the child's strengths as well as areas of vulnerability! This is especially the case when extreme deficits are observed in developmental profiles. When areas of strength, as well as strategies that helped elicit skills, are outlined in the report, this helps clinicians who will subsequently be treating the child to know effective strategies to try during intervention.

Specifically, while Johnny was observed to vocalize and produce some consonant sounds, he did not consistently babble, jabber, or produce any word approximations, nor was he observed to use communicative gestures. Johnny also had difficulty understanding language, such as responding to simple verbal directions (e.g., "Where is the door?") and gestures (e.g., responding to an open hand for "give me"). In addition, his fine motor skills fell below average, which could be a reflection of his limited imitation skills in that he did not always follow the examiner's models. Despite these vulnerabilities, Johnny was very inquisitive and put forth strong effort in completing tasks, particularly those that involved objects or pictures on which to focus. He understood the nature of contingency (e.g., first do ___, then get ___) and he responded well to direct instruction. Thus, with the exception of his limited imitation skills, his basic learning-readiness skills were strong.

Assessment of Adaptive Behavior

In order to assess Johnny's adaptive skills, Johnny's mother completed the *Vineland Adaptive Behavior Scales, Second Edition, Survey Form* (*Vineland-II*). The *Vineland-II* is an individual assessment of adaptive behavior, which can be defined as day-to-day activities necessary to take care of oneself and get along with others. Adaptive behavior reflects what a child actually does in an independent manner, as opposed to what the child is capable of doing. Johnny's scores on the *Vineland-II* are listed in Table 8.2. Domain scores are provided as *Standard Scores* that have a *Mean of 100* and *Standard Deviation of 15*. Each domain has subdomain scores that are reported in *V-Scores* that have a *Mean of 15* and *Standard Deviation of 3*.

Results of the *Vineland-II* interview indicate that Johnny's Adaptive Behavior Composite score falls in the Moderately Low range relative to age-based comparisons. When comparing the different Vineland domains, Johnny's adaptive profile is quite scattered. He exhibited strengths in Written Communication and Motor skills, whereas many of his other areas of adaptive functioning range from Moderately Low to Low, designating areas of delay.

Johnny's overall adaptive Communication score on the *Vineland-II* was in the Moderately Low range for his age, with a relative strength in Written Communication compared to significant delays in Receptive and Expressive Communication. His level of adaptive Daily Living skills was also variable in that his Personal and Domestic scores

Table 8.2. Vineland Scores

Subdomain/ Domain	V-Scores and Standard Scores	Age Equivalent (years-months)	Percentile Rank	Adaptive Level
Receptive	9	0-9		Low
Expressive	9	0-11		Low
Written	16	1-10		Adequate
Communication	75		5	**Mod. Low**
Personal	11	1-2		Mod. Low
Domestic	11	1-2		Mod. Low
Community	14	1-4		Adequate
Daily Living	79		8	**Mod. Low**
Interpersonal	9	0-9		Low
Play/Leisure Time	9	0-10		Low
Coping	12	1-2		Mod. Low
Socialization	65		1	**Adequate**
Gross Motor	15	1-8		Adequate
Fine Motor	12	1-3		Mod. Low
Motor	85		16	**Mod. Low**
Adaptive Behavior Composite	75		5	**Mod. Low**

were moderately delayed, but his Community score was within age expectations. His overall Socialization score fell in the Low range, highlighting his significant vulnerabilities in social interaction and play. Lastly, Johnny's overall Motor domain reflects age-level gross motor abilities and moderately delayed fine motor skills—similar to results from the developmental assessment.

Speech, Language, and Communication Assessment

Tests Administered

Communication and Symbolic Behavior Scales-Developmental Profile (CSBS)

Behavioral Observations

Johnny was evaluated on the second day of his visit, and the assessment lasted approximately 45 minutes. Johnny was very active throughout the assessment and required significant physical redirection to attend to activities. Johnny's mother assisted in the assessment by sitting Johnny on her lap and redirecting his attention, as needed. Johnny's mother commented that his level of communication during the *CSBS* was consistent with his general presentation at home. Therefore, the following results appear to be an accurate reflection of Johnny's current speech and language skills.

Johnny's communication skills were assessed using the *Communication and Symbolic Behavior Scales—Developmental Profile (CSBS)*. The *CSBS* engages the child in a variety of activities in which the examiner "tempts" the child to communicate, and it provides three composite scores in the Social, Speech, and Symbolic domains. Johnny's scores on the *CSBS* appear in Table 8.3 (Scaled Scores have a Mean of 10 and Standard Deviation of 3).

Results of the *CSBS* revealed significant delays across domains of functioning, which is consistent with results from the developmental assessment. Johnny produced no words or word approximations during the administration, and overall, he was relatively quiet. When he did vocalize, his vocalizations consisted of vowel sounds (e.g., "ah," "ooh," "uh"), grunts and whines, and he only produced four vocalizations containing consonant sounds (e.g., "mmm," "tititi," "dododo," "gogogo"). Furthermore, a large proportion of his vocalizations revealed unusual resonance (e.g., hyponasality). Johnny was observed to use a few conventional gestures (e.g., reaching, pushing) when making requests or protesting, but no pointing or descriptive gestures were observed, and he tended not to integrate eye contact with his gestures or vocalizations. At times, he would pair a vocalization with a

Table 8.3. CSBS Scores

Clusters	Subscales	Scale Score	Percentile Rank
Social Scales	Emotion and Gaze	7	16th
	Communication	4	2nd
	Gestures	6	9th
Social Composite		**5**	**5th**
Speech Scales	Sounds	7	16th
	Words	7	16th
Speech Composite		**7**	**16th**
Symbolic Scales	Understanding	6	9th
	Play	6	9th
Symbolic Composite		**5**	**5th**

gesture, but in general, Johnny was more apt to attempt completion of an activity on his own (e.g., trying to open up a jar containing a snack) rather than requesting help from another person. Thus, many of his vocalizations were not used communicatively.

Johnny's play skills were also delayed. He briefly showed interest in a picture book and stacked blocks after the examiner's model, but no symbolic or pretend play was observed. He did, however, imitate the examiner feeding a stuffed doll after several prompts.

Diagnostic Assessment

Tests Administered: The Autism Diagnostic Observation Scale, Module 1(ADOS, Module 1)

The *Autism Diagnostic Observation Schedule, Module 1* (ADOS) was administered in order to obtain standard observations of Johnny's social communication, behavioral, and play skills. The ADOS is a clinical procedure that places the child in social and playful situations that are unstructured, providing no guidelines to the child as to how to respond. In this way, a sample of naturalistic social and communicative behaviors can be obtained. Johnny was tested with the ADOS on the first day of the evaluation in the presence of his mother. Overall, Johnny's mother reported that the behaviors observed during this session were generally consistent with Johnny's presentation at home.

Social Communication

Similar to his presentation during the developmental assessment, Johnny's vocalizations were limited to vowel sounds and only a few consonant blends. On occasion, his vocalizations were directed toward the examiner and his mother for the purposes of requesting and to express interest, although his overall use of eye contact was inconsistent. He was more likely to use eye contact as a means of sharing his excitement in an activity by looking to the examiner or his mother and smiling. When making requests, Johnny's primary strategy for communicating involved moving the examiner's hand from items he desired and crying without directed facial expression. Johnny did not always respond to vocal attempts to gain his attention, including responding to his name, and it was difficult to gain his attention without touching him. Johnny was not observed to point to objects in the distance, use communicative gestures (e.g., wave, clap, nod/shake his head), or give objects as a means of communication.

≋ Rapid Reference 8.3

In the social communication section, comment on the following:
- Frequency of communicative attempts
- Quality of communicative attempts
- Nonverbal communication (gestures, eye contact, facial expressions)
- Initiation of social bids to others
- Responsivity to the social bids of others
- Ability to sustain a reciprocal social interaction

≡ Rapid Reference 8.4

In the play section, comment on:
- Functional play skills
- Reciprocal play skills
- Symbolic and pretend play skills
- Capacity for abstraction (in preschool-aged and school-aged children)
- Ability to create narrative storyline (in preschool-aged and school-aged children)

Play and Interaction

Although Johnny enjoyed engaging in novel activities that included an action toy (e.g., mechanical bunny, bubble machine), his functional play skills were limited to rolling a ball back and forth and pushing a car. He was more likely to engage in cause-and-effect play, such as repeatedly pressing buttons on a musical phone and playing with a pop-up toy. Of notable importance, however, Johnny thoroughly enjoyed physical routine games with his mother, such as when she tickled him or threw him in the air. No emerging symbolic or pretend play skills were observed.

Restricted and Repetitive Behaviors

Throughout the play session, Johnny was observed to engage in repetitive motor behaviors, such as flapping his arms and bouncing. He also exhibited an unusually strong interest in utensils, preferring to hold them in each hand, and he evidenced some distress when these

≡ Rapid Reference 8.5

The behavior section includes:
- Presence of unusual and repetitive behaviors or compulsive behaviors
- Sensory-oriented behaviors
- Perseverative behaviors or circumscribed interests

utensils were removed. His mother reported these behaviors to be present at home as well.

Summary

Johnny is an 18-month-old boy who received a multidisciplinary evaluation upon referral from his pediatrician regarding concerns about his limited language and socialization skills.

Summary of Developmental Assessment

Results of the developmental assessment indicate that Johnny's visual processing and gross motor skills fall within age expectations, whereas his receptive and expressive language skills are significantly delayed for his age. His fine motor skills are currently below average. Johnny fares better on structured tasks that involve objects that he can physically manipulate and colorful pictures on which to focus. He has more difficulty engaging in language-based tasks. Johnny's adaptive skills are also significantly delayed, particularly in the areas of receptive and expressive communication and interpersonal and play skills.

Summary of Communication Assessment

Results of the communication assessment also reveal delays in Johnny's receptive and expressive language, as well as in his social communication and play skills. His speech is limited to minimal vocalizations and word approximations, and he fails to compensate for his limited language through the use of communicative gestures. He also has difficulty responding to the language of others. Nevertheless, in the context of highly motivating and preferred activities (e.g., blowing bubbles), Johnny is better able to make communicative bids, such as requesting, and to share his enjoyment in the activity through eye contact. Johnny's play skills are currently limited to cause-and-effect

≡ *Rapid Reference 8.6*

....

The Diagnostic Formulation ties all of the findings together and then provides the diagnosis. Prior to this section, there is no discussion of a specific diagnosis; rather, only behavioral descriptions are provided. Although cognitive and language testing results can certainly highlight specific cognitive and language delays, the diagnoses of, for example, Intellectual Disability, Nonverbal Learning Disability, Receptive and Expressive Language Disorder, etc., should be saved for the Diagnostic Formulation section.

play with toys. He is not yet engaging in true functional or symbolic play, although he does appear to enjoy reciprocal social games that involve a physical component, such as rolling a ball back and forth and tickling games.

Diagnostic Formulation

Johnny's current profile of symptoms that include language, communication, and social vulnerabilities, along with the presence of atypical behaviors, meets criteria for a diagnosis of autism spectrum disorder (ASD). It should be emphasized that in very young children, the diagnosis of ASD is provisional and can only be confirmed through continuous monitoring of Johnny's development and rate of change in response to intervention over the next few years. Developmental outcomes of young children who present with ASD symptoms early in life differ greatly from child to child. Therefore, there should be no limitation on what is expected of Johnny, and intensive intervention is indicated so that Johnny can begin to build on

CAUTION

....

In children under the age of 3, it is very difficult to differentiate among the pervasive developmental disorders (i.e., autistic disorder, PDD-NOS, Asperger syndrome). For this reason, it is common practice to use the broad diagnosis of autism spectrum disorder, or ASD, with clarification provided at a later age. Given that the forthcoming *DSM-5* is proposing to eliminate autism subtyping, this is all the more reason to use this terminology.

the emerging repertoire of skills that he possesses. Based on the results of this evaluation, the following recommendations are made.

Recommendations

Therapeutic Programming

Early and intensive intervention services are indicated for children with autism spectrum disorders. Two resources that outline best practices in intervention include the book *Educating Children with Autism* (National Research Council, National Academy of Sciences, 2001) and the National Standards Project (National Autism Center, 2010). For children under the age of 3, service provision is often recommended in the home environment, with the following specific specialized services dependent on the needs of the child.

Specialized Services/Evaluations

The results of the comprehensive evaluation will determine the specialized services and/or additional assessments that are required for each child based on individual needs. The following specialized services are often indicated:

- Speech and language therapy
- Occupational therapy/evaluation
- Physical therapy/evaluation
- Behavioral interventions/assessments
- Developmental/play therapy
- Medical evaluations (e.g., neurology, genetics, hearing, feeding)

Conceptual Development

When specific developmental delays are identified, then recommendations for specific skills to build on can be provided. Common skills important for conceptual development include the following:

- Basic learning readiness skills (e.g., sitting, attending, following adult-led instructions)
- Imitation skills (e.g., motor imitation; verbal imitation)

- Matching/sorting/sequencing objects and pictures
- Visual and verbal memory

Developmental Play Skills

When delays or deficits are identified in play development, then specific recommendations to build on the child's repertoire of play skills are indicated. Recommendations can follow the natural stages of play development based on the identified needs of the child:

- Functional play
- Symbolic play
- Imaginative play

Parent Training and Education

When a child is initially diagnosed with an ASD, parents need a great deal of education and support in regards to coping with the diagnosis and setting up an appropriate and effective intervention program for their child. Specific recommendations on local services and support networks, as well as specific strategies that can be taught within the home, can be extraordinary resources for parents.

Follow-Up Evaluation

Given the provisional nature of any ASD diagnosis in children under the age of 3, follow-up evaluations are indicated. The time frame depends on the age and specific needs of the child; however, for a child under the age of 2, it is often recommended to reevaluate that same child at the age of 3 or 4 for diagnostic confirmation.

Parent and Professional Resources

It is often helpful to provide a short list of suggested readings and/or websites of resources that the clinicians consider to be relevant based on the needs of the child assesses. Common resources for initial diagnoses of ASD include:

- References for standards of best practice for treatment and intervention (e.g., *Educating Children with Autism*, National

Research Council, 2001; National Standards Project, www
.nationalautismcenter.org/nsp/)
- National websites with information on ASD (e.g., Autism Speaks, www.autismspeaks.org)
- Local and national parent support networks (e.g., Autism Society of America, www.autism-society.org)
- Local agencies for intervention services (e.g., departments of education; early intervention; social services; etc.)
- Governmental informational websites (e.g., Centers for Disease Control and Prevention: Learn the Signs. Act Early, www.cdc .gov/ncbddd/actearly/index.html)

References

National Research Council. (2001). *Educating children with autism.* Committee on Educational Interventions for Children with Autism. Division of Behavioral and Social Sciences and Education. Washington, DC: National Academy Press. www.nap.edu

National Autism Center (2010). National Standards Project. Randolph, MA. www .nationalautismcenter.org/about/national.php

CASE SAMPLE: SCHOOL-AGED CHILD WITH ASD

Reason for Referral

William is a 6-year, 9-month-old boy who was seen at the clinic for a multidisciplinary diagnostic evaluation. This evaluation was requested by William's school system in order to provide diagnostic clarification regarding his current presentation, as well as to obtain recommendations for his educational and therapeutic programming. The evaluation included assessments of William's cognitive, language, and behavioral skills; extensive review of his prior records; and interviews with William's parents. The evaluation took place over the course of two consecutive days.

History

The following information was gathered from William's parents, who were both interviewed during the course of the evaluation.

Developmental History

William was born three days after the expected due date following an uncomplicated pregnancy and labor. In the first year of life, there were no concerns regarding William's development. In terms of motor skills, William sat up without support at 6 months, crawled at 8 months, and walked alone at 15 months. He smiled at 3 months and seemed to enjoy interacting with his parents.

William said his first words between 9 and 10 months, and at 18 months he had approximately 25 words, but he was still not putting words together. His parents became concerned at 24 months because he still was not speaking in phrases and was not playing with toys in an appropriate fashion. In contrast, William knew his numbers and letters at 18 months, and he could read at an early age. However, his reading comprehension level did not match his decoding skills. Furthermore, his parents noted that during the second year of life, William did not pick up toys to show others in order to demonstrate his interest, nor did he point to things in the environment that interested him. As a baby and toddler, he was very upset by the sound of babies or other children crying.

With regards to social interactions, currently, William is quite interested in interacting with adults and other children, but he may not always know how. He may ask the same question or make the same comment repeatedly, so that other children get annoyed. He has trouble in a small group setting figuring out what the game is or what he should do. At these times he tends to drift off and go to play on his own.

William also struggles with self-regulation, for example, knowing where his body is in space or containing extraneous movements when he is excited. His parents note that he may become upset if something is not going as he expected (e.g., going to an unfamiliar restaurant). Once he is upset, it is difficult to soothe him.

Medical History

William is generally healthy. He has had a basic hearing test that showed normal hearing. William has a great deal of difficulty with sleep; it often takes him over an hour to fall asleep at night, and he wakes frequently during the night.

Family History

There is no family history of autism spectrum disorders or developmental delays.

Educational History

William is in a mainstream kindergarten classroom with 16 children. It is a full-day program. He receives the following special education supports: academic support in a resource room, speech and language, and occupational therapy. He reportedly does well academically but has difficulty with maintaining social relationships, as described previously.

Psychological Assessment

Prior Psychological Evaluations

William was first evaluated when he was 3 years, 6 months old by a clinical psychologist, Dr. Jones, Ph.D. William received the *Mullen Scales of Early Learning*, which revealed significant delays in nonverbal problem-solving, fine motor, and receptive language skills. These skills fell at about the two-and-a-half-year age level. His expressive language skills, though, were in the average range for his age. Dr. Jones also administered the *Vineland Adaptive Behavior Scales*, which indicated mild to moderate delays in adaptive functioning, particularly in socialization and motor

DON'T FORGET

Prior evaluation data provides information about:
- Any previous baseline of functioning, as well as profile of strengths and weaknesses
- The level of progress the child has made
- The history and course of the child's delays, which is relevant to diagnostic clarification

skills. Lastly, Dr. Jones reported that William had significant social and communication vulnerabilities. He had delays in pragmatic language, he used echolalia and repetitive phrases, he was reluctant to follow adult-led activities, he did not engage in joint attention, and he did not engage in age-appropriate imaginative play. The diagnosis provided in Dr. Jones' report was pragmatic language disorder.

Behavioral Observations

William came to the evaluation accompanied by his parents. He was appropriately dressed and groomed. When the evaluators greeted William, he was playing with toys in the waiting room. When he saw the evaluators, he looked up, made eye contact, and said "hi." William separated easily from his parents, entered the evaluation room with the evaluator, and sat down when instructed.

At the start of the session, William asked many questions about what he would be doing during the day and when he would be able to play with the toys. The evaluator then created a schedule of the day's activities, which he could reference. With this schedule in place, he did not ask any further repetitive questions, and he seemed much more comfortable and at ease with the demands.

Overall, William was very cooperative and compliant with the testing. He followed the evaluator's instructions and worked diligently. He sustained his effort and attention on the tasks for about 45 minutes. He then asked for a break. Following a short break, he readily transitioned back to the testing room and resumed working for the remainder of the structured testing session, which was about another 20 minutes. With regards to his approach to tasks, William attempted all of the tasks that the evaluator presented, tolerated frustration, persevered through tasks that were challenging for him, and was generally careful and reflective in his response style. At times, he was mildly impulsive and responded quickly without first considering his answer, although he responded immediately to reminders to work carefully.

In terms of William's language, he spoke in complex sentences and used his language for a variety of purposes, such as to request, to seek information, and to relay information about his past experiences and interests. For example, during the breaks between subtests, William told the evaluator that he finished school and would be attending camp during the summer. William did, however, evidence some unusual qualities to his language, such as recurrent grammatical errors (e.g., when asked to define an umbrella, he said, "you do it in the rain, for rain").

With regards to his behavior, William sat appropriately at the table, although he was quite fidgety in his seat. His level of motor activity did not, however, impact his performance, as he was able to attend and respond appropriately despite his movements. Also, William repetitively jumped and flapped his hands when he got excited.

William's parents reported that the skills and behaviors he demonstrated were generally consistent with their expectations. Given this information, coupled with William's effort and compliance, the following results are thought to be reliable and valid measures of his current ability.

Cognitive Testing

William's intellectual abilities were assessed using the *Wechsler Intelligence Scale for Children, Fourth Edition* (WISC-IV). The WISC-IV comprises a variety of subtests that taken together provide estimates of ability in various domains of cognitive functioning. The battery is divided into four indices: Verbal Comprehension, Perceptual Reasoning, Working Memory, and Processing Speed. The instrument also yields a global score, the Full-Scale IQ, which is a composite of the four indices and indicates overall level of intellectual functioning. These

> **CAUTION**
>
> Choose an instrument that is appropriate for the child. The WISC-IV was selected for this child because it includes a global measure of functioning as well as domain scores for verbal, nonverbal reasoning, working memory, and processing speech, which is relevant for children with ASD, who often have discrepant abilities between and within the domains.

Table 8.4. WISC-IV Index and Full-Scale IQ Scores

Index	IQ Standard Score	Confidence Interval	Percentile
Verbal Comprehension (VCI)	89	83–96	23
Working Memory (WMI)	97	90–105	42
Perceptual Reasoning (PRI)	115	106–121	84
Processing Speed (PSI)	80	73–91	9
Full Scale	**94**	**89–99**	**34**

scores are reported as standard scores, with an average of 100 and standard deviation (SD) of 15. William's performance on these scales is summarized in Table 8.4.

General Cognitive Abilities William's cognitive profile showed significant scatter, with a 35-point difference between his highest and lowest Index scores (Perceptual Reasoning and Processing Speed). The magnitude of the difference was significant and unusual, occurring in less than 1% of the standardization sample. William also showed significant and unusual discrepancies between his verbal and nonverbal abilities and within both the verbal and nonverbal reasoning indices (Verbal Comprehension and Perceptual Reasoning). Therefore, his Full-Scale IQ score should be interpreted with caution, as it represents the average of a diverse set of cognitive strengths and weaknesses. Rather, a more complete appreciation of his cognitive profile is obtained from a description and analysis of both his Index scores and individual subtest scores, which is provided as follows.

The WISC-IV provides Scaled Scores based on individual subtests in this test battery in

CAUTION

It is common for children with ASD to evidence a high level of scatter between cognitive processes, so often the full-scale score is not interpretable, because it is not a true representation of the child's abilities.

Table 8.5. WISC-IV Subtest Scores

Subtest	Score	Subtest	Score
Verbal Comprehension subtests		*Perceptual Reasoning subtests*	
Similarities	12	Block Design	15
Vocabulary	9	Picture Concepts	7
Comprehension	3	Matrix Reasoning	15
Working Memory subtests		*Processing Speed subtests*	
Digit Span	11	Coding	6
Letter-Number Sequencing	8	Symbol Search	7

order to examine specific cognitive functions. William's subtest Scaled Scores (Mean = 10, SD = 3) are reported in Table 8.5.

Verbal Expression, Understanding, and Reasoning The Verbal Comprehension (VC) Index of the WISC-IV represents a general measure of verbal knowledge and understanding obtained both informally and through formal education. William's score on this index fell in the Low Average range relative to his same-aged peers (Verbal Comprehension Index, 23rd percentile), but his component subtest scores were significantly discrepant from each other, ranging from the Above Average to Impaired range. Specifically, his scores on the Similarities and Vocabulary subtests were significantly greater than his score on the Comprehension subtest, which represents a significant weakness within his cognitive profile. The Similarities and Vocabulary subtests assessed his knowledge of verbal concepts and word knowledge, respectively. The

≡ Rapid Reference 8.7

Children with ASD often exhibit relative strengths in rote verbal tasks and difficulty with tasks that measure social judgment and intuitive reasoning.

Comprehension subtest provided a measure of William's formulation and expression of reasoned solutions involving social judgment and commonsense reasoning or everyday problem-solving abilities.

Auditory-Verbal Attention and Memory The Working Memory Index (WMI) of the WISC-IV comprises two verbal subtests (Letter-Number Sequencing and Digit Span). William's overall score on this index fell in the Average range (Working Memory Index, 42nd percentile). His component subtest scores were significantly different from each other, yet both fell within the Average range. For the Digit Span subtest, William listened to and then recalled a series of digits forward and then a series of digits backward, and his scores on these tasks were consistent with each other. Both components of the Digit Span subtest required attention and rote memorization, and the digit span backward portion of the subtest also involved working memory. For the Letter-Number Sequencing subtest, William was required to listen to a series of mixed letters and numbers and then recall them correctly after mentally rearranging them into a sequential order. This task required working memory and mental control.

Visual Analysis and Nonverbal Reasoning The Perceptual Reasoning (PR) Index of the WISC-IV represents a diverse set of skills for organizing visually perceived material (Block Design) and nonverbal reasoning (Picture Concepts and Matrix Reasoning). On these visually based problem-solving tasks, William's overall score was in the Above Average range (Perceptual Reasoning Index, 84th percentile), but his component subtests were significantly different from each other. His scores on the Block Design and Matrix Reasoning subtests were significantly higher than his score on the Picture Concepts subtest. The Block Design subtest involves spatial and visualization components, as it requires analyzing and synthesizing visual information to perceive ("see") as well as construct the whole. The Matrix Reasoning subtest requires pattern completion and analogic reasoning, as William was asked to identify the pattern via viewing the relationships among the parts of the design. The Picture Concepts subtest is a nonverbal conceptual reasoning task, as he was asked to identify pictures from an array that were conceptually similar. On this task, William had trouble maintaining the mental set or rules for the task, even when given frequent reminders. Specifically, he was asked to choose one picture from each of two rows, and he was often drawn to pictures on the same row that were physically similar (as opposed to ones that may be conceptually related).

> ### CAUTION
>
> Children with ASD often have weaker skills on Coding than Symbol Search because of the greater graphomotor demands on Coding. If this is the case, the Processing Speed domain score should not be interpreted as a unitary reflection of a child's speed of processing.

Speed of Processing The Processing Speed (PS) Index of the WISC-IV involves scanning and responding to simple or routine visual material without making errors in a rapid manner (Coding, Symbol Search). Performance in this domain also requires attention and concentration and is sensitive to impulsive responding. William's overall score in this domain was in the Below Average range (Processing Speed Index, 9th percentile), and his component subtest scores were consistent with each other. On both subtests, William maintained his attention and effort throughout the tasks and was careful and reflective in his approach, but he worked at a slow, fixed pace.

Assessment of Executive Functioning

In order to gauge William's attentional and regulatory behaviors as they pertain to his day-to-day functioning, William's parents were asked to complete the *Behavior Rating Inventory of Executive Functioning* (BRIEF). This questionnaire presents a list of 86 behaviors and asks respondents to rate the frequency with which the child manifests each one in the more naturalistic environment of the home. Behaviors generally fall into one of two domains: (1) *behavioral regulation*, which reflects the child's ability to inhibit inappropriate behavior, adapt to changes in his routine or environment, and regulate his emotions, and (2) *metacognition*, which characterizes the child's capacity to organize, coordinate, plan, and direct his mental activity in order to complete an activity.

Ratings are then used to derive index scores for each of these broad areas as well as several subscales within each domain; an overall estimate of executive functioning is also obtained in the form of the Global Executive Composite. Scores are reported as T-scores with a mean of 50 and a standard deviation of 10, with higher scores indicating areas of greater difficulty. T-scores of 65 or greater indicate clinically significant difficulty. William's scores on the BRIEF are presented in Table 8.6.

The validity indices of the BRIEF, which measure consistency across similar test items as well as any tendency to respond in

Table 8.6. BRIEF Scores

Index/Scale	T-Score
Global Executive Composite	**65**
Behavioral Regulation Index	**69**
Inhibit	67
Shift	70
Emotional Control	64
Metacognition Index	**60**
Initiate	58
Working Memory	65
Plan/Organize	54
Organization of Materials	53
Self-Monitor	63

a wholly negative way, were within normal limits, indicating a valid profile.

The overall index, or Global Executive Composite, on the BRIEF was elevated, as was the Behavioral Regulation Index,

> **CAUTION**
>
> As with the cognitive testing, it is important to comment on the validity of the results. The BRIEF provides two validity scales for this purpose.

indicating that William has significant difficulties with a range of behaviors related to executive functioning in his everyday life. William's Metacognitive Index, however, was within the normal range.

William's mother's responses indicated that William has significant difficulty with behavioral regulation. In particular, the Inhibit and Shift Scales were significantly elevated. This indicates that William has trouble with changes in his routine, making transitions, flexibly solving problems, and changing focus from one topic to another. Additionally, she indicated that William often acts impulsively and without thinking, acts wild and silly, and has trouble staying seated. Also, within the Metacognition Index, William's mother reported that William has weaknesses in working memory. For example, he has trouble following multistep directions and completing tasks involving more than one step.

Assessment of Adaptive Behavior

William's mother provided information necessary for completing the *Vineland Adaptive Behavior Scales, Second Edition, Survey Form* (Vineland-II). The Vineland-II is an individual assessment of adaptive behavior, which can be defined as day-to-day activities necessary to take care of oneself and get along with others. Scores on the Vineland-II indicate what skills an individual performs *independently* within daily contexts, not merely

> **DON'T FORGET**
>
> Include examples of behaviors with which the child has difficulty to help with understanding of the results and intervention planning.

Table 8.7. Vineland Scores

Subdomain/ Domain	V-Scale and Standard Score	Age Equivalent (years-months)	Percentile Rank	Adaptive Level
Receptive	10	2-5		Mod. Low
Expressive	13	4-6		Adequate
Written	13	5-1		Adequate
Communication	**81**	—	**10**	**Mod. Low**
Personal	11	4-0		Mod. Low
Domestic	11	2-2		Mod. Low
Community	12	4-5		Mod. Low
Daily Living Skills	**77**	—	**6**	**Mod. Low**
Interpersonal	11	2-10		Mod. Low
Play/Leisure Time	10	2-9		Mod. Low
Coping	10	2-3		Mod. Low
Socialization	**74**	—	**4**	**Mod. Low**
Gross Motor	12	4-5		Mod. Low
Fine Motor	12	4-9		Mod. Low
Motor Skills	**81**	—	**10**	**Mod. Low**
Adaptive Behavior Composite	**75**	—	**5**	**Mod. Low**

what the individual is capable of performing. William's scores on the Vineland-II are provided in Table 8.7.

Results of the Vineland-II interview indicate that William's overall adaptive skills fall in the Moderately Low range relative to age-based comparisons, and he exhibits a discrepancy between his adaptive skills and level of cognitive functioning, as measured using the WISC-IV. The discrepancy between his cognitive abilities and his adaptive skills indicates that he is not able to independently apply his repertoire of cognitive

> **DON'T FORGET**
> ....
> Despite strong cognitive capacities, individuals with ASD often struggle to apply their abilities to real-world situations.

skills to daily routines and contexts. This discrepancy may also suggest that William performs better in environments that are highly structured as opposed to more informal or naturalistic settings.

In the adaptive Communication domain, William's scores range from Moderately Low to Adequate. However, a review of his age equivalencies indicates that he is functioning behind his chronological age level in all subdomains. His adaptive Receptive language score is at an age equivalency of 2:5; he has difficulty listening to and following instructions. His adaptive Expressive Language skills are at a 4:6 age equivalency; he is stating information about himself such as his birthdate and home address, and is using present and past-tense verbs; however, he has difficulty telling the basic parts of a story or television show plot, consistently telling about his experiences in detail, and modulating the volume of his voice appropriately. His adaptive Written skills are at a 5:1 age equivalency; he is identifying all printed letters of the alphabet and copying his own first name, but he is not reading at least 10 words aloud or printing at least three simple words.

Within the Daily Living Skills domain, William's scores are consistently Moderately Low, although a review of his age equivalencies suggests some variation. His adaptive Domestic skills are at an age equivalency of 2:2; he is not independently demonstrating caution around hot or sharp objects, clearing items from his place at the table, or

> **CAUTION**
> ....
> Many children with ASD evidence a relative strength in Written Communication that falsely inflates their overall domain score.

participating in basic household chores. His adaptive Personal and Community Daily Living skills are at age equivalencies of 4:0 and 4:5, respectively; he dresses himself, including putting on shoes and using fasteners, understands the function of money and a clock, but he has difficulty using utensils appropriately and does not consistently use caution when near streets and cars.

In the Socialization domain, William's scores are quite uniform, and his age equivalencies fall within the 2- to 3-year range. Within the adaptive Play and Leisure domain, William initiates activities with peers and engages in make-believe activities; however, he has trouble sustaining play activities and taking turns and following the rules in games. His adaptive Coping skills are at an age equivalency of 2:3; he responds appropriately when introduced to strangers and is sometimes using verbal manners; however, he has difficulty with transitions at home and some changes in routine. William's Moderately Low Interpersonal Relationships score (yielding an age equivalency of 2:10) emphasizes the extent of his social difficulties and the need for additional support in this domain. He has a best friend and answers when adults make simple small talk (e.g., "How are you?"), but he does not yet recognize the likes and dislikes of others, show happiness or concern for others, or talk with others about shared interests.

William's adaptive Motor skills are Moderately Low. He runs, catches a large ball, rides a bicycle with training wheels, makes recognizable letters and numbers, and draws shapes while looking at examples; however, he is not yet skipping, holding a pencil in the proper position, or coloring in simple shapes.

Overall, William's profile of Vineland scores shows delays in multiple areas of adaptive behavior. These results emphasize the importance of implementing adaptive skills instruction directly within his intervention program.

DON'T FORGET

....

Providing examples of adaptive skills the child can and cannot perform is helpful for treatment planning. Also, age-equivalent scores can be helpful for those who are less familiar with standard scores.

Speech, Language, and Communication Assessment

Tests Administered

The *Clinical Evaluation of Language Fundamentals, Fourth Edition* (CELF-4) was administered to gain information regarding William's receptive and expressive language skills. Subtests for this standardized measure have a mean of 10 and a standard deviation of 3. Thus, *CELF-4* subtest standard scores ranging between 7 and 13 are considered to fall within the range of average. Additionally, the *CELF-4* provides composite standard scores for Core Language, Receptive Language, Expressive Language, Language Content, Language Memory, and Working Memory. Composite standard scores have a mean of 100 and a standard deviation of 15; thus, scores ranging between 85 and 115 are considered to be average. William's scores on the CELF-4 are provided in Table 8.8.

Table 8.8. CELF-4 Scores

Subtests/Composites	Standard Score	Percentile Rank
Concepts and Following Directions	12	75
Word Structure	12	75
Recalling Sentences	6	9
Formulated Sentences	12	75
Word Classes—Receptive	8	25
Word Classes—Expressive	7	16
Word Classes—Total	7	16
Sentence Structure	9	37
Expressive Vocabulary	13	84
Core Language	*102*	*55*
Receptive Language	**98**	**45**
Expressive Language	**99**	**47**
Language Content	**104**	**61**
Language Structure	**98**	**45**

Test Results

William's *CELF-4* composite standard scores were solidly average, with no statistically significant discrepancies among them. The Receptive Language Score is a measure of listening and auditory comprehension. The Expressive Language Score is an overall measure of expressive language skills. The Language Content Score is a measure of various aspects of semantic development, including vocabulary, concept and category development, comprehension of associations and relationships among words, interpretation of factual and inferential information presented orally, and the ability to create meaningful semantically and syntactically correct sentences. The Language Structure Score is an overall measure of receptive and expressive components of interpreting and producing sentence structure.

Overall, William's performances across *CELF-4* subtests revealed average to above average receptive and expressive syntactic (i.e., grammar) and semantic (i.e., vocabulary/word meaning) recognition. However, there was a statistically significant discrepancy between his one Borderline Impaired score (Recalling Sentences) and his other Average to Above Average scores.

It is important to note that William's low score on Recalling Sentences suggests that his listening skills declined when auditory information was presented in absence of visual information. When he needed to respond to complex directions by pointing to pictures, he achieved an Above Average standard score. In contrast, when he was required to repeat sentences of increasing length and complexity without visual information to support his understanding, William's standard score dropped significantly. This discrepancy suggests that he fares better with contextual listening tasks when provided with supplemental visual cues. For example, in the classroom he will benefit when verbal instructions are presented together with a written checklist.

DON'T FORGET

Provide an explanation of the testing scores and how the child's profile may impact his functioning within the context of his daily life.

Pragmatic Language Abilities

Although William obtained age-appropriate scores on standardized measures of language and verbal cognition, his ability to use language for the purposes of effective social interaction and communication with others was variable. During the communication assessment, he was observed to use basic pragmatic skills, including the following: he returned social greetings, including a handshake; he used and responded to social amenities; he used language to get his needs and wants met; he offered responses to concrete questions; he posed questions to gain information; he understood the concept of conversational volley; and he requested repetition when confused. Nevertheless, William struggled in his use of language as a tool for establishing shared meaning and interpersonal connection with a conversational partner. In addition to having poor eye contact, in many instances, he appeared to talk "at" rather than "with" the examiner. His prosody was atypical, with a monotone quality, and he did not use intonation as a tool for emphasizing key points. He introduced topics with inaccurate assumption of listener background knowledge; he did not consistently attend to nonverbal cues offered by his partner; and he did not effectively respond to listener bids for background information, details, and clarification. He rapidly shifted topics, without attending to his partner's confusion regarding these shifts. He also struggled to pick up on his partner's bids. Additionally, William struggled to sequence his spoken comments so that his language was organized and clear for a conversational partner. He vacillated between offering too few and too many details while speaking, at times shifting from one topic to the next without alerting his partner of this change.

Diagnostic Assessment

Tests Administered

The Autism Diagnostic Observation Schedule (ADOS) is a semistructured play and interview session that assesses social, communicative, and emotional responses. William was assessed using the ADOS, Module 3, to gain understanding of his social and communicative style. The assessment took place following the cognitive assessment, and William's father was present for the duration of the session, which allowed opportunities for more naturalistic interactions between William and a familiar adult.

Social Communication and Interaction

During interactive activities, William clearly enjoyed interacting with both the evaluator and his father. He made comments about his activities and directed facial expressions for the purpose of sharing his experiences and enjoyment. He also showed some interest in the evaluator as a social partner, as he posed questions about her interests and experiences. Furthermore, William was generally responsive to the adult's social bids. He answered the evaluator's questions and allowed her to engage with him in his play.

Although William exhibited appropriate basic social skills, he still presented with vulnerabilities. For example, even though he initiated many interactions, some of his overtures were unusual. He asked atypical questions, and he made repetitive statements and asked repetitive questions. For instance, he repeatedly asked if the evaluator was going to talk about his favorite subject, and then when given an opportunity to talk about it (art class), he did not show a great interest in the topic. Overall, it seemed that he made these unusual and

≡ Rapid Reference 8.8

In the Social Communication section, comment on:
- Interactions with clinician, frequency and quality
- Quality of language, including unusual qualities
- Conversation skills
- Narrative language skills
- Nonverbal communication

repetitive comments because he was motivated to interact and engage in reciprocal conversations but was not yet skilled enough to do so fluidly and adeptly. William also made off-topic comments without appropriate segues or transitions, and at times, he ignored the evaluator's bids or provided simple curt responses (e.g., "Yeah" without any further elaboration). Additionally, of note, William often misinterpreted the social context of the materials (e.g., a book, cartoon, and complex social picture). For example, when describing a cartoon where a cat stole a fish, William said that the cat was hugging the fish. Similarly, he misinterpreted the character's affective expressions and reactions.

With regards to William's language, he spoke in complex sentences, and he used his language for a variety of purposes, such as to request, decline, and comment. Of note, William frequently made grammatical errors and used some unusual language, such as "the guy banged tree," and when looking at a picture of a sailboat, "that's a day sailing on the boat." William's reciprocal conversation skills were variable. He clearly understood the concept of a conversational volley, but he had difficulty executing it fluidly. He was most adept at topics of his own designation, and he had more difficulty with topics that the evaluator introduced. Even with his own topics, he changed topic abruptly and did not monitor his partner's understanding or interest. Lastly, William had difficulty with narrative language. When relaying experiences, he tended to describe them in fragmented details and did not provide his conversational partner with sufficient context or background. Also, he required high levels of support and scaffolding from the adults (e.g., What happened then? What did you do next? etc.) to describe any of the details of his experiences.

In terms of the nonverbal aspects of communication, William's eye contact was inconsistent. When his attention was caught deliberately (i.e., when the evaluator called his name), he made eye contact, but he did not make eye contact to modulate social interactions. William's use of gestures was also limited. He did use some gestures, but they were often idiosyncratic and overly dramatic.

≡ Rapid Reference 8.9

In the Social and Emotional Awareness section, comment on:
- Identification and description of friendships and relationships
- Understanding of one's own role in relationships
- Insight and awareness into one's own social and emotional experiences

Social and Emotional Awareness

When asked about his friends, William said that he had "lots of friends" and proceeded to list the children in his class in alphabetical order. The evaluator then inquired about a best friend, and he was able to provide names of two children. He talked about the activities that he and the children do together, but he was not able to describe the children or their individual interests. Furthermore, William's understanding of social relationships was elementary. He described a friend to be "someone you care about and love," but he was not able to differentiate between friends and acquaintances at school. When asked, he said that all of the children at his school were his friends. His father then indicated that William does, in fact, know all of the names of the children in his school, as he has studied the yearbook.

William's insight into his own emotional experiences seemed to be emerging. He was able to define and then describe situations that make him feel happy, scared, and sad, but he was not able to talk, even in general terms, about the physiological reactions to these emotions or describe any ways to cope with negative emotions. Though he could describe ways in which his peers can irritate and annoy him, William did not acknowledge his role in relationships or how his actions might impact others.

Play and Imagination Skills

When given a set of miniature figurines, William was able to create an imaginative story where the parents took care of a baby. The story was simple, but it was clearly creative. He also willingly allowed the evaluator to join him in his play, and he was able to engage in

≡ *Rapid Reference 8.10*

When evaluating the play skills of a school-age child, assess for the following:

- Ability to independently develop a play scheme
- Use of objects/figurines as agents
- Creativity in play versus fixation on topics of interest
- Flexibility in play (e.g., does the child allow for the introduction of new themes?)
- Reciprocity and engagement with the evaluator

appropriate reciprocal play with her. Additionally, when asked to create a story using several objects, William was quickly able to create a pretend story, where the characters were independent agents. His story definitely showed his capacity for abstraction, but it was simple and somewhat repetitive.

Unusual Behaviors/Interests

William exhibited a few unusual behaviors. When excited, he flapped his hands and jumped. Also, he seemed to evidence a compulsive style and approach to some tasks. For example, when asked to describe a book and a cartoon, he insisted on starting at the beginning, even though the evaluator already described those pages/cards, and when working on a picture, he had trouble stopping in the middle and strongly desired to finish it. These behaviors, however, were quite subtle and did not interfere with his functioning or ability to participate fully in the assessment. William did not exhibit any unusual or intense interests, although his parents reported that at home, he is quite interested in music, specifically one particular children's band.

Summary and Interpretations

William is a 6-year, 9-month-old boy who was seen for a multidisciplinary evaluation to (a) assess his current functioning, (b) obtain diagnostic clarification, and (c) obtain observations of his behaviors to inform his current educational program and treatment planning.

Summary of Psychological Assessment

Results of the cognitive assessment indicate that William's overall cognitive abilities fall in the Average range of functioning. Importantly, he evidences a significant level of variability within his cognitive profile that is relevant to his learning. Namely, his nonverbal abilities are significantly greater than his verbal abilities. However, even within the verbal domain, William's abilities are quite discrepant. He is more successful at tasks that require minimal verbal responses. When he has to formulate more elaborate and longer responses, he has significant difficulty, particularly with organizing his responses and determining the most salient information. Additionally, he exhibits a significant weakness on tasks requiring social reasoning and judgment, and his speed of processing is impaired.

Finally, William exhibits moderate delays in his adaptive functioning, with areas of relative weakness in receptive communication, domestic daily living skills, and play and social interaction. These delays are beyond what would be expected based on William's cognitive abilities, and thus suggest that he is struggling to independently apply his repertoire of skills to daily contexts and routines.

Testing results also indicate that William experiences significant difficulties with a range of behaviors related to executive functioning, specifically with cognitive shifting, working memory, and inhibition. Additionally, William can, at times, be rigid in his behavior and thinking, as exhibited by difficulty with transitions between activities and conversational topics. He also has trouble modulating his level of motor activity and can be quite active.

Summary of Communication Assessment

Results of the communication assessment indicate that William has scattered communication skills. As indicated by standardized testing, his receptive and expressive syntactic (i.e., grammar) and semantic (i.e., vocabulary/word meaning) skills are average to above average. It is important to note, however, that his listening skills decline significantly when auditory information is presented in the absence of visual cues. Thus, he will be better able to follow directions and respond to classroom information that is presented in conjunction with visual cues and concrete materials.

William's pragmatic language skills, or social uses of language, fall well below those that might be reasonably expected based on his age and cognitive ability. His eye contact is poor, as are his responses to nonverbal cues offered by conversational partners. He uses spoken language merely to get his needs and wants met (e.g., he poses questions, makes choice, requests, declines, inquires); however, he does not use language as a tool for establishing shared meaning and interpersonal connection with others. Although he is capable of maintaining a conversational volley, the majority of William's utterances are brief. He does not attempt to build on comments and topics posed by his partner, nor does he attempt to understand or share his partner's ideas and perspectives.

Diagnostic Formulation

William currently presents with a strong repertoire of cognitive and language skills, but he also evidences significant vulnerabilities in his social communication and interaction skills. Specifically, he is quite motivated to engage with others, yet he does not have the skills needed to consistently do so appropriately. He has difficulty thinking about himself and others in an intuitive manner; he misreads social cues, does not take others' perspectives into account, and has limited insight into and understanding of social relationships. William struggles to analyze and connect his personal observations in order to generate and share his own cohesive narrative and develop shared meaning and experiences with his listener. Therefore, at present, his narratives consist of fragmented, concrete, and at times, nonsalient details without an appropriate level of detail or context.

Given William's vulnerabilities in social communication and interaction, coupled with his history of delayed language and play skills, and the presence of unusual and focused interests, his current presentation is consistent with a diagnosis of Autistic Disorder. William's diagnosis necessitates intensive intervention services, and his strong repertoire of cognitive and language skills will be assets to utilize within his educational program to build upon his more vulnerable skills. Given the results of this comprehensive evaluation, the following recommendations are provided.

Recommendations

School Setting

It is recommended that William be placed in an educational setting that includes typically developing peers for social modeling and interaction within the context of structured and intensive support services.

Special Education

It is recommended that William receive services from a special education teacher to support his understanding of curricular material (specific academic subjects can be outlined based on individual needs).

Speech and Language

It is recommended that William receive direct services from a speech and language pathologist to help the development of his social communication skills, including conversation skills and narrative language. Facilitated instruction in naturalistic settings with typical peers is indicated.

Social Skills

Participation in a social skills group is recommended where William can explicitly learn social skills and then practice his new skills in a supported, yet naturalistic setting with peers. We recommend that this group include at least one trained typical peer model who can help facilitate naturalistic interactions.

Extended Time

William's speed of processing is a weakness within his profile, so it is recommended that he have additional time to complete his school-work, particularly on timed tests and tasks. Use of a visual timer can be helpful in offering William a concrete resource for better understanding the concept of time.

Adaptive Skills Instruction

Although William possesses a broad range of cognitive and language skills, he struggles to independently apply his skills to daily contexts and routines. For this reason, specific instruction to build on functional skill development and application is indicated.

Communication Between Home and School

We recommend that William be provided with a notebook that can be exchanged between William's school team and parents regarding skills on which William is working and ways his parents can foster skill development at home. Frequent meetings to address William's

≡ *Rapid Reference 8.11*

Failed items on the Vineland II that are within an individual's level of capability and, more importantly, that are essential for independence, can be placed directly into the recommendations for adaptive skills instruction as skills on which to build. It can be useful to break down the adaptive skills recommendation into the specific areas of the Vineland as follows:

Adaptive Communication Skills

Adaptive Daily Living Skills

Adaptive Socialization Skills

Adaptive Motor Skills

progress and how his parents can help support his skills at home to foster generalization.

Follow-Up Evaluation

William's parents are suggested to seek a follow-up evaluation in 2 to 3 years to monitor William's development and response to intervention. If any concerns arise, such as a plateau or regression in his development, it is recommended that they seek an evaluation sooner.

Recommended Resources for Parents and Professionals

Resources will depend on the age, level of functioning, and needs of the child. Sample categories for resources include:

- Contact information for local governmental agencies for special education services (e.g., departments of early intervention, educational, social services)
- National websites for autism information and support
- Local websites for autism information and support
- Websites for assistive technology and software supports
- Books with informational resources on specific strategies recommended
- Local professionals/clinics that provide recommended services

Annotated Bibliography

Carrow-Woolfolk, E. (1999). *Comprehensive Assessment of Spoken Language (CASL)*. Circle Pines, MN: American Guidance Services.

The CASL is a comprehensive language battery, which includes subtests for measuring supralinguistic skills. The CASL offers information regarding an individual's abilities to understand nonliteral spoken language, such as indirect questions, figurative language, and sarcasm, infer meaning of an unknown word from an oral linguistic context, initiate conversations, and describe the importance of turn-taking routines.

Chawarska, K., Klin, A., & Volkmar, F. R. (2008). *Autism spectrum disorders in infants and toddlers: Diagnosis, assessment, and treatment.* New York, NY: Guilford Press.

This edited book is an essential for clinicians and researchers focusing on the early markers of autism spectrum disorders in infancy and young childhood. The book offers detailed information on the assessment, diagnosis, and treatment of infants and toddlers based on the expertise of top clinical researchers in the field. There is also an extremely informative chapter on supporting families upon initial diagnosis.

Constantino, J. N., & Gruber, C. P. (2005). *Social Responsiveness Scale (SRS)*. Torrance, CA: Western Psychological Services.

The SRS is a questionnaire that inquires about the child's social interactions with others. All 65 items are rated on a scale from 0 (not true) to 3 (almost always true), based on the frequency of the behavior. The SRS can be completed by a parent or other adult who routinely observes the child's social interactions with peers and adults.

Elliot, C. D. (2007). *Differential Ability Scales, Second Edition: Introductory and technical handbook.* San Antonio, TX: Harcourt.

The DAS-II is a broadly based measure of cognitive abilities that yields standard scores in verbal, nonverbal reasoning, and spatial domains. This is often the test of choice for children with ASD who have impaired language skills for the following reasons: (1) the subtests offer teaching items that allow for examiners to model and correct item responses; (2) there are extended norms for the Early Years battery to age 8 years, allowing for more impaired older children to complete easier tasks while still obtaining standard scores; and (3) there are alternative stopping points so that examiners can determine the appropriate place to end a subtest based on the child's ability.

Fenson, L., Dale, P. S., Reznick, J. S., Thal, D., Bates, E., Hartung, J. P., Pethick, S., & Reilly, J. S. (1993). *The MacArthur Communicative Development Inventories: User's guide and technical manual (CDI)*. San Diego, CA: Singular Publishing Group.

The CDI is a parent report instrument containing scales applicable for children ages 8 to 37 months that measure expressive vocabulary, receptive vocabulary, gestures, and early word combinations.

Lord, C., Rutter, M., DiLavore, P., & Risi, S. (1999). *Autism Diagnostic Observation Schedule (ADOS)*. Los Angeles, CA: Western Psychological Services.

The ADOS is a standardized observation of social and communicative behavior that is carried out directly with the individual. The ADOS is organized in four overlapping modules according to the expressive language level of the individual and it is considered one of the gold standard measures for the diagnosis of ASD.

Mullen, E. (1995). *Mullen Scales of Early Learning*. Circle Pines, MN: American Guidance Service.

The Mullen is a developmental test that yields age equivalents and T-scores in five areas of development: gross motor, fine motor, visual perception, receptive language, and expressive language. It has norms for infants and children from birth through 5 years.

Robins, D. L., Fein, D., Barton, M. L., & Green, J. A. (2001). The Modified Checklist for Autism in Toddlers: An initial study investigating the early detection of autism and pervasive developmental disorders. *Journal of Autism and Developmental Disorders, 31*(2), 131–144.

The M-CHAT is a 23-item parent report checklist to detect behaviors that are most at risk for ASD in toddlers between the ages of 16 and 30 months. For children who fail key items on the M-CHAT, there is a follow-up interview that can be conducted with the parent that reduces the false positive rate for ASD. The M-CHAT is widely used and well researched as an autism-based screener, and both the M-CHAT and the follow-up interview are available online for free download at www2.gsu.edu/~psydlr/DianaLRobins/Official_M-CHAT_Website.html

Rutter, M., Bailey, A., & Lord, C. (2003). *Social Communication Questionnaire (SCQ)*. Torrance, CA: Western Psychological Services.

The SCQ is a questionnaire to evaluate communication skills and social functioning in individuals ages 4 years and older (including adults). It is completed by a parent or other primary caregiver and includes Current and Lifetime versions, each with 40 yes-or-no questions.

Rutter, M., LeCouteur, A., & Lord, C. (2003). *Autism Diagnostic Interview, Revised (ADI-R)*. Torrance, CA: Western Psychological Services.

The ADI-R is a comprehensive interview that assesses for both current and historic autism-specific symptomatology. It is administered to the individual's caregiver and there is an algorithm keyed to DSM-IV criteria for autism.

Semel, E., Wiig, E. H., & Secord, W. A. (2003). *Clinical Evaluation of Language Fundamentals, Fourth Edition (CELF-4)*. San Antonio, TX: Pearson.

Semel, E., Wiig, E. H., & Secord, W.A. (2004). *Clinical Evaluation of Language Fundamentals—Preschool, Second Edition (CELF-Preschool-2)*. San Antonio, TX: Pearson.

The CELF-4 is a comprehensive language battery that provides an overview of receptive and expressive syntactic and semantic skills. The CELF-4 and CELF-Preschool-2 give specific information regarding the amounts and types of information the child understands (i.e., abilities with words, word groups, word problems, phrases, sentences, heard narratives) and is capable of using (i.e., single words, phrases, sentences, syntax).

Sparrow, S. S., Cicchetti, D. V., & Balla, D. A. (2005). *Vineland Adaptive Behavior Scales, Second Edition*. San Antonio, TX: Pearson.

The Vineland-II is a standardized measure of personal and social self-sufficiency that is conducted with the child's parents or caregivers. It assesses adaptive functioning in the domains of communication, daily living skills, and socialization skills from birth to adulthood, as well as motor skills through age 6.

Volkmar, F. R., Paul, R., Klin, A., & Cohen, D. (2005). *Handbook of autism and pervasive developmental disorders, Third Edition, Volumes 1 & 2*. Hoboken, NJ: Wiley.

This edited book is one of the most comprehensive textbooks on autism spectrum disorders to date that includes contributions from world-renowned clinicians and researchers in the field. Volume 1 covers diagnosis, development, neurobiology, and behavior, and Volume 2 covers assessment, interventions, and policy.

Wechsler, D. (2003). *Wechsler Intelligence Scale for Children, Fourth Edition: Technical and Interpretive Manual*. San Antonio, TX: Pearson.

Wechsler, D. (2008). *Wechsler Adult Intelligence Scale, Fourth Edition: Technical Manual*. San Antonio, TX: Pearson.

The Wechsler scales are the most researched and widely used measures of intelligence. The scales measure broad intellectual abilities, as well as cognitive skills in the areas of verbal comprehension, perceptual reasoning, processing speed, and working memory.

Wetherby, A., & Prizant, B. (2001). *Communication and Symbolic Behavior Scales Developmental Profile—Preliminary Normed Edition (CSBS)*. Baltimore, MD: Paul H. Brookes.

The CSBS-DP is a play-based assessment that provides information about functional communication between ages 6 months and 24 months. Examines frequency, means, and range of communicative intent using toys and interactions to gain information regarding skills, such as gesture, sounds, words, and object use.

Wetherby, A., & Prizant, B. (2002) *Communication and Symbolic Behavior Scales-Developmental Profile, Infant-Toddler Checklist.* Baltimore, MD: Paul H. Brookes.

The CSBS-DP Infant-Toddler Checklist is a broadband screener that is useful for detecting at-risk behaviors for general developmental delays in children between the ages of 6 and 24 months. It is a parent-report measure that is very efficient to administer and can be extremely useful in detecting developmental and communication delays in children who are at risk for ASD.

ABOUT THE AUTHORS

Celine Saulnier, Ph.D., is the Clinical Director for Research at the Marcus Autism Center, Children's Healthcare of Atlanta, and an Assistant Professor in the Division of Autism and Related Disorders, Department of Pediatrics at Emory University School of Medicine. She obtained her doctorate in Clinical Psychology from the University of Connecticut under the mentorship of Dr. Deborah Fein. She then completed a postdoctoral fellowship at the Yale Child Study Center under the mentorship of Dr. Ami Klin before joining Yale's faculty. At Yale, Dr. Saulnier was both the Clinical Director and the Training Director for the Autism Program, where she oversaw, conducted, and supervised multidisciplinary diagnostic evaluations on individuals with ASD from infancy through young adulthood. At the Marcus Autism Center, Dr. Saulnier is overseeing the development of a diagnostic assessment core for clinical research within one of the nation's largest clinical care facilities for autism spectrum and related disorders. Her research focuses on adaptive behavior profiles in ASD.

Pamela Ventola, Ph.D., is a faculty member in the Autism Program at the Yale Child Study Center. She earned her doctorate in Clinical Psychology from the University of Connecticut under the mentorship of Dr. Deborah Fein. She completed her postdoctoral training at the Yale Child Study Center. Dr. Ventola has vast experience conducting psychological and neuropsychological assessments on children with autism and other developmental disabilities. Her current research focuses on neuropsychological processes in children with autism as well as response to intervention in preschool-aged children with ASD. Dr. Ventola has written numerous scholarly journal articles and book chapters on developmental disabilities.

AUTHOR INDEX

Achenbach, T. M., 61, 70, 138
Almond, P., 90
Aman, M. G., 61, 70
Arick, J., 90

Bailey, A., 90, 95
Balla, D. A., 64, 66, 69
Baron-Cohen, S., 88
Barton, M. L., 89
Bayley, N., 16, 18, 51
Beck, A. T., 61, 138, 143, 147
Booth, L., 39–58
Boyle, M. H., 68
Bracken, B. A., 23, 28
Brown, C., 91
Brown, G. K., 61, 143, 147
Brown, L., 23, 28
Brown, T. E., 61
Bruininks, R. H., 66, 70
Bryant, B. R., 134
Bryson, S. E., 68, 119, 120
Burd, L., 132

Calhoun, S. L., 23, 25
Canitano, R., 141
Carrow-Woolfolk, E., 51, 54
Carter, A., 50, 67

Chawarska, K., 1, 17
Cicchetti, D. V., 27, 64, 65, 66, 67, 69
Conners, C. K., 29, 30, 61, 70
Constantino, J. N., 90, 95
Coon, H., 68
Coonrod, E. E., 89

Delis, D., 29, 30
DeVincent, C. J., 136
DiLavore, P., 116
Duku, E. E., 68
Dunn, D. M., 52
Dunn, G., 68
Dunn, L. M., 52
Dunn, W., 91

Edith, K., 30
Ekstrom, L., 143
Elliott, C., 18, 21, 22, 34
Emilsson, B., 143
Engstrom, I., 143

Farley, M. A., 68
Fein, D., 29, 30, 89
Fenson, L., 51
Field, C. J., 61

Filipek, P. A., 128, 129
Flanagan, H. E., 68
Freeman, N. L., 68

Gadow, K. D., 136
Gillberg, C., 3
Gilliam, J. E., 90, 96
Gilliam, R. B., 51, 53
Gillot, A., 137
Gilotty, L., 30
Gioia, G. A., 30, 31
Goode, S., 68
Goodman, W. K., 139
Gotham, K., 117
Goudreau, D., 67
Gould, J., 3
Green, J. A., 89
Grigorenko, E. L., 132
Gruber, C. P., 51, 90, 95
Gupta, V. B., 78
Guthrie, W., 117
Guy, S. C., 30, 31

Harris, J. C., 129
Harrison, P., 66, 70
Heaton, R. K., 30
Hill, B. K., 66
Howlin, P., 68, 141, 143
Hutton, J., 68

Isquith, P. K., 30, 31

Johnsen, S. K., 23, 28
Joseph, R. M., 27

Kamphaus, R. W., 61, 139
Kanne, S. M., 68
Kaplan, E., 29, 30
Kaufman, A. S., 21, 22, 134

Kaufman, N. L., 21, 22, 134
Keelan, J., 78
Kemp, S., 30
Kenworthy, L., 30, 31
Kerbeshian, J., 132
Kirk, U., 30
Klin, A., 3, 17, 27, 50, 68, 132
Koenig, K., 8, 9
Korkman, M., 30
Kovacs, M., 61, 143, 147
Kramer, J., 29, 30
Krug, D. A., 90

LeCouteur, A., 87, 96
Loncola, J. A., 8
Lord, C., 27, 87, 90, 95, 96, 116, 120
Love, S. R., 90
Luyster, R., 117

Marans, W. D., 50
Mather, N., 21, 23
Mayes, S. D., 23, 25
McCallum, R. S., 23, 28
McGrew, K. S., 19, 21, 23
Miller, L., 23, 28
Morris, R., 29, 30
Mullen, E., 16, 18
Muris, P., 137

Oakland, T., 66, 70
Ober, B. A., 29, 30
Offit, P. A., 78
Osterreith, P., 29, 30
Ousley, O. Y., 89

Paul, R., 39
Pearson, N. A., 51, 53
Perry, A., 68
Pomeroy, J., 136

Pond, R. E., 51
Prizant, B., 51, 52, 89, 95

Rescorla, L. A., 138
Rey, A., 29, 30
Reynell, J. K., 51
Reynolds, C. R., 61, 139
Risi, S., 116
Robertson, G. J., 134
Robins, D. L., 89, 90, 95
Roeper, T. W., 51
Roid, G. H., 18, 21, 22, 23, 28
Rourke, B. P., 27, 130, 131
Rutter, M., 68, 87, 90, 95, 96, 116

Saulnier, C., 3
Scahill, L., 61, 140
Schopler, E., 90, 96
Secord, W. A., 51, 52, 53, 55
Semel, E., 51, 52, 53
Seymour, H. N., 51
Sherbenou, R., 23, 28
Shtayermann, O., 137, 141
Singh, N. N., 61
Sparrow, S. S., 27, 50, 64, 65, 66, 67, 68, 69, 70
Standen, P. J., 137
State, M., 8, 9
Steer, R. A., 61, 143, 147

Steiner, V. G., 51
Stewart, A. W., 61
Stone, W. L., 89
Streiner, D. L., 68
Szatmari, P., 68

Tager-Flusberg, H., 27

Van Acker, E. Y., 8
Van Acker, R., 8
Van Bourgondien, M. E., 90
Villiers, J., 51
Vivanti, G., 141
Volkmar, F., 8, 9, 27, 50, 67, 132

Weatherman, R. F., 66
Wechsler, D., 18, 22, 34, 134
Wellman, G. J., 90
Wetherby, A., 51, 52
Wetherby, A. M., 89, 95
Wiederholt, J. L., 134
Wiig, E., 51, 52, 53, 55
Wilkinson, G. S., 134
Williams, K. T., 54
Wilson, K., 78
Wing, L., 3
Woodcock, R. W., 21, 23, 66

Zimmerman, I. L., 51

SUBJECT INDEX

ABAS-II *(Adaptive Behavior Assessment System, Second Edition)*, 66, 67, 70
ABC *(Aberrant Behavior Checklist)*, 61, 70
Abstraction, 110, 113
Abstract language, 47, 50
Academic performance, 82–83
Adaptive behavior, 8, 17, 30, 50, 59, 125
   assessment of, 64–69, 161–162
   and change, 69
   comparison of measures of, 66
   defined, 64
   importance of assessment, 70
   and IQ, 68
   school-aged child case study, 181–184
Adaptive Behavior Assessment System, Second Edition. See ABAS-II
Adaptive deficits, 65
ADHD (attention deficit hyperactivity disorder), 135–137, 147
ADI-R *(Autism Diagnostic Interview, Revised)*, 87–88, 96, 116

Adolescents:
   direct diagnostic assessment, 114–116
ADOS *(Autism Diagnostic Observation Schedule)*, 116–119, 120, 164–167, 187–191
Adults:
   cognitive measures, 22–23
   and differential diagnosis, 148
   direct diagnostic assessment, 114–116
   psychiatric conditions in, 143–146
Affect, 40
Aggression, 19, 59, 62, 86, 87, 126, 137
Agoraphobia, 137, 138
Antecedent, 62–63
Anxiety, 5, 59, 60, 87
Anxiety disorders, 137–139, 147
AOSI *(Autism Observation Scale for Infants)*, 119, 120
Appetite, 142
Arithmetic subtest, 24–25, 27
Articulation, 40
ASD (autism spectrum disorders). *See also* Asperger syndrome; Autism and anxiety disorders, 138

ASD (*Continued*)
  assessing level of functioning,
    13–37
  associated medical conditions,
    128–130
  atypical communicative behaviors
    observed in, 41
  case study of school-aged child,
    171–196
  challenges in assessing, 14
  and coding skills, 179
  common features with
    intellectual disability, 126
  comparison between *DSM-IV*
    and *DSM-5*, 7
  and deductive thought, 23
  defined, 1
  and depression, 141–143
  diagnosis of children under age
    3, 168
  diagnostic criteria, 2
  distinctions from ID
    characteristics, 127–128
  and environmental agents, 78
  and family functioning, 86
  importance of communication
    evaluation, 39
  and mood disorders, 5
  overview, 1–12
  prevalence, 1
  proposed change in diagnosis in
    DSM-5, 10
  and repetitive behaviors, 139
  use of behavior as means of
    communication, 45–46
  and Wechsler scales, 23
Asperger syndrome, 2. *See also* ASD
    (autism spectrum disorders);
    Autism
and circumscribed interests, 139
common misconceptions about, 4
diagnosis of, 3
distinctions from other PDDs, 6
interaction with peers, 4–5
and nonverbal learning disability,
  130
and nonverbal skills, 27
overview, 3–5
and speech development, 101
and vocabulary, 24
WISC-IV profiles, 26–27
Assessment:
  of adaptive behavior, 64–69,
    161–162, 181–184
  of anxiety disorders, 138–139
  audiological, 80, 94
  of behavior, 60–61
  of behavioral profiles, 59–73
  of child's strengths and
    weaknesses, 160
  choosing appropriate
    instruments, 14–16, 34
  cognitive, 19–28, 34
  of communication, 39–58,
    185–187, 192–193
  developmental, 16–19, 104–109,
    152–162, 167
  diagnostic, 164–167, 187–191
  direct diagnostic, 99–122
  executive functioning, 179–181
  functional behavior (FBA),
    61–64, 87, 108
  of hyperlexia, 133–134
  language, 39–58, 101, 185–187
  level of functioning, 13–37
  neuropsychological, 28–31, 34
  nutritional, 94
  play-based, 100–101, 101–102

psychiatric, 94
psychological, 94, 192
semistructured measures for,
    116–119
of speech, 39–58, 163–164,
    185–187
tools, 16–18
of verbal communication,
    104–105
At-risk behaviors, 89
Attention, sustained, 30, 32
Attention deficit hyperactivity
    disorder. *See* ADHD (attention
    deficit hyperactivity disorder)
Attention to task, 32, 34
Atypical behaviors, 59, 86
Audiological assessment, 80, 94
Auditory processing, 20
Auditory-verbal attention and
    memory, 178
Autism, 2. *See also* ASD (autism
    spectrum disorders); Asperger
    syndrome
    assessment of symptomatology,
        75
    diagnostic criteria in *DSM-IV-TR*,
        95
    and expressive language skills,
        43
    and nonverbal skills, 27
    regressive, 9
    WISC-IV profiles, 26–27
Autism Behavior Checklist, 90
Autism Diagnostic Interview, Revised
    (ADI-R). *See* ADI-R *(Autism
    Diagnostic Interview)*
Autism Diagnostic Observation Schedule.
    See ADOS *(Autism Diagnostic
    Observation Schedule)*

Autism Observation Scale for Infants.
    See AOSI *(Autism Observation
    Scale for Infants)*
Autism Society of America, 171
Autism Speaks, 171
Autism spectrum disorders. *See*
    ASD (autism spectrum
    disorders)
Avoidant personality disorder, 145

Background information, 41, 50
BAI *(Beck Anxiety Inventory),* 61,
    138, 147
BASC-2 *(Behavior Assessment Scale for
    Children, Second Edition),* 61,
    139
Bayley-III *(Bayley Scales of Infant and
    Toddler Development, Third
    Edition),* 16, 17–18, 51
BCBA (Board Certified Behavior
    Analyst), 61
BDI-II *(Beck Depression Inventory,
    Second Edition),* 61, 143, 147
Beck Anxiety Inventory. See BAI
    (Beck Anxiety Inventory)
*Beck Depression Inventory, Second
    Edition. See* BDI-II *(Beck
    Depression Inventory)*
*Beery-Buktenika Tests of Visual-Motor
    Integration. See* VMI
Behavior:
    adaptive *(see* Adaptive behavior)
    in autism, 2
    challenging, 19
    changing, 64
    consequence of, 63–64
    internalizing, 59, 147
    as means of communication,
        45–46

Behavior (*Continued*)
milestones, 79
problems as presenting concerns,
77
regulating others', 50
regulation of, 40, 126, 179–180
repetitive/unusual in young
children, 107–108
standardized assessments of,
60–61
that negatively impacts learning,
50
unusual in school-aged children,
113–114
Behavioral dysregulation, 86–87
Behavioral observations:
school aged-child case study,
174–175
toddlers, 158–159, 163–164
Behavioral presentation, 85–87
Behavioral profiles, 59–73
Behavioral specialist, 61
*Behavior Assessment Scale for Children,
Second Edition. See* BASC-2
*Behavior Rating Inventory of Executive
Functioning. See* BRIEF
Block Design subtest, 24, 26, 29, 178
Board Certified Behavior Analyst
(BCBA), 61
BRIEF (*Behavior Rating Inventory of
Executive Functioning*), 30–31,
179–181
Brown Attention-Deficit Disorder Scales,
61
Bullying, 85, 112

California Verbal Learning Test. See
CVLT (*California Verbal
Learning Test*)

Cancellation subtest, 26, 27
CARS-2 (*Childhood Autism Rating
Scale, Second Edition*), 90, 95–96
Case conceptualization, 153–196
Case samples, 155–196
CASL (*Comprehensive Assessment of
Spoken Language*), 51, 54
Cattell-Horn-Carroll theory. *See*
CHC (Cattell-Horn-Carroll)
theory
Cause-and-effect play, 107
Cause-effect toys, 47
CBCL (*Child Behavior Checklist*), 61,
70, 138
CDD (Childhood Disintegrative
Disorder), 2, 8–9
CDI-2 (*Children's Depression Inventory,
Second Edition*), 61, 143, 147
CDI (*Communication Development
Inventory*), 51
CELF-4 (*Clinical Evaluation of
Language Fundamentals*), 43, 51,
53, 185–187
CELF-P-2 (*Clinical Evaluation of
Language Fundamentals, Preschool,
2nd edition*), 51, 52–53
Centers for Disease Prevention and
Control, 171
CHAT (*Checklist for Autism in
Toddlers*), 88
CHC (Cattell-Horn-Carroll) theory,
19–20
Checklist for Autism in Toddlers. See
CHAT (*Checklist for Autism in
Toddlers*)
Child Behavior Checklist. See CBCL
(*Child Behavior Checklist*)
*Childhood Autism Rating Scale, Second
Edition. See* CARS-2

(Childhood Autism Rating Scale)

Childhood Disintegrative Disorder. *See* CDD (Childhood Disintegrative Disorder)

Children. *See* School-age children; Toddlers; Young children

Children's Depression Inventory, Second Edition. See CDI-2 (Children's Depression Inventory)

Children's Yale-Brown Obsessive Compulsive Scale for Pervasive Disorders. See CYBOCS-PDD

Choosing language, 40

Circumscribed interests, 3, 6, 86, 139

Circumstantial speech, 145

Clinical Evaluation of Language Fundamentals. See CELF-4

Clinical Evaluation of Language Fundamentals, Preschool, 2nd edition. See CELF-P-2

Clinical interview, 76–87, 87–88

CVLT *(California Verbal Learning Test),* 29

Coding subtest, 25, 27, 29, 179

Cognition, 19–20

Cognitive ability, 17, 125
   in preschool children, 18
   school aged-child case study, 175–179

Cognitive assessments, 19–28, 34

Cognitive delays, 14

Cognitive impairment, 125

Cognitive processes, 15

Colloquialisms, 47, 114

Communication:
   aspects of skills, 40–41
   assessment of, 39–58, 167–168, 185–187, 192–193

atypical behaviors observed in ASD, 41

impairments in, 2, 129, 134–135

nonverbal, 40, 105, 135

social (*see* Social communication)

spontaneous social, 103

standardized measures to assess skills, 52–55

using behavior, 45–46

verbal assessment of, 104–105

Communication and Symbolic Behavior Scales. See CSBS

Communication and Symbolic Behavior Scales, Developmental Profile. See CSBS-DP

Communication Development Inventory. See CDI (Communication Development Inventory)

Comorbidity, 123–151

Compensatory strategies, 105

Complex imaginative play, 107, 113

Comprehension subtest, 25, 26, 177

Comprehensive Assessment of Spoken Language. See CASL

Compulsivity, 60, 86, 113, 139

Concept formation, 30

Conceptual development, 169–170

Conners, Third Edition (Conners 3), 61, 70

Conners' Continuous Performance Test, Second Edition, 29

Consequence, 63–64

Contextual language, 44, 47, 103–104
   contextual, 44, 47, 103–104

Contingencies, 32

Continuous Performance Tests. See CPT (Continuous Performance Tests)

Conversational language, 40–41, 43
   assessing in young children, 106

Conversations, one-sided, 41
Coping skills, 137
CPT *(Continuous Performance Tests)*, 29, 30
Creativity, 113
Critical judgment, 132
Crying, 19
CSBS *(Communication and Symbolic Behavior Scales)*, 51, 52
CSBS-DP *(Communication and Symbolic Behavior Scales, Developmental Profile)*, 89, 95, 163–164
CVLT *(California Verbal Learning Test)*, 30, 31
CYBOCS-PDD *(Children's Yale-Brown Obsessive Compulsive Scale for Pervasive Disorders)*, 61, 140

DAS-II Early Years *(Differential Ability Scales, Second Edition)*, 18, 21–22, 27, 34
Decision-making, 132
Decoding skills, 133, 134, 179
Deductions, 23
Delis-Kaplan Executive Functioning System. See D-KEFS
Delusions, 144
DELV *(Diagnostic Evaluation of Language Variation)*, 50, 51
Depression, 5, 59, 87, 141–143, 147
Developmental assessments, 16–19, 158–162
Developmental history, 4, 77–80, 157, 172–173
Developmental milestones, 78, 79
Developmental processes, 15

Diagnosis:
    case example of initial toddler diagnosis, 156–171
    criteria for autism, 2
    formulation of findings, 51, 55
Diagnostic and Statistical Manual, Fourth Edition. See DSM-IV
Diagnostic assessment, 99–122. *See also* Clinical interview
    of adolescents and adults, 114–116
    goal of, 100
    primary areas to evaluate, 101
    purpose of, 99
    sample activities for, 109
    of school-aged children, 109–114, 187–191
    semistructured measures for, 116–119
    structuring, 102–104
    toddler case study, 164–167
Diagnostic differentials:
    and comorbidity, 123–151
Diagnostic Evaluation of Language Variation. See DELV
Diagnostic formulation:
    school-aged child case study, 193–194
    toddler case study, 168–169
Differential Ability Scales, Second Edition. See DAS-II Early Years
Differentials, diagnostic. *See* Diagnostic differentials
Differentiated instruction, 133
Digit Span subtest, 24, 27, 178
Direct diagnostic assessment. *See* Diagnostic assessment
Direct observation, 99–100
Distractibility, 60

D-KEFS *(Delis-Kaplan Executive Functioning System)*, 30
Down syndrome, 129
Drawing conclusions, 50
DSM-5 *(Diagnostic and Statistical Manual, Fifth Edition)*, 3, 6, 7, 9–11, 65
DSM-IV *(Diagnostic and Statistical Manual, Fourth Edition)*, 2, 65, 95
  and Asperger syndrome, 3
  comparison with *DSM-5* for ASD, 7
Dysregulation, behavioral, 60, 126

Early intervention, 17, 82
Early Reading Diagnostic Assessment, Second Edition. See ERDA
Early SB5 *(Stanford-Binet Intelligence Scales for Early Childhood)*, 18
Echolalia, 6, 40, 41, 43, 45
Educating Children with Autism (National Research Council), 169, 170–171
Education, parent, 170
Education history, 82–83, 173
Emotional awareness, 190
Emotional control, 30
Emotional development, 17
Emotional experiences, 112
Environmental agents, 78
ERDA *(Early Reading Diagnostic Assessment, Second Edition)*, 134
Escape/avoidance behavior, 19
Evidence-based practices, 153
EVT *(Expressive Vocabulary Test)*, 54
Executive functioning, 30–31, 34, 129
  school-aged child case study, 179–181

Exploratory play, 106–107
Explosive behavior, 19, 59
Expressive formulation, 134
Expressive language, 8, 17, 40, 43, 44–46, 134, 186
Expressive Vocabulary Test. See EVT *(Expressive Vocabulary Test)*
Externalizing behaviors, 59
Eye contact, 32, 50, 89, 129, 165, 189
Eye gaze, 40, 48, 50

Facial expressions, 40
Family and ASD, 86
Family history, 80–82, 173
FBA (functional behavior assessment), 61–64, 87, 108
Figures of speech, 41, 50, 114
Findings, 51, 55
Fine motor skills, 17
Flexibility, 30, 32, 86
Fluency, atypical, 41
Fluid reasoning, 20, 113
Formal language, 40
Fragile X syndrome, 129
Freedom from Distractibility Index, 20, 23, 24
Friendships, 84, 112
Frustration tolerance, 32
Functional behavior assessment (FBA), 61–64, 87, 108
Functional play, 107
Functioning:
  assessing level of, 13–37

GADS *(Gilliam Asperger Disorder Scale)*, 90, 96
GARS-2 *(Gilliam Autism Rating Scale, Second Edition)*, 90, 96

Gastrointestinal procedures, 94
Generalizability of skills, 103–104
Genetic syndromes, 8, 128, 129
Genetic testing, 94, 129, 130
Gestalt, 132
Gestures, 40, 41, 48
Gilliam Asperger Disorder Scale. See GADS *(Gilliam Asperger Disorder Scale)*
Gilliam Autism Rating Scale, Second Edition. See GARS-2 *(Gilliam Autism Rating Scale)*
Global Executive Composite, 181
GORT-4 *(Gray Oral Reading Test, Fourth Edition),* 134
Graphomotor abilities, 29
Gray Oral Reading Test, Fourth Edition. See GORT-4 *(Gray Oral Reading Test, Fourth Edition)*
Gross motor activities, 17, 47

Hallucinations, 144
Halstead-Reitan test, 29
Hand-over-hand gestures, 40, 41
Head circumference, 8
Hearing loss, 80
Helplessness, 87, 141
High-functioning individuals, 124, 125
Hopelessness, 87, 141
Humor, 41, 47, 114
Hyperactivity, 59, 60, 136
Hyperlexia, 132–134
Hypersensitivity, 91

ID. *See* Intellectual disability (ID)
IDD (intellectual developmental disorder), 124

Idioms, 41, 47
Idiosyncratic speech, 40, 41
IEP (individualized education program), 83, 92, 93
IFSP (individualized family service plan), 83, 92
Imaginative play, 107, 113, 190–191
Imitation, 32, 40, 48, 89
Impulsivity, 59, 60, 132, 136
Inattention, 60, 136
Independent living skills, 30, 114, 115
Individualized education program. *See* IEP (individualized education program)
Individualized family service plan. *See* IFSP (individualized family service plan)
Inefficiency, 32
Infants. *See also* Young children assessment tools, 16–17
Inferencing, 41, 50
Information collection, 87–94
Information subtest, 26
Inhibition, 30
Inhibit Scale, 181
Integrated report writing, 153–196
Intellectual Developmental Disorder (IDD), 124
Intellectual disability (ID), 65, 124–130
and autism, 127–128
Intelligence, 20, 21
Intelligence test, nonverbal, 27–28
Intent, 45
Interests, restricted, 85, 113–114
Interfering behaviors, 33
Internalizing behaviors, 59, 147

Intervention:
  agencies offering services, 171
  and anxiety disorders, 138
  history, 82–83
  strategies, 155
  toddler case study, 169
  tracking progress, 65
Interview, clinical, 76–87
Intonation, atypical, 40, 41, 50
Intuitive reasoning, 177
IQ score, 20, 68, 124, 176
Irony, 41, 47
Irritability, 87, 142
Isolation, 5

Joint attention, 40, 48, 89
Judgment, 132, 177

KABC-II (Kaufman Assessment Battery
    for Children, Second Edition), 21, 22
KAIT (Kaufman Adolescent and Adult
    Intelligence Test), 21, 22
KTEA-II (Kaufman Test of
    Educational Achievement, Second
    Edition), 134

Language:
  assessment of, 39–58, 101,
      163–164, 185–187
  comprehension, 60
  conversational, 40–41
  delays, 6, 80, 128
  development, 17
  expressive, 8, 17, 40, 43, 44–46,
      186
  impaired skills, 6, 126
  nonliteral, 41
  observing in young children,
      102–103

pervasive impairments, 27–28
  pragmatic, 47–48
  rate of acquisition, 48
  receptive, 8, 17, 40, 42–44, 186
  responsivity to, 48
  skills, 40–41, 79
  social, 44
  social-pragmatic, 40
  as social tool, 134
  stages of development, 48–51
Learning:
  behaviors that negatively impact,
      60
  difficulties, 83
  disabilities, 130–132
  profiles, 130–134
  readiness, 32–33, 60
Leiter International Performance Scale,
    Revised, 23, 28
Letter-Number Sequencing subtest,
    24, 27, 178
Limitation skills, 60
Linguistic stage, 49–51
Low-functioning individuals, 124,
    125
Luria-Nebraska test, 29

Made-up speech, 40
Marriage, 115–116
Matrix Reasoning subtest, 24, 26,
    178
M-CHAT (Modified Checklist for
    Autism in Toddlers), 89, 95
Medical history, 80, 157–158, 173
Meltdowns, 86–87
Memory, 34
  short-term, 20
Mental age, 126
Mental retardation, 65, 124

Mercury, 78
Metacognition, 180–181
Metalinguistic skills, 51
Metaphors, 41, 47
Modified Checklist for Autism in Toddlers. See M-CHAT
Mood disorders, 5, 87, 141–143, 147
Mood lability, 142
Motivation:
  limited, 60
  social, 4–5, 85, 146
Motor Coordination subtest, 29–30
Motor skills, 8, 17, 20, 79, 128
Mullen Scales of Early Learning, 16, 17, 18, 51, 158, 159–169, 173

Name, responsivity to, 89
National Database for Autism Research, 17
National Standards Project, 171
Negative punishment, 63–64
Negative reinforcement, 64
Neologisms, 40, 41, 145
NEPSY-II, 29, 30, 50
Neurodevelopmental disorders, 124
Neuroimaging, 130
Neuropsychological assessments, 28–31, 34
Neuropsychological processes, 15
NLD (nonverbal learning disability), 130–132, 147
Noncompliance, 62
Nonliteral language, 41, 47
Nonverbal cognitive skills, 6, 23, 27
Nonverbal communication, 40, 50, 105, 135
Nonverbal learning disability (NLD), 30, 130–132, 147

Nonverbal reasoning, 178
Nonverbal signals, 50
Nutritional assessment, 94

Objectives, 93
Observation:
  direct, 99–100
  qualitative, 25, 31–33, 50
Obsessive behaviors, 113
OCD (obsessive-compulsive disorder), 137, 139–140
OCPD (obsessive-compulsive personality disorder), 146
One-sided conversations, 41
Organization, 30
Overfocused attention, 136

Pain, 91
Panic disorder, 137
Parent conferences, 153–154
Parent reports, 103, 108
  case sample, 156–158
Parent training, 170
Passivity, 6, 59
PDD-NOS (Pervasive Developmental Disorder, Not Otherwise Specified), 2, 5–6, 168
PDD (Pervasive Developmental Disorders), 2, 6, 7, 136
Peabody Picture Vocabulary Test. See PPVT-4 (Peabody Picture Vocabulary Test)
Pedantic speech, 40, 41
Peers:
  interest in, 4–5, 84
  and school-aged children, 111–112
Perception, visual, 29

Perceptual Organization Index, 20, 23
Perceptual Reasoning Index, 20, 24, 26, 175, 176, 178
Perseveration, 25–26, 32, 85–86
Perseverative interests, 6
Perseverative play, 107
Personality disorders, 145–146, 148
Perspective taking, 40, 47, 50
Pervasive Developmental Disorder, Not Otherwise Specified. *See* PDD-NOS
Pervasive Developmental Disorders. *See* PDD (Pervasive Developmental Disorders)
Pharmacological treatments, OCD, 140
Picture Concepts subtest, 26, 178–179
Planning, 30
Planning, transitional, 155
Plateauing, 128
Play-based assessments, 100–101, 101–102
Play skills, 8
  assessing in young children, 106–107
  development of, 83–85
  school-aged child case study, 190–191
  stages of development, 108
  toddler case study, 166, 170
PLS-5 *(Preschool Language Scale)*, 51
Positive punishment, 64
Positive reinforcement, 63–64
PPVT-4 *(Peabody Picture Vocabulary Test)*, 52
Pragmatic language, 47–48, 187
Precocious reading, 133
Predicting, 50

Prelinguistic stage, 48–49
Preoccupation, 3
Pre-school children. *See* Young children
Preschool Language Scale. See PLS-5 (Preschool Language Scale)
Presenting concerns, 76–77
Pretend play, 84
Problem-solving, 50
Processing speed, 25, 179
Processing Speed Index, 20, 23, 25, 27, 175, 176, 179
Pronoun reversal, 40, 41
Prosody, 40, 41, 50
Protesting language, 40
Psychiatric assessment, 94
Psychiatric conditions, 143–146, 148
Psychological assessment, 94
  school-aged child case study, 173–179, 192
Psychomotor development, 8
Psychosis, 148
Psychosocial stressors, 8–9
Psychotic disorders, 143–145
Punishment, 63–64
Purdue Pegboard test, 29

Qualitative observations, 25, 31–33, 50

Rating scales, 90, 95–96
RDLS *(Reynell Developmental Language Scales)*, 51
Reading, 132, 133
Reality, grounding in, 144
Reasoning:
  fluid, 20
  intuitive, 177
  nonverbal, 178

Receptive language, 8, 17, 40, 42–44, 186
Receptive understanding, 134
Reciprocal social interaction, 5–6
Reciprocity, 50
Recommendations, 155
  school-aged child case study, 194–196
  toddler case study, 169–171
Record review, 91–94
Regression, 78, 128
Regressive autism, 9
Regressive disorders, 8–9
Reinforcement, 19, 63–64
Repetitive behaviors, 2, 3, 85–86, 139
  toddler assessment case study, 166–167
  in young children, 107–108
Report writing, integrated, 153–196
Representational thought, 110
Requesting language, 40
Resources for parents, 170–171
Response inhibition, 32
Responsibility, 114
Responsivity, social. See Social responsivity
Restricted behaviors, 2, 3, 85, 139
  toddler assessment case study, 166–167
Rett's disorder, 2, 8–9
Reynell Developmental Language Scales. See RDLS
Rey-O (Rey Osterreith Complex Figure Test), 29, 30, 31
Rigidities, 60, 86
Rituals, 86
Romantic relationships, 115–116

Rote facts, 23, 177
Rote verbal skills, 6, 23, 24
Routines, 86

Sadness, 87
Sarcasm, 41, 114
SB5 (Stanford-Binet Intelligence Scales, Fifth Edition), 21, 22
Scales of Independent Behavior, Revised. See SIB-R (Scales of Independent Behavior)
Schizoid personality disorder, 145–146
Schizophrenia, 143–145
Schizotypal personality disorder, 146
School-aged children:
  ASD case study, 171–196
  and Asperger syndrome, 4–5
  assessment of social communication and interaction skills, 110–111
  capacity for abstraction, 113
  case study summary and interpretations, 191–194
  cognitive measures, 22–23
  direct diagnostic assessment with, 109–114
  emotional experiences, 112
  observation of, 100
  and peers, 111–112
  strengths and weaknesses, 82
  unusual behaviors/interests, 113–114
School observations, 100
SCQ (Social Communication Questionnaire), 90, 95
Screaming, 19
Screening measures, 88–90

Screening Tool for Autism in Two-Year-Olds. See STAT *(Screening Tool for Autism)*
Scripting, 6, 40, 41, 45, 86, 144
Seizure disorders, 128–129
Self-advocacy, 31, 32
Self-awareness, 5
Self-evaluation, 32
Self-expression, 46
Self-injury, 19, 59, 86, 87, 126, 137
Self-management skills, 114
Self-monitoring, 30, 32
Self-regulation, 31, 32, 172
Semantic skills, 44
Sensitivity, sensory, 108
Sensorimotor play, 106–107
Sensorimotor processing, 34
Sensory-oriented behavior, 86
Sensory processing, 91, 108
Sensory Profile, 91
Sensory sensitivities, 108
Separation anxiety, 137, 138
Sexual relationships, 115–116
Shift Scale, 181
SIB-R *(Scales of Independent Behavior, Revised)*, 66, 70
Similarities subtest, 26, 177
Simons Foundation Autism Research Initiative, 17
Sitting, 32
Slang, 47
Sleep, 142
SLI (specific language impairment), 134–135
Smile, social, 89
Social awareness, 5, 111–112, 190
Social challenges, 85
Social communication, 47–48, 55, 129, 135

in school-aged children, 110–111, 188–189
in toddlers, 165
Social Communication Questionnaire. See SCQ *(Social Communication Questionnaire)*
Social development, 17, 83–85
Social disabilities, 10, 138, 147
Social initiation, 105
Social interaction, 6
and Asperger syndrome, 3, 4–5
impairments in, 2
and nonverbal learning disability, 131–132
and PDD-NOS, 5–6
school-aged child case study, 188–189
in school-aged children, 110–111
Socialization skills, 79
Social judgment, 177
Social language, 44
Social motivation, 4–5, 85, 146
Social passivity, 6
Social-pragmatic language, 40
Social relationships, 145–146
Social Responsiveness Scale. See SRS *(Social Responsiveness Scale)*
Social responsivity, 105–106
Social skills, 8
Social smile, 89
Social vulnerabilities, 138
Sound, hypersensitivity to, 91
Special education services, 92, 169
Specific language impairment (SLI), 134–135
Speech:
aspects of skills, 40–41
assessment of, 39–58, 163–164, 185–187

Speech (*Continued*)
  atypical development, 40
  deficits, 129
  delayed, 6, 101
  precocious, 6, 101
  and psychiatric conditions, 145
Speech-language pathologist, 42
SRS (*Social Responsiveness Scale*), 90,
  95
SSRI medications, 140
*Stanford-Binet Intelligence Scales, Fifth
  Edition. See* SB5
*Stanford-Binet Intelligence Scales for
  Early Childhood. See* Early SB5
Staring spells, 129
STAT (*Screening Tool for Autism in
  Two-Year-Olds*), 89
Stereotyped behaviors, 2, 3, 6, 60,
  62, 86, 129
Support networks, 171
Sustained attention, 30
Symbolic play, 84, 107
Symbol Search subtest, 25, 27, 179
Syntax, 40, 44

Tactile input, 91
Tangential speech, 145
Tantrums, 19, 59, 86–87
Task demands tolerance, 60
Teasing, 85, 112
Temperament, 84
Test of Language Competence. See TLC
  (Test of Language Competence)
Test of Narrative Language. See TNL
  (Test of Narrative Language)
*Test of Nonverbal Intelligence, Fourth
  Edition. See* TONI-4
Theory of mind, 40, 50
Thimerisol, 78

Thought disorders, 144, 145
Tic behaviors, 113, 140–141
Time, concept of, 25
Time constraints, 25
TLC (*Test of Language Competence*),
  51, 55
TNL (*Test of Narrative Language*), 51,
  53–54
Toddlers. *See also* Young children
  assessment of speech, language,
    and communication, 163–164
  assessment tools, 16–18
  case example of initial diagnosis,
    156–171
  diagnostic assessment case study,
    164–167
Toileting skills, 8
TONI-4 (*Test of Nonverbal Intelligence,
  Fourth Edition*), 23, 28
Topic control, 41
Topic recognition/maintenance, 41,
  50
Touch, 91
Tourette's disorder, 140–141
Training, parent, 170
Transitional planning, 155
Transition difficulties, 60
Tuberous sclerosis complex, 129
Turn-taking, 40, 50

UNIT (*Universal Nonverbal Intelligence
  Test*), 23, 28
Unusual behaviors, 107–108
  in school-aged children,
    113–114, 191

Vaccines, 78
Validity statements, 159, 181
Verbal association tasks, 23

Verbal communication assessment, 104–105
Verbal Comprehension Index, 20, 23, 26, 175, 176, 177
Verbal expression, 62
Verbosity, 3–4, 6, 24, 101
Victimization, 85, 112
Videotape, 100
Vineland II (Vineland Adaptive Behavior Scales, Second Edition), 65–66, 69, 70, 158, 161–162
case study, 173–174, 181–184
domain and subdomain scores, 67
failed items on, 196
standard scores, 68
Visual analysis, 178
Visual-Motor Integration subtest, 29
Visual-motor skills, 25
Visual perception, 29
Visual Perception subtest, 29–30
Visual reception, 17
Visual-spatial processing, 20
VMI (Beery-Buktenika Tests of Visual-Motor Integration), 29
Vocabulary subtests, 24, 26, 177
Vocal intensity, 50

WAIS-IV (Wechsler Adult Intelligence Scale, Fourth Edition), 20, 22, 34
WCST (Wisconsin Card Sorting Test), 30
Websites, autism information, 171
Wechsler Adult Intelligence Scale, Fourth Edition. See WAIS-IV
Wechsler Individual Achievement Test, Third Edition. See WIAT-III

Wechsler Intelligence Scale for Children, Fourth Edition. See WISC-IV
Wechsler Preschool and Primary Scales of Intelligence, Third Edition. See WPPSI-III
Wechsler scales, 20, 23, 29, 34
WIAT-III (Wechsler Individual Achievement Test, Third Edition), 134
Wide Range Achievement Test, Fourth Edition, 134
WISC-IV (Wechsler Intelligence Scale for Children, Fourth Edition), 20, 22, 26–27, 29, 30, 34
case study, 175–179
Wisconsin Card Sorting Test. See WCST (Wisconsin Card Sorting Test)
WJ-III (Woodcock-Johnson Tests of Cognitive Abilities, Third Edition), 21, 23
Word Reasoning subtests, 24
Working memory, 30
Working Memory Index, 20, 24, 27, 175, 178
WPPSI-III (Wechsler Preschool and Primary Scales of Intelligence, Third Edition), 18, 20
Written report, 154–155
case samples, 155–196

Yale-Brown Obsessive Compulsive Scale. See Y-BOCS (Yale-Brown Obsessive Compulsive Scale)
Y-BOCS (Yale-Brown Obsessive Compulsive Scale), 139–140
Young children. See also Infants; Toddlers
and Asperger syndrome, 43

Young children (*Continued*)
  assessing conversational skills in,
    106
  assessing play skills in, 106–107
  assessing social initiation in, 105
  assessing social responsivity in,
    105–106
  assessing unusual/repetitive
    behaviors in, 107–108
  developmental areas to assess,
    104–109
  direct diagnostic assessment of,
    101–109
  measuring cognitive skills in, 18
  nonverbal communication,
    105
  screening for risk of ASD,
    88–89